Metaheuristics for Air Traffic Management

AF720955

Metaheuristics Set

coordinated by
Nicolas Monmarché and Patrick Siarry

Volume 2

Metaheuristics for Air Traffic Management

Nicolas Durand
David Gianazza
Jean-Baptiste Gotteland
Jean-Marc Alliot

iSTE

WILEY

First published 2016 in Great Britain and the United States by ISTE Ltd and John Wiley & Sons, Inc.

Apart from any fair dealing for the purposes of research or private study, or criticism or review, as permitted under the Copyright, Designs and Patents Act 1988, this publication may only be reproduced, stored or transmitted, in any form or by any means, with the prior permission in writing of the publishers, or in the case of reprographic reproduction in accordance with the terms and licenses issued by the CLA. Enquiries concerning reproduction outside these terms should be sent to the publishers at the undermentioned address:

ISTE Ltd
27-37 St George's Road
London SW19 4EU
UK

www.iste.co.uk

John Wiley & Sons, Inc.
111 River Street
Hoboken, NJ 07030
USA

www.wiley.com

© ISTE Ltd 2016
The rights of Nicolas Durand, David Gianazza, Jean-Baptiste Gotteland and Jean-Marc Alliot to be identified as the authors of this work have been asserted by them in accordance with the Copyright, Designs and Patents Act 1988.

Library of Congress Control Number: 2015955801

British Library Cataloguing-in-Publication Data
A CIP record for this book is available from the British Library
ISBN 978-1-84821-810-9

Contents

Introduction

Metaheuristics are methods designed to address difficult optimization problems[1]. The term "metaheuristic", coined by Glover when introducing his tabu search method, refers to high-level strategies guiding lower-level heuristics in the search of optimal or near-optimal solutions. Today, metaheuristics cover a wide range of methods that can be categorized in many different ways: population-based or single-solution, mono-objective or multi-objective, nature- or physics-inspired algorithms, hybrid metaheuristics, etc. These categories may overlap. Population-based metaheuristics, for example, include some nature-inspired methods, such as genetic algorithms or particle swarm optimization algorithms. The simulated annealing algorithm, inspired by the annealing process in metallurgy, is an example of metaheuristic iterating on a single individual. Other examples of single-individual metaheuristics include the tabu search, iterated local search and variable neighborhood search.

Many metaheuristics are iterative stochastic methods, in the sense that they rely on some kind of random walk to explore the search space. They also implement a form of "intelligent bias" toward good solutions, based on the evaluation of the objective function at the points sampled during the search. A typical example is the selection of the best-fit individuals in evolutionary algorithms. Another example is the deterministic selection in the differential evolution algorithm: a candidate individual (trial vector) replaces the current individual only if this improves the evaluation of the objective function. Such a mechanism can be viewed as a "greedy" strategy whose aim is to find a better solution as quickly as possible. In addition to randomness and greediness, a third component that may appear in metaheuristics is memory. The promising zones encountered during the search can be memorized so as to intensify the search in these areas. Conversely, non-promising zones can be

1 Large-scale and/or NP-hard problems. In computational complexity theory, the abbreviation NP refers to "non-determistic polynomial-time".

forbidden, as in the tabu search, so as to force the algorithm to explore other areas (diversification).

Beyond the mind-catching analogies with real-world phenomena such as the natural evolution, annealing process, bee swarms, ant colonies or bacterial foraging, it is the right mix of these three components – randomness, greediness and memory – that allows metaheuristics to find a good balance between intensification and diversification of the search. As opposed to exact optimization methods, metaheuristics do not guarantee the optimality of the solutions found. They are, however, powerful tools to tackle difficult problems where other methods fail.

Air traffic management (ATM) is an endless source of challenging optimization problems. Between the moment passengers board the aircraft and the moment they arrive at their destination, a flight goes through several phases: pushback at the gate, taxiing between the gate and the runway threshold, takeoff and initial climb following standard instrument departure procedure, cruise, final descent following standard terminal arrival route, landing on the runway and taxiing to the gate. During each phase, the flight is handled by air traffic control organizations: airport ground control, approach and terminal control and en route control. These control organizations provide services ensuring a safe and efficient conduct of flights, from departure to arrival.

The core of the air traffic controllers' activity is to facilitate the traffic flow through the airspace sectors and on the airport ground surfaces under their responsibility, while avoiding collisions between aircraft. To satisfy this essential safety constraint, they must detect and solve conflicts between trajectories. Such conflicts may occur at any time of the flight, during taxi, takeoff, climb, cruise, descent or landing. The underlying constrained optimization problem is to minimize the deviations from the nominal trajectories while maintaining horizontal or vertical separations between conflicting aircraft. For an airborne aircraft, the air traffic controller can order different types of maneuvers to pilots: horizontal deviations, vertical maneuvers, modified rate of climb or descent or speed adjustments. Conflicts related to runway occupancy can be solved only by optimizing the landing and takeoff sequences. When aircraft are taxiing on the ground, conflict resolution can be achieved by choosing different paths or by making aircraft wait on some taxiways. An additional constraint may then occur: flights must respect their takeoff slots. These slots are traffic regulations enforced by ATM so as to avoid congestion in en route sectors or terminal areas, or at the destination airport. Congestion is actually related to excessive controller workload in some parts of the ATM system. This workload can be alleviated or balanced by several means. One of them is to delay departing flights by allocating takeoff slots. Another is to reroute some flights so as to avoid the congested areas. In addition, the airspace sectors and airways can be designed and managed so as to facilitate traffic flows and alleviate controller workload as much as possible. Strategic activities such as airspace and air route network design are conducted months before the day of operation. The assignment of airspace sectors to controller working positions and the traffic regulation measures – slot allocations and traffic rerouting – can be prepared hours in advance, but they must be adapted in real time considering the effective workload undergone by the controllers.

Several optimization problems have been evoked in this short introduction to ATM: optimal sector design and airways positioning, optimal allocation of airspace sectors to controller working positions, takeoff slot allocation, runway sequencing, conflict resolution for taxiing or airborne aircraft. They are often difficult to model and hard to solve. When building models, one must consider the complexity of the system and the multiple sources of uncertainties (e.g. weather, unknown aircraft parameters and unexpected delays). The problems to solve are not always easy to formulate because they are often complex combinations of interdependent subproblems. In many cases, the size and complexity of the problems being addressed make them hard or even impossible to solve with exact methods.

In this book, we present several applications of metaheuristics to difficult ATM problems. Although metaheuristics applied to ATM is the main focus of this book, we have also tried to present a few cases where specific ATM problems can actually be addressed using other methods, such as computational geometry, clustering techniques, exact tree-search methods and machine learning approaches. We hope this will highlight the advantages and limitations of the different approaches proposed in the literature and by the authors of this book. This should also bring the reader a broader view of what kind of methods can be applied to what problem, sometimes with different problem formulations. In several cases, researchers have proposed hybrid methods combining metaheuristics with exact or heuristic methods to tackle specific problems. Although metaheuristics are not supposed to be problem-specific in general, we will see that real-world problems do sometimes require to replace standard operators – such as mutation or crossover for example, in the case of a genetic algorithm – by problem-specific and possibly hybrid operators.

The book is organized as follows. Chapter 1 describes the ATM context in more detail. The other chapters deal with the different categories of ATM problems being addressed: optimization of air routes (Chapter 2), airspace management (Chapter 3), departure slot allocation (Chapter 4), airport traffic management (Chapter 5) and conflict detection and resolution for airborne aircraft (Chapter 6).

1

The Context of Air Traffic Management

This chapter is a short introduction to the air traffic management operational context.

1.1. Introduction

The aim of this chapter is to present clearly and concisely the current air traffic management (ATM) system, so that readers who are not familiar with it can understand the problems being addressed in this book. More detailed information on the rules and organization in ATM can be found in specific documentations such as [INT 01, INT 08], published by the International Civil Aviation Organization (ICAO).

ATM covers a wide range of activities, including air traffic control (ATC) in which ground-based controllers monitor aircraft and issue instructions to pilots in order to avoid collisions. Between the moment passengers board the aircraft and the moment they arrive at their destination, a flight goes through several phases: push back at the gate, taxiing between the gate and the runway, takeoff and initial climb following standard instrument departure procedure, cruise, final descent following standard terminal arrival route, landing on the runway and taxiing to the gate. During each phase, the flight is handled by ATC organizations: airport ground control, approach and terminal control and en route control. These control organizations provide services ensuring a safe and efficient conduct of flights, from departure to arrival.

The ATM system is highly complex. It handles a huge number of flights and involves many actors: airlines, air navigation service providers (ANSP), airports, national and international regulatory authorities, etc. In 2013, the ATM system controlled 9.6 million flights operating under instrumental flight rules (IFR) in

Europe and 15.1 million in the United States. The Federal Aviation Administration estimates that its National Airspace System is in charge of 4,000–6,000 flights simultaneously[1] during peak hours.

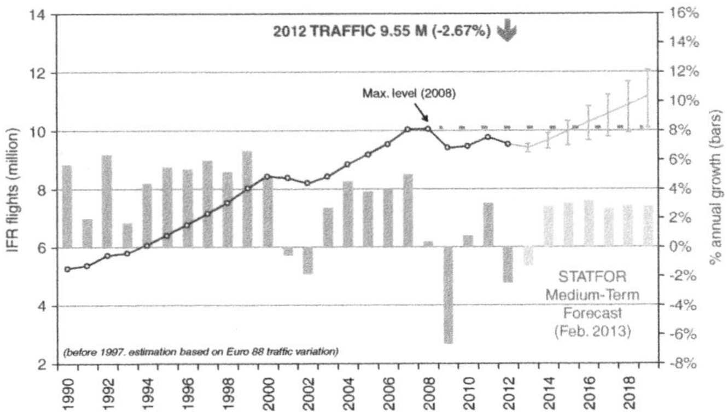

Sources Eurocontrol/Statfor (ESRA2008).

Figure 1.1. *Air traffic forecast in Europe*

In terms of future evolutions, the Asia-Pacific region is anticipated to undergo a rapid growth in traffic volume. In North America and Europe, the growth rate is expected to weaken. However, the global trend still points toward a traffic increase, as shown in Figure 1.1.

1.2. Vocabulary and units

The aviation community uses specific units and a specific vocabulary that needs to be introduced before describing the ATM system. An index of acronyms can be found at the end of the book.

Altitudes are expressed in feet (ft), or in flight levels (FL), with 1 FL $=$ 100 ft. There are several definitions of altitude, but the most widely used is the geopotential pressure altitude, computed from the static air pressure p measured onboard the aircraft. FL are defined in reference to the isobar surface $p_0 = 1,013.25$ hPa.

Distances are expressed in nautical miles (NM), with 1 NM $= 1,852$ m. Velocities are expressed in knots (kts), with 1 kts $=$ 1 NM/h.

The aircraft speed in the air is measured through dynamic pressure sensors. The true airspeed (TAS) is the actual aircraft speed in the air. The calibrated airspeed

1 http://www.fly.faa.gov/Products/Information/information.html.

(CAS) is the TAS that would be necessary at mean sea level to obtain the same dynamic pressure than that measured onboard the aircraft. If we neglect the instrument errors, the CAS is the speed used by pilots when operating their flight, together with the Mach number, which is the ratio of the TAS and the speed of sound in the air. Typically, a climbing aircraft will follow several climb segments at constant CAS, followed by a climb segment at constant Mach number, at high altitudes.

Aircraft fly in the air, and the air is in movement above the Earth's surface. We also define velocity relative to the Earth's surface, called the ground speed, expressed in knots.

1.3. Missions and actors of the air traffic management system

The objective of ATM is to ensure safe and efficient flights, from departure to arrival. This mission is carried out by a number of national or international organizations that provide different services to the airspace users.

There are different kinds of airspace users. General air traffic includes commercial flights, private flights for leisure or for affairs, special flights for geographic data collection, meteorological studies or any other scientific study, drones, gliders, aeromodelling, etc. Military air traffic includes flights with specific missions such as flight combat training, surveillance and in-flight refueling, and other military missions.

Several kinds of services can be provided to the users:

– ATC services: 1) prevent collisions between airborne aircraft; 2) on the ground between aircraft and obstacles; 3) organize and expedite air traffic flows;

– flight information services provide useful information and advice to ease safe and efficient traffic;

– alerting services notify relevant organizations regarding aircraft in need of search and rescue aid, and assist such organizations as required.

While information services are not responsible for trajectory separation, control services are. Therefore, air traffic controllers issue instructions to pilots to maneuver the aircraft laterally, vertically or by adjusting speed or rate of climb/descent. When only the flight information service is provided, pilots take charge of collision avoidance.

The control, information and alert services are provided to users by ANSP. There are many actors interacting with one another in the ATM system: airports, air traffic control centers (ATCCs), airline operators, national and international regulatory authorities, military control centers and authorities, meteorological services, etc.

In order to avoid airspace or airport congestion, it is necessary to organize and regulate the traffic flows. This continental-scale network management is carried out in Europe by the Eurocontrol Network Management Operations Center (NMOC) that enforces air traffic flow management (ATFM) regulations when required so by ATC units anticipating overloads. In the United States, this regulation takes the form of ground delay programs (GDPs) concerning each one or several airports in a same area. These GDPs are coordinated by the Air Traffic Control Strategic Command Center (ATCSCC). Similar organizations exist in other parts of the world where the traffic is dense enough to require such flow regulations.

1.4. Visual flight rules and instrumental flight rules

Flights can be separated into two categories, depending on the level of equipment of the aircraft and level of qualification of the pilots. A flight may operate under visual flight rules (VFR) or instrumental flight rules (IFR).

Under VFR, the pilot must maintain a sufficient distance to the neighboring clouds and obstacles. He/she can fly only if the meteorological conditions are compatible with VFR, especially concerning the visibility. These flight rules are designed for light aviation, where the basic "see and avoid" principle is applied to maintain separation from other aircraft.

IFR are less hampered by degraded meteorological conditions. Because IFR flights are allowed to fly in low visibility conditions, they are generally controlled by an ATC unit that is in charge of ensuring separation from other IFR or VFR flights.

1.5. Airspace classes

Several classes of airspace (from A to G) determine which services are provided to which types of flight. For example, only IFR flights can fly in Class A airspace, where the ATC service is provided to all IFR flights. In Class B airspace, IFR and VFR flights are admitted. The control service is provided to all flights and separation from other aircraft in ensured for all flights (IFR and VFR). Both IFR and VFR flights are allowed to fly in Class C airspace. However, separation from other aircraft is only ensured for IFR/VFR or IFR/IFR pairs. VFR flights are separated from IFR flights, but they only receive flight information relative to the other VFR flights and must ensure their own separation from these VFR flights. The following classes are similarly defined, with less and less services provided to flights. In Class G airspace, only the flight information service is provided and only for the flights that request it.

1.6. Airspace organization and management

1.6.1. *Flight information regions and functional airspace blocks*

Flight information regions (FIRs) are managerial divisions of the airspace into large regions where the air navigation services (control, information, alerting) are provided to airspace users. FIRs cover the totality of the Earth's atmosphere. In some countries, there is only one FIR covering all the airspace within their borders. This is not always the case, however. Some countries may have their national airspace included in a wider FIR covering neighboring countries. Other countries have divided their airspace into several FIRs. This is the case in France, for example, where the national airspace is divided into five FIRs. Figure 1.2 shows the airspace partitioning into FIRs in Europe.

Source Eurocontrol

Figure 1.2. *FIRs in Europe*

The FIR boundaries are designed by the national authorities. Some FIRs are split vertically. In such cases, the lower part keeps the name FIR whereas the upper part is called an upper information region (UIR).

As a consequence of Europe's history, a great number of FIRs cover the European territory. The Single European Sky legislative package aims at harmonizing the ATM system, making it less dependent on the national boundaries. For that purpose, FIRs covering different national airspaces are grouped into larger units, called functional airspace blocks (FABs). Figure 1.3 shows the FABs in Europe. For the time being, the different FIRs within an FAB are not fully integrated yet, but there is a closer coordination of the ANSP within a same FAB.

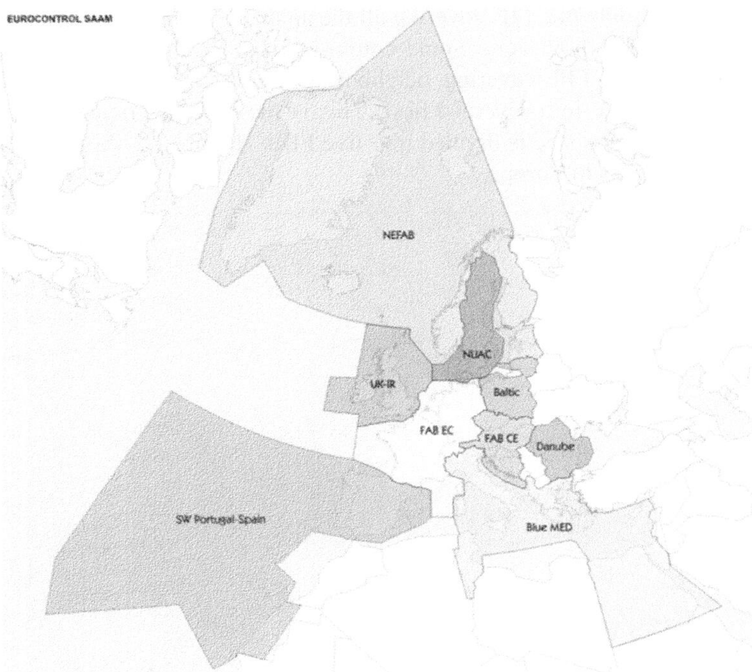

Source Eurocontrol

Figure 1.3. *Functional airspace blocks in Europe. For a color version of the figure, see www.iste.co.uk/durand/atm.zip*

1.6.2. *Lower and upper airspace*

In Europe, the airspace is split vertically, defining a lower airspace and an upper airspace. The boundary between upper and lower airspace is usually at FL 195, which means a pressure altitude of 19, 500 above isobar 1, 013.25 hPa. However, in some countries, lower and upper airspace may be divided at a different FL. For example the UIR of the Maastricht control center, which is in charge of the airspace above Belgium, Luxembourg and the north west of Germany, starts at FL 245. In France, there is only one UIR, above FL 195, and five FIRs below FL 195, although in practice the portion of upper airspace above each FIR is controlled by the ATCC in charge of this FIR. In the United States, there is no UIR but the upper airspace sectors start at FL 240.

1.6.3. *Controlled airspace: en route, approach or airport control*

In the airspace where control services are provided to users, some volumes are dedicated to aircraft flying in the vicinity of airports, and some others are dedicated to en route flight between departure and destination.

The airspace volume around the airport is a control zone (CTR) for aircraft flying at low altitude, close to the airport runway. Above the CTR, a larger zone called terminal maneuvering area (TMA) in Europe or terminal control area (TCA) in the United States is dedicated to aircraft following arrival or departure procedures. It may cover several airports, in dense areas. Figure 1.4 shows the Paris TMA, as an example of such zones, with top and side views illustrating the airspace classes for each volume of airspace in the TMA.

The TMA (or TCA) is a transition between airports and the network of airways defined in the en route airspace. To summarize, there are different types of control activities, depending on the airspace volume being controlled:

– airport control, which includes tower control for runway operations and ground control for aircraft taxiing on the airport surface;

– approach control, for departure and arrival procedures;

– en route control, for flights following airways from departure to destination.

These three kinds of control activities are illustrated in Figure 1.5, where some radio-navigation aids, radars and communication equipment are also shown. A control tower and an en route ATCC are also represented. The control tower is in charge of aircraft separation in the neighborhood of the runway. It sequences takeoffs and landings, and prevents collisions of aircraft taxiing between the gates and the runway. The ATCC is in charge of en route traffic. The approach control service can be provided by an ATC unit located on or near the airport, for big airports, or the regional ATCC center, for small airports.

1.6.4. *Air route network and airspace sectoring*

Aircraft flying in the lower or upper en route controlled airspace follow predefined airways. The air route networks might be different in the upper and lower airspaces. Aircraft can deviate from their intended routes when instructed so by air traffic controllers, in order to keep separation with other aircraft or to avoid convective weather.

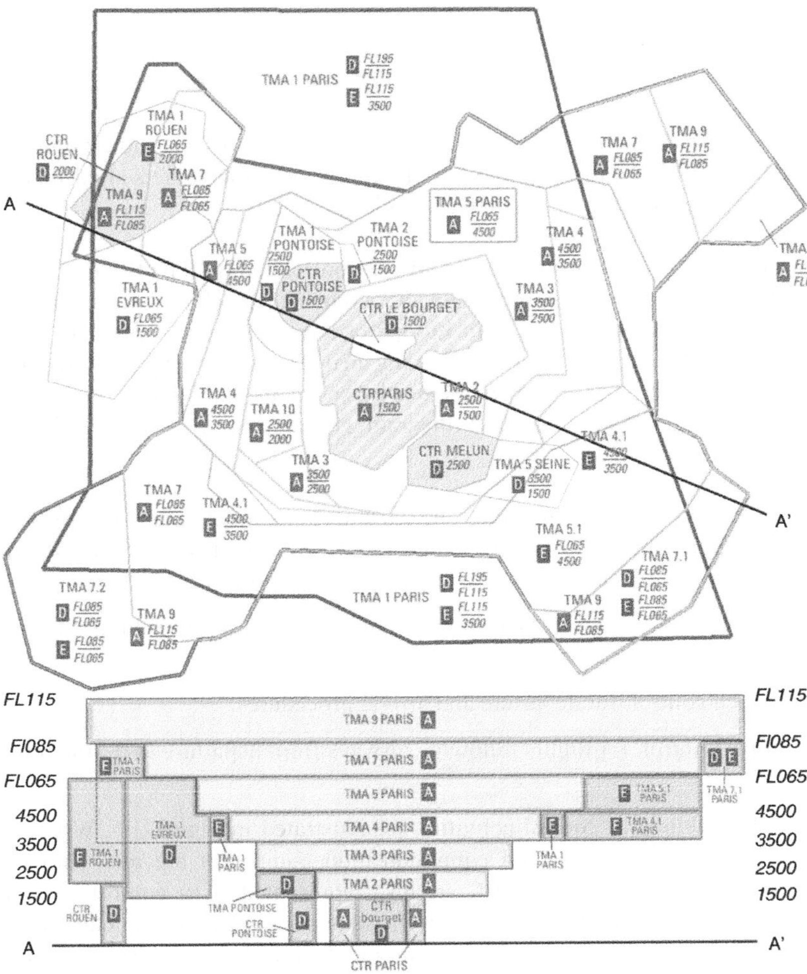

Source DGAC/SIA

Figure 1.4. *Top and sectional view of Paris TMA (2011). For a color version of the figure, see www.iste.co.uk/durand/atm.zip*

As a human controller can only handle a limited amount of traffic, the airspace is divided into sectors, which can be seen as the smallest airspace unit. An air traffic controller is only in charge of the traffic flying through the airspace sectors assigned to its working position.

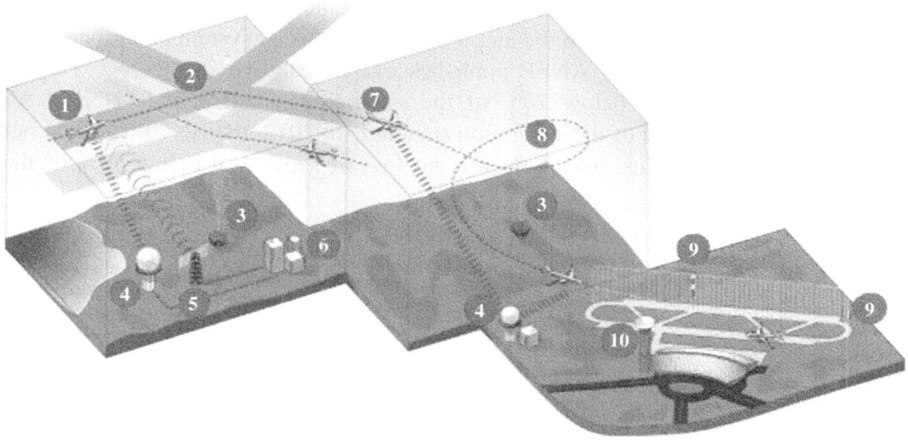

Source http://www.developpement-durable.gouv.fr/Controle-aerien,10109.html

1 Aircraft entering an en route sector
2 Airway
3 Radio-navigation aid
4 Mono-pulse radar
5 Two-way radio transmitter
6 ATCC
7 Aircraft entering an approach sector
8 Holding stack
9 Instrument landing system (ILS)
10 Control tower and ground radar

Figure 1.5. *En route, approach and airport control. For a color version of the figure, see www.iste.co.uk/durand/atm.zip*

Figure 1.6 shows both the air route network and the airspace sectors in Europe, in the upper airspace.

1.7. Traffic separation

1.7.1. *Separation standard, loss of separation*

One of the core tasks of the air traffic controller is to avoid collisions between aircraft. For that purpose, he/she must make sure that all aircraft are separated at all times by a distance greater than a given distance, called the separation standard. Any pair of aircraft must maintain a lateral separation of at least δ_ℓ, or a vertical separation of at least δ_z. These separation standards can take different values, depending for example on the radar and radio coverage in the airspace where the aircraft fly.

Typical values for the radar separations in the European en route airspace is 5 NM laterally and $1,000$ ft vertically. These separations, which may look large, consider the position uncertainties due to radar detection, the navigation errors and the delays in the processing of the radar information, between the actual radar detection and the position display on the controller's screen.

Losses of separations are critical events in ATC. When they occur such events are analyzed by the authorities, with the aim to improve the ATC system and procedures. As an example, the French ANSP publishes every year two indicators, "HN70" counting the separations below 70% of the separation standard and "HN50" for separations less than half of the separation standard. In 2012, the HN70 was 0.64 per 100,000 controlled flights, and there was no loss of separation below 50% of the separation standard.

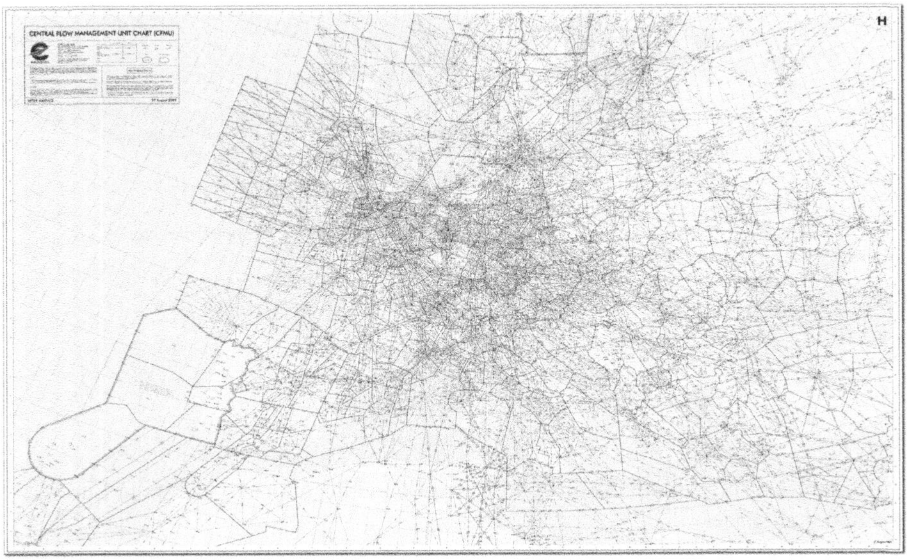

Source Eurocontrol

Figure 1.6. *Routes and airspace sectors in Europe (2009), in the upper airspace. For a color version of the figure, see www.iste.co.uk/durand/atm.zip*

Safety culture is widespread in the civil aviation environment. When they consider that the safety of a flight has been put at risk, controllers or ground-based agents can file a report. Pilots can also file "airprox" reports. These incidents are systematically processed and analyzed by the authorities in order to continuously improve the procedures and the air traffic safety. In 2012, the French ANSP reported 1 airprox per 100,000 flights, involving at least one IFR flight and no military aircraft, and 0.3 airprox per 100,000 flights, involving a military and a civil aircraft.

1.7.2. *Conflict detection and resolution*

In order to avoid losses of separation, air traffic controllers monitor aircraft trajectories and give instructions to pilots to maneuver the aircraft when they anticipate a loss of separation. A conflict can be defined as an anticipated loss of separation between the future trajectories of two aircraft, as illustrated by Figure 1.7. Mathematically, two aircraft i and j are in conflict when $\exists t$ such that:

$$d_\ell(i,j,t) \leq \delta_\ell \quad \wedge \quad d_z(i,j,t) \leq \delta_z$$

where δ_ℓ and δ_z are the lateral and vertical separation standards (e.g. 5 NM laterally and 1,000 ft vertically).

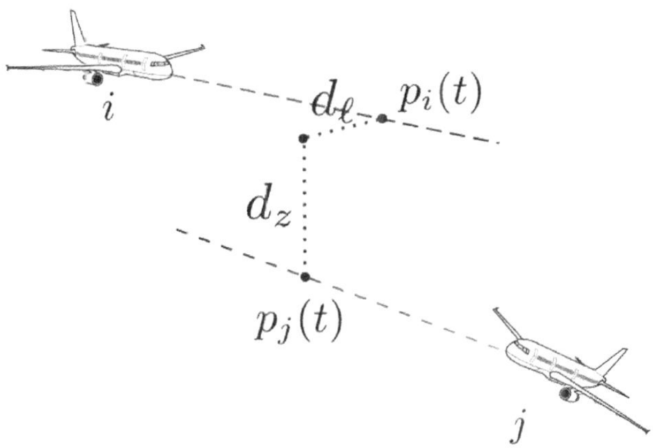

Figure 1.7. *Aircraft conflict*

In practice, the notion of conflict can cover traffic situations involving more than two aircraft (see Figure 1.8), for example when an aircraft is in conflict with another, which is itself in conflict with a third aircraft. Such situations are called n-aircraft conflicts, assuming n is the number of aircraft involved. Such extended conflicts can be formalized as closures of the relationship "is in conflict with". In some publications, the term conflict denotes only a potential loss of separation between two aircraft, whereas the "n-aircraft conflicts" are called clusters, so as to make a clear distinction between the two notions.

The maneuvers instructed to pilots by controllers can be of several types: heading or altitude change, climb/descent interruption at an intermediate level, speed regulation, holding pattern start at a given position, etc. These instructions are transmitted to pilots by radio.

1.7.3. *The distribution of tasks among controllers*

The "radar controller" (R-side) monitors aircraft trajectories on a "radar display" and gives instructions to pilots. He is also called "tactical controller", or "executive controller". He/she is assisted by a "planning controller", or "data controller" (D-side), who predetects potential conflicts between incoming flights and coordinates flights with adjacent sectors.

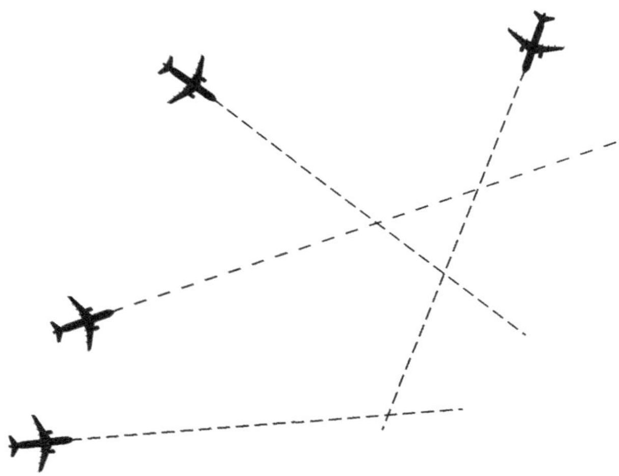

Figure 1.8. *An example of 4-aircraft conflict (cluster)*

In several countries, radar and planning controllers operate in tandem on the same ATC sector. With the emergence of new technologies and new computer-assisted control tools that are being developed, a new distribution of tasks is being discussed in the European and American modernization programs of the ATM/ATC systems. One of the possibilities being discussed is to introduce a "multisector planner" that could either act as a planning controller for several radar controllers or organize the traffic in advance for the benefit of several ATC sectors, using short- to medium- term traffic and workload forecasts.

1.7.4. *The controller tools*

The controller uses a number of tools to perform his/her tasks. One of them is the radar screen where the aircraft positions and velocities are displayed, together with the sector boundaries, routes and other relevant information. Controllers also use strips containing all necessary information relative to a flight: departure and arrival airport, route, times over waypoints, etc. Former paper strips are now being replaced by electronic strips or stripless environment. The other equipment that can be found on a controller working position are radiocommunication and telephone equipment, some input/output devices allowing the controllers to receive, display and modify flight data and screens displaying meteorological data and other relevant information.

A radio frequency is allocated to each airspace sector. Telephone lines and radio frequencies can be switched from one controller working position to another, allowing the control room manager to dynamically assign airspace sectors to controller working positions.

1.8. Traffic regulation

A key issue for air traffic safety is to avoid overloading air traffic controllers. The traffic level in any opened ATC sector should remain acceptable for a human being. This constraint determines the capacity of the ATM system to accommodate the traffic demand in a given environment (meteorological conditions, level of equipment, type of traffic, etc.). In this section, we briefly introduce the different measures and procedures that aim at avoiding overloads while trying to match capacity and demand as much as possible.

These measures and procedures are applied in advance, before the aircraft enter the ATC sector that might get overloaded, with an advance notice depending on the type of measure being taken. Strategic planning is mostly concerned with the route network and airspace design, and takes place well in advance. Pre-tactical planning, such as staff changes and flow regulation measures, usually takes place one or two days before, or a few hours in advance. Tactical measures such as flight rerouting due to severe weather are decided in real time.

1.8.1. *Capacity and demand*

Capacity and demand are defined as follows in the ICAO documentation [INT 08]:

– *Capacity*: The maximum number of aircraft that can be accommodated in a given time period by the system or one of its components (throughput).

– *Demand*: The number of aircraft requesting to use the ATM system in a given time period.

With these definitions, capacity and demand can be quantified in a number of different ways, depending on the context. The mathematical expression of the capacity will not be the same when considering the ATM subsystems at various geographical scales (airspace sector, FIR, FAB) and with different time periods (e.g. one hour, one day or one year). As a consequence, there is a multitude of formal definitions for capacity, depending on the context and purpose.

Among the multiple uses of this rather vague notion of capacity, let us cite the strategic design of airspace sectors and FABs, or the performance evaluation of ANSP. In pre-tactical applications, the notion of capacity can be used to regulate the traffic flows by allocating delays to departing aircraft so as not to exceed capacity in airspace sectors. The ATCC capacity can also be adapted to better match the demand by modifying the staff roster. Capacities can also be used and adjusted in real time, for example when an airport capacities (arrival and departure rates) are decreased due to bad weather.

These few examples show the diversity of objectives, of geographical and temporal scales, in the use of the notion of capacity. A direct consequence of this diversity is that there is no unique mathematical definition of capacity.

The same remark is true for the traffic demand, which can be quantified in many ways: density (number of aircraft within the sector boundaries at time t), entry counts (number of aircraft entering the sector in a given time period), occupancy counts (number of flights occupying the sector in a given time period), number of repetitive flight plans over a year, number of aircraft requesting takeoff, or landing, etc.

At the beginning of this section, we have outlined the need to avoid overloading air traffic controllers. However, the notion of workload is not explicitly mentioned in the ICAO definition of capacity, although we can guess that there is a relationship between the workload perceived by controllers and the maximum number of aircraft that can be accommodated, as mentioned in the ICAO definition. The reason why workload is not explicitly mentioned is related to the difficulty to quantify the actual controller workload. We shall see in section 1.8.2 that several factors, such as the traffic complexity or the sector complexity, impact the controller workload. Considering these factors when estimating workload and capacity has been a recent development in ATM research, with the aim to introduce more accurate metrics. Currently, very simple metrics are still being used in operations to roughly adjust the traffic variable to the capacity constraints.

The ATM organizations in charge of traffic flow regulation use declared capacities, provided by the ATCCs or airports, to enforce ATFM measures (in Europe) or GDPs (in the United States). Such measures consist of delaying departing aircraft or rerouting some flights so as to avoid to exceed the capacities declared by the ATC units. This declared capacity can be seen as an acceptable compromise between the delays imposed to the airlines and the workload incurred by air traffic controllers.

1.8.2. *Workload and air traffic control complexity*

Capacity is related to a workload threshold that should not be exceeded by air traffic controllers. Controller workload can be defined as the amount of physical and mental work done by the controller to perform his/her tasks [MAJ 02]. In this same publication [MAJ 02], Majumdar and Ochieng wrote that the term "controller workload" is subject to confusion, and to a multitude of definitions, models and metrics proposed in the literature.

In practice, the controller workload can vary significantly, for a same number of flights, depending on dynamic factors related to the traffic and static factors related to the sector geometry and route network. An additional factor is the operational procedures that air traffic controllers must follow when handling the traffic in their sector.

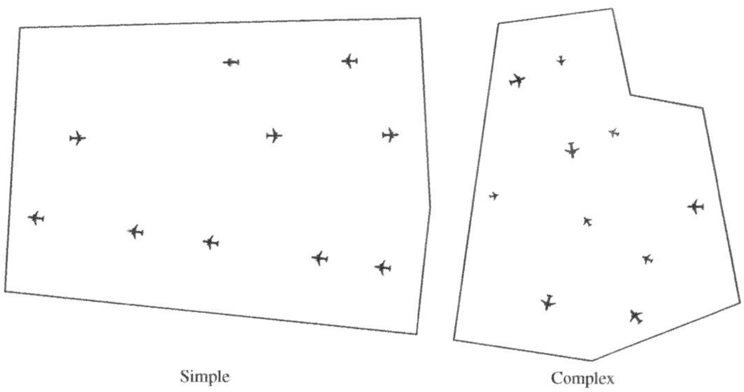

Figure 1.9. *Intuitive approach of ATC complexity*

The influence of traffic and sector complexity is illustrated in Figure 1.9, assuming the aircraft size in this figure is related to its speed. Intuitively, we can expect the traffic situation on the left, with aircraft at the same speed following routes that do not cross, to be much easier to handle than the traffic situation on the right, with various speeds and many crossing trajectories. Adding the vertical dimension, we can also have all flights cruising at separate constant FL, or we can have many climbing or descending aircraft that cross other traffic cruising at a constant FL.

Other factors related to the human operator and its environment can impact the controller workload. Figure 1.10, taken from [MOG 95], shows how controller workload is affected by source factors related to ATC complexity and mediating factors related to the controller and its equipment. Mogford *et al.* [MOG 95] defined ATC complexity as "a multidimensional construct that includes static sector characteristics (sector complexity) and dynamic traffic patterns (traffic complexity)". The reader can refer to [MOG 95, HIL 04] and their bibliography for a literature review on ATC complexity.

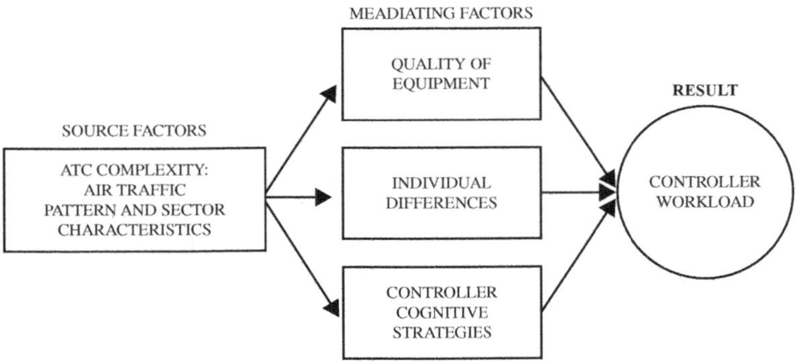

Source Mogford et al. [MOG 95]

Figure 1.10. *Factors impacting the air traffic controller workload.*

1.9. Airspace management in en route air traffic control centers

1.9.1. *Operating air traffic control sectors in real time*

Several adjacent airspace sectors can be grouped together and assigned to a controller working position. Depending on the context, the term "sector" is used in the ATM community with different meanings: it may refer either to an "airspace sector", which is an elementary unit of airspace, or a "control sector" (or ATC sector), which is a volume of airspace made up of one or several airspace sectors and operated on a controller working position.

Controllers can alleviate their workload, when it becomes excessive, by transferring some of their airspace sectors to another working position. This sector splitting can be done either by opening a new working position or by merging some of the airspace sectors of the initial ATC sector with a neighboring ATC sector that is less loaded. This is possible only when the initial ATC sector is made up of several airspace sectors, and when there is enough staff to open a new position, if necessary. Conversely, when workload is low, the control room manager can decide to merge several ATC sectors that are under loaded and assign them to a single working position.

These sector merging/splitting operations give some flexibility in the capacity to accommodate the traffic demand, in real time. Of course, when an ATC sector is made up of only one airspace sector and when this ATC sector is overloaded, some other measures must be taken (traffic reroutings, for example).

Dividing the airspace sectors into even smaller sectors can alleviate the workload. However, there is a lower limit to the size of airspace sectors that can be actually operated as ATC sectors. If the sector is too small, the radar controller has not enough time and space to maneuver the aircraft, and the coordination workload of the planning controller becomes excessive.

1.9.2. *Anticipating sector openings (France and Europe)*

The duty roster and the provisional sector opening scheme are usually built in advance. They can be adapted in real time by splitting or merging sectors as explained before, but it is essential to anticipate as much as possible if staffing will be sufficient, or if some overloads are expected. Anticipating such situations well in advance allows the traffic flow managers to prepare and take preventive measures, such as delaying departing aircraft or rerouting flights, if necessary.

In order to better understand the choice of metrics that are still being used nowadays to evaluate the traffic demand and capacity in this context, it is useful to go back in time. Before 1995 in France and in other European countries, the pre-tactical planning phase used to take place one or two days in advance, in each ATCC. It consisted of collecting the list of repetitive flight plans filed by the airlines, manually counting the flights entering any given sector to estimate the traffic load in a given period of time (one hour or half-an-hour). Candidate sector configurations were then compared, and the sector opening scheme that seemed to best fit the traffic demand was then transmitted to the organization in charge of traffic flow management. At the time, it was a national flow management team, which was soon replaced by the Eurocontrol Central Flow Management Unit (CFMU), now baptized NMOC.

After 1995, when CFMU became fully operational, the preparation of sector opening schemes was done by the flow management positions (FMPs) installed in each European ATCC. Some computer tools replaced the pen and paper that were used before. The Human Machine Interface (HMI) of a prototype of such tools is shown in Figure 1.11. This HMI displays a table where the columns are time slices of one hour, and the lines are ATC sectors. There are two numbers in the cells associated with ATC sectors that are planned to be opened: the number of flights entering the sectors in the hour (left) and the sector capacity (right).

Actually, Figure 1.11 does not show a provisional sector opening scheme. It matches the sector openings that actually occurred that day with the initial traffic demand. The first two lines of the table show the number of controller working positions that were actually opened (first line) and the number that was planned in the provisional sector opening scheme (second line) transmitted to the CFMU. We can observe that there are big differences between these numbers. If we look more closely at the colored cells representing ATC sectors that were actually opened, we can see that several of them are red or black, which indicates that the traffic demand, expressed as the flow of aircraft entering the sector within the hour, exceeds the declared sector capacity, which is a threshold value that should not be exceeded, in theory. This comparison shows the difference between what was planned and what actually occurred on that day. It questions the quality of the prediction that was made concerning the sector opening scheme based on the incoming traffic flows and sector capacities.

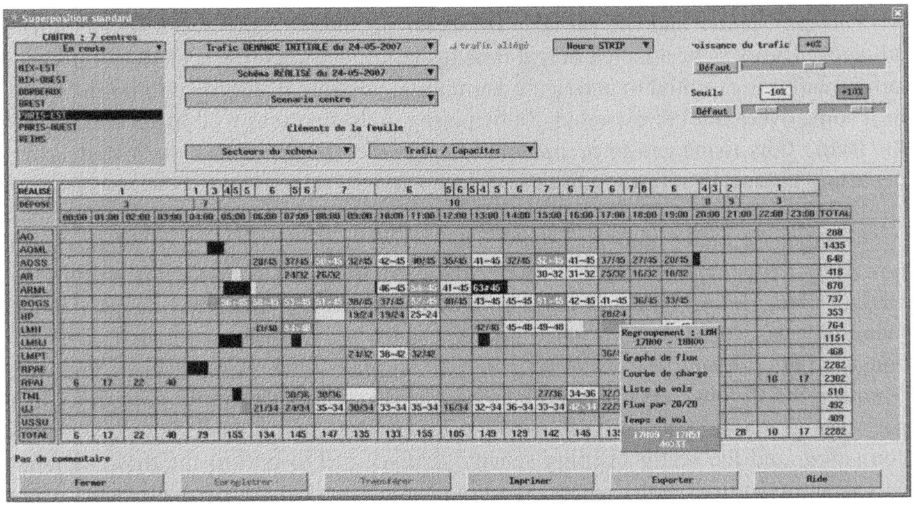

Source DGAC/DSNA

Figure 1.11. *Example of an HMI displaying sector opening schemes. For a color version of the figure, see www.iste.co.uk/durand/atm.zip*

Since 2011, a few other metrics have been introduced in the new tools for short-term ATFM used by the FMP operators. In addition, instead of a unique capacity, there are now several monitoring values representing different kinds of thresholds (peak, average, etc.), as shown in Figure 1.12 for the occupancy count.

This recent evolution is probably just the consequence of the recent awareness that incoming flows and sector capacities are poor indicators of the actual controller workload. This is well known by air traffic controllers. This may also be the result of a slow dissemination of the research works on ATC complexity and air traffic controller workload.

However, the current method to build sector opening schemes remains manual, although it is assisted with some computer tools. The FMP operator still chooses the successive ATC sector configurations among a small number of predefined configurations. Figure 1.13 gives an example of a provisional sector opening scheme for the ATCC of Zagreb (Croatia), which is made up of such predefined configurations. The FMP selects the configurations on the basis of his/her previous experience of similar traffic situations and considering the duty roster constraints.

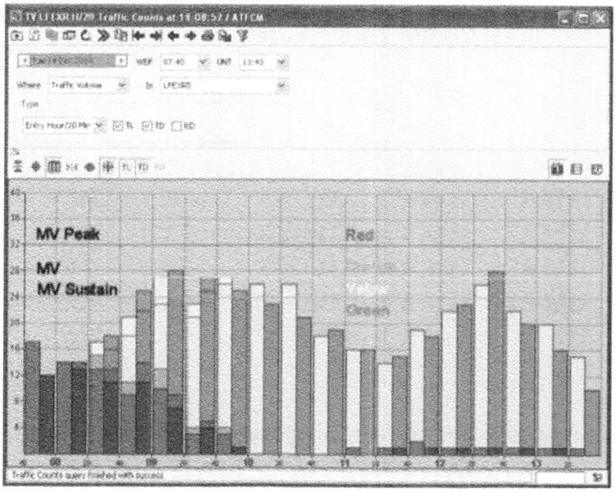

Source Eurocontrol

Figure 1.12. *"Monitoring values" for the "occupancy count" metric*

1.10. Air traffic flow management

In Europe, ATFM consists of delaying departing aircraft or rerouting flights in order to satisfy the capacity or flow constraints that have been enforced in congested areas. These traffic regulations are requested by ATC units so as to stay below the runway capacity of congested airports, for example, or to remain below the capacity of overloaded en route ATC sectors, when the workload cannot be alleviated simply by splitting or merging sectors (see section 1.9).

To be efficient, such measures must be taken well before the flights enter the areas where congestion is anticipated. They are enforced at the European level by a single actor, the European NMOC, in coordination with the FMPs of each ATCC. The network managers use the capacities declared by the ATCCs and the airports to regulate the traffic. These capacities may change across the day, depending on weather conditions, military activity, equipment failures, etc.

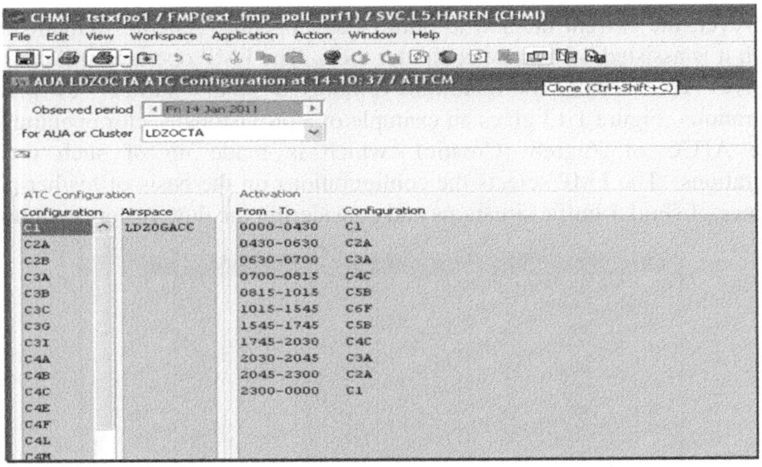

Source Eurocontrol

Figure 1.13. *Eurocontrol CHMI/CIFLO interface for FMPs*

Historically, in Europe, the en route airspace was subject to more congestion than airports. This was due to the scattering of the European airspace into a number of national airspaces, subject to a number of constraints (national borders, military areas, etc). In the United States, congestion was mostly observed at the airports whose capacities can be highly impacted by convective weather, in the airspace around the biggest metroplex. These differences can explain that researchers in Europe and in the United States sometimes focus on different subjects. This also explains why, in the United States, traffic flow management is more centered on GDPs that concern each a specific airport or terminal area, these different GDPs being coordinated by the ATCSCC.

Since the 1990s, however, these differences between Europe and the United States have tended to fade away, as airports have also become congested in Europe. The European air route network and en route airspace also follow a continuous process of harmonization and optimization, impulsed by the Single European Sky legislation, making the en route airspace comparatively less congested than it was before.

1.11. Research in air traffic management

1.11.1. *The international context*

Two major programs have taken the lead in the worldwide modernization of the ATM system: NextGen in the United States (also called NGATS for Next Generation

Air Transportation System) and SESAR (Single European Sky ATM Research) in Europe. These programs define new operational concepts based on 4D-trajectory management. They aim at harmonizing and modernizing the ATM systems, at a continental scale. They introduce new concepts such as the "business trajectory" that would be negotiated between ATC and pilots, enabling a more flexible and efficient use of the airspace while maintaining or improving the current level of safety of the ATM system.

In the proposed operational concept (see [CON 07] and [SWE 06]), the 4D-trajectory is defined as a contractual 4D-volume in which the aircraft would be free to fly, which would be negotiated between the ground control and the airline operators and pilots. The concept does not say how such conflict-free trajectories can be computed.

The implementation of this 4D-trajectory concept and other operational concepts is mainly an opportunity to involve all the actors (airlines, ANSP, industrial partners, regulatory authorities) in discussions on how to improve the current ATM system, and in the specification and development of the future tools to be deployed in the ATCCs and NMOC. In this context, scientific research on ATM problems is a marginal activity, carried out mostly in work package E "Innovative research," for the SESAR program.

1.11.2. *Research topics*

Through the quick description of the ATM system made in this chapter, we have introduced a number of topics that can be addressed as optimization problems: route network design, airspace sectoring, takeoff slot allocation, airport traffic optimization, conflict resolution.

These problems are complex and not always easy to formulate explicitly for the ATM actors, for several reasons. First, all these problems are related to one another, and ideally they should all be answered at once. For example we can avoid airspace congestion by smoothing the traffic (e.g. by delaying departing flights), but we can also address this by dynamically reassigning airspace sectors to working positions or by addressing both problems simultaneously. This gives us three different formulations for the same general problem (airspace congestion). Second, ATM relies on complex systems involving many actors from different domains, operating at different temporal horizons. Airlines, ANSP, and airports conduct different activities on the short, medium or long term. Finally, these activities undergo many uncertainties: predicting an aircraft trajectory is difficult because of errors generated by uncertainties on the weather, pilot intents and aircraft parameters. Before departure, missing luggage or passengers can generate unexpected delays on takeoffs. Dealing with uncertainties requires complex models that must be robust and reactive.

Modeling ATM problems is a difficult task in this context: if the model is too simple, it cannot handle realistic hypotheses, if it is too complex, it becomes impossible to optimize. Furthermore, when problems are correctly modeled, they are often hard to solve with exact methods because of their huge sizes.

For all these reasons, metaheuristics are generally good candidates to answer many ATM optimization problems. We will see in some examples that, sometimes, they can be less efficient than exact methods, and in some other examples that they are the best known methods.

2

Air Route Optimization

2.1. Introduction

The air route network, as it exists today, is the result of successive modifications that were made across time, taking into account some geographic and technical constraints. In the recent past, every air route was defined as a sequence of segments starting and ending at *waypoints* that had to be located at the geographic coordinates of ground-based radio-navigation aids. This is not the case anymore, as modern navigation systems can handle waypoints located almost anywhere. However, other constraints remain on the positioning of the network nodes[1]. Typically, the crossing point of two secant routes should not be too close to a sector boundary, so that there is room enough for lateral maneuvers in the vicinity of this crossing point.

The overall continuous increase of traffic since the beginning of commercial aviation has often led to rethink and redesign the routes network, at a local or global scale, and even to propose new concepts for the operation of air routes and airspace sectors. An example of such a new concept, that has been proposed several times for air traffic, is to define airways dedicated to the most important traffic flows [MAU 98, HER 05]. Such a concept is similar to the highways for ground traffic that accommodate flows of car traffic between big cities. The problem of optimally separating these airways (or 3D-tubes) in 3 dimensions is a difficult optimization problem, quite different from those associated with the 2D-representation of the route network.

We see that optimizing the air route network is a problem that can be formulated and addressed in several ways. Let us list a few of them:

– nodes and edges positioning. The route network can be seen as a planar graph in 2 dimensions for which the edges must not cross;

1 The waypoints are here considered as the nodes of the air route network. Note that a dual representation where route segments are nodes and waypoints are edges is also possible.

– nodes positioning only. Starting from an initial network (e.g. a regular grid), we can move the nodes in order to optimize a given criterion related to the traffic flow routing, while maintaining the planar graph property;

– optimal positioning of 2D-routes for the biggest traffic flows;

– in the 3rd dimension, optimal placement of separated "3D-tubes," for the biggest origin–destination flows.

2.2. 2D-route network

2.2.1. *Optimal positioning of nodes and edges using geometric algorithms*

In current operations, air traffic controllers solve conflicts occurring within the airspace volumes (sectors) of which they are in charge. The airways followed by aircraft must take this sector constraint into account: crossing points should not be near sector boundaries, and there must be enough space around each crossing point to allow for lateral maneuvers. In addition, the network must be designed so as to minimize trajectory lengthening, when compared with direct routes. Ideally, big traffic flows should be less deviated from their direct routes than small flows.

The horizontal projection of the air route network can be seen as a planar graph whose nodes are route intersections, and whose edges are route segments. The objective, when building such a network, is to position the nodes and edges so as to satisfy a distance constraint between nodes while minimizing the trajectory lengthenings for aircraft flying on the network.

The method addressing this problem, that we are now going to present, is not metaheuristic. It consists of first applying a *clustering* method to the crossing points between direct routes, then a geometric triangulation algorithm to build route segments joining the barycenters of the clusters. This method was introduced by Mehadhebi in [MEH 00] (see also [GIA 04a], in French, for the application of a similar method). It does not aim to find a global optimum to the positioning problem. However, this method can actually build a network satisfying the node separation constraint, and the solutions are of good quality, by construction, because the method is applied to an initial situation where routes are direct from origin to destination. As such, this method could be used as a baseline, in future works, when trying to apply metaheuristics to the node and edge positioning problem. This is why it is worth mentioning it here.

The aim of the *clustering* method is to position the network nodes, considering the traffic demand, so that they satisfy a minimum separation distance between nodes. For this purpose, the crossing points between direct routes are first computed, using for example a *sweep line* geometric algorithm. Then, the crossing points are clustered according to proximity criteria, so that the cluster barycenters are distant from at least a distance d_1 and that the points that are closer to a barycenter than a distance d_2 belong to the corresponding cluster. Typically, a variant of the *k-means* method can be used to compute the clusters. When computing the barycenter, weights related to the traffic flows passing through the crossing points can be used. Such weighing of the crossing points avoids moving nodes with heavy traffic too much. Figures 2.1 and 2.2 illustrate this *clustering* process, applied to the French airspace.

Once the network nodes are computed, the edges are positioned so that they do not cross (otherwise the graph would not be planar), using a geometric triangulation method. Figures 2.3 and 2.4 show the results obtained by applying the Fortune algorithm [FOR 95] to the barycenters of the clusters. This algorithm computes both a Delaunay triangulation of the set of points, and its dual graph, a Voronoï diagram.

Each polygonal cell of the Voronoï diagram is such that the points inside the cell are closer to the cell's center (i.e. a network node) than to any other barycenter. This interesting side effect of this geometric method allows us to associate a cell of airspace with each node of the network. The surface of this cell gives an indication of how much room is available in the vicinity of the node for the lateral maneuvers of conflicting aircraft.

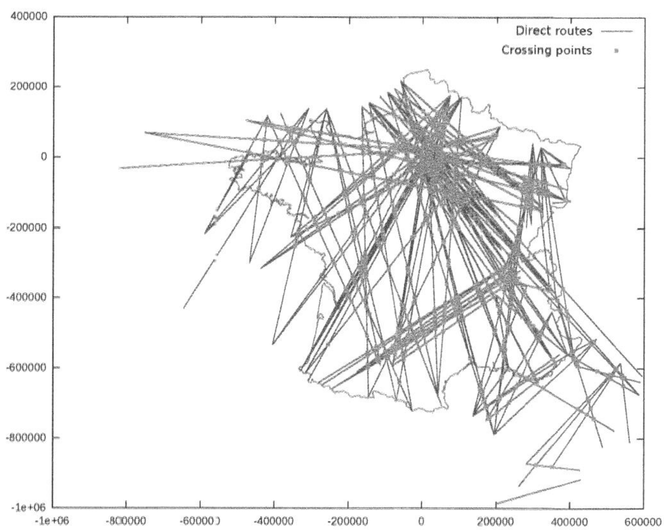

Figure 2.1. *Crossing points of the direct routes of traffic flows above 10 flights per day. For a color version of the figure, see www.iste.co.uk/durand/atm.zip*

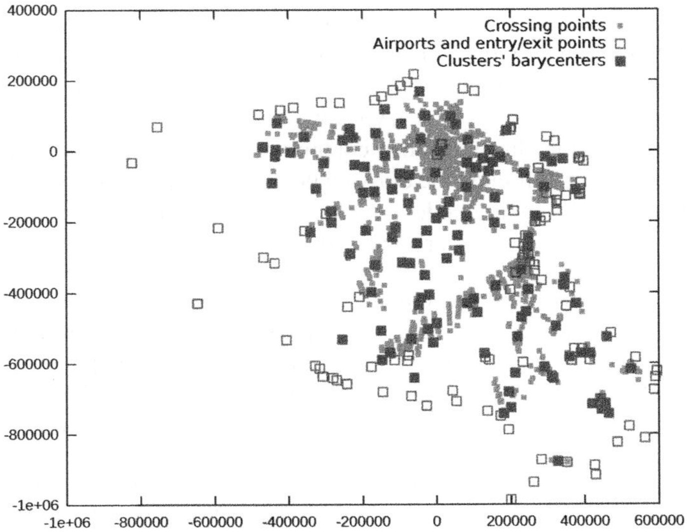

Figure 2.2. *Clustering process applied to crossing points. For a color version of the figure, see www.iste.co.uk/durand/atm.zip*

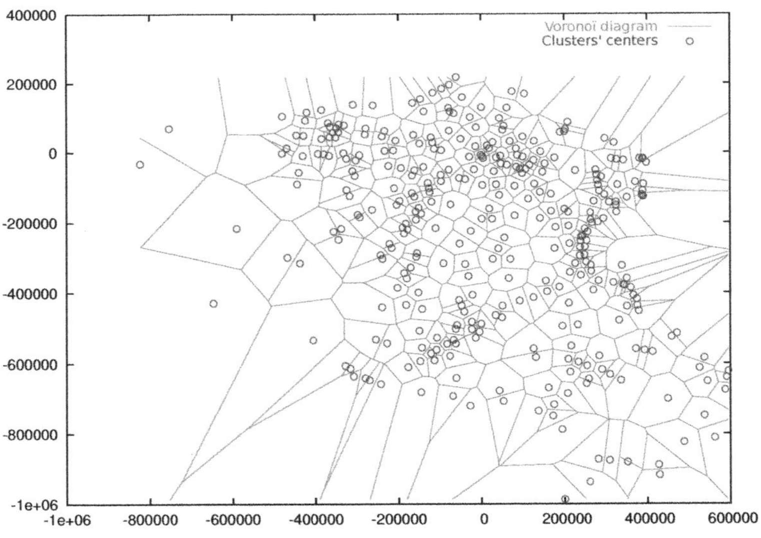

Figure 2.3. *Voronoï diagram applied to the clusters barycenters. For a color version of the figure, see www.iste.co.uk/durand/atm.zip*

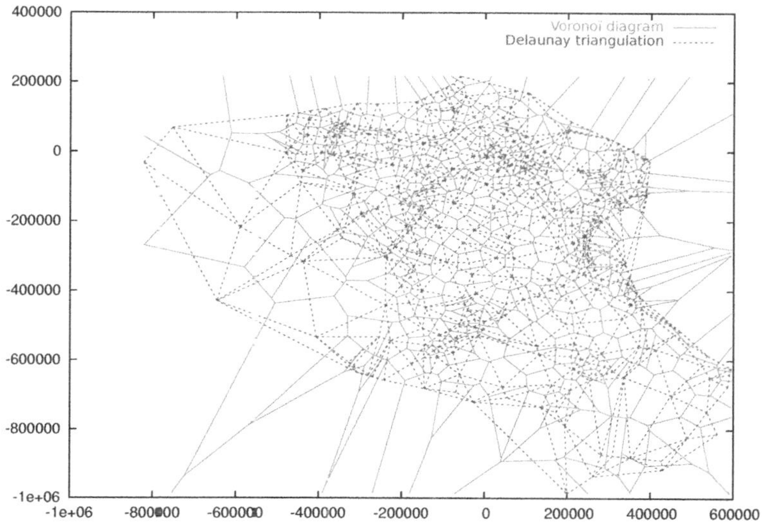

Figure 2.4. *Delaunay triangulation of the clusters barycenters. For a color version of the figure, see www.iste.co.uk/durand/atm.zip*

In [MEH 00], Mehadhebi uses the cell's surface to measure the density of conflicts. He builds a network with the aim to avoid excessive densities in the considered airspace. For each crossing point, the density is obtained by computing the ratio of a number quantifying the conflicts[2] at this crossing point and the surface of the Voronoï cell associated with the crossing point. In a dense area, moving the crossing points apart has the effect to increase the cell surfaces, thus decreasing the density. The optimization method used by Mehadhebi is not detailed in [MEH 00]. It seems to be an iterative method that locally smoothes the density in congested areas.

Once the full network (nodes and edges) is defined, the flights can choose a path in this network, from the departure airport to the destination airport. These paths must take into account a constraint on the angle between successive route segments. For any route to be actually flown by aircraft, the angle between successive segments should not be too acute. This constraint is handled differently in [MEH 00], where it is satisfied as best as possible in the *clustering* phase, and in [GIA 04a] where it is examined afterward, when searching the shortest path in the network, for each flight.

2 This conflict quantification can be for example the number of conflicts at the crossing point, weighed by the difficulty of each conflict.

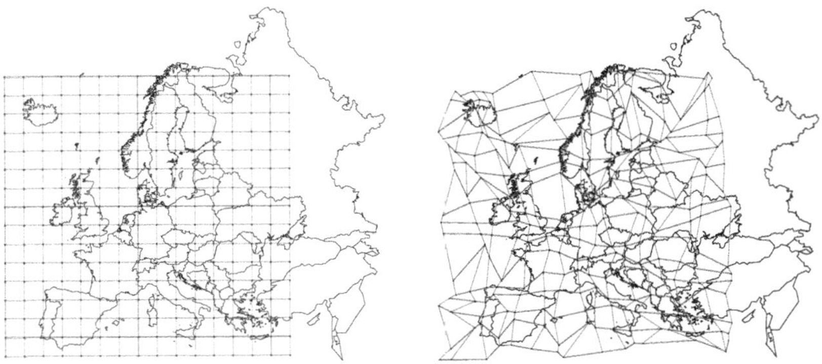

Figure 2.5. *Air route network found by a simulated annealing (right), starting from an initial regular grid (left)*

2.2.2. *Node positioning, with fixed topology, using a simulated annealing or a particle swarm optimization algorithm*

In [RIV 04], Rivière focuses on a different problem where the network topology is already fixed, and where only the node positioning problem is addressed. Starting from an initial regular grid over the European airspace, he uses a simulated annealing algorithm [KIR 83] to modify this grid, minimizing the sum of trajectory lengthenings between origin and destination. This optimization process takes account of a minimum distance that must be maintained between crossing points.

The evaluation of the trajectory-lengthening criterion requires the computation of the shortest paths in the network, between all origin–destination pairs. This is done using the Floyd–Warshall algorithm, taking account of an angle constraint between two successive route segments: this angle should not exceed 90°.

As the objective function being minimized requires the computation of the shortest paths in the network, the gradient of the objective function cannot be computed and gradient descent methods cannot be used. We must use derivative-free methods, and metaheuristics such as the simulated annealing used in [RIV 04] or the particle swarm optimization used in [CAI 12] (that we shall see later on) are a good option.

Starting from an initial point, the simulated annealing algorithm explores the search space by randomly choosing a next point in the neighborhood of the current point. The move is accepted if the new point improves the objective function. It can also be accepted if it does not, with a probability decreasing with the number of iterations (annealing scheme). In the route network design problem, a point in the search space is a route network, and a local move in the neighborhood of the current point is a random change in this network. The left part of Figure 2.5 shows the initial grid, and the right part the final grid obtained with the simulated annealing algorithm.

In more recent works [CAI 12], Cai *et al.* use an approach similar to the one of Rivière [RIV 04], but on the Chinese airspace and with a multiobjective optimization problem formulation. Two criteria are minimized in this work. The first criterion is related to the trajectory lengthenings, as in [RIV 04]. The second criterion, taken from [SID 73], is the sum over all crossing points of the average number of potential conflicts per unit of time.

The metaheuristic used in [CAI 12] is a hybrid method combining a variant of particle swarm optimization (CLPSO: comprehensive learning particle swarm optimization), introduced in [LIA 06]) and an *ad hoc* method relying on local moves of the crossing points to improve the optimized criteria.

In its canonical version, the particle swarm optimization algorithm iteratively moves a population of particles, characterized by their positions and velocities, in the search space, memorizing the best positions found by each particle. Each particle is moved in the direction of its velocity vector. After each move, the speed vector is updated, combining several directions: the current velocity vector (i.e. inertia of the particle), the direction to the best position found by the particle, and the direction to the best position found by the whole swarm (or a subset of the population). The CLPSO variant uses all the best positions found by the particles to update the velocity vector, in order to avoid a premature convergence toward a local minima.

The hybrid algorithm proposed by [CAI 12] is similar to the CLPSO, except that a local optimization is performed after updating the particles' positions and velocities. For each particle (i.e. an air route network), the local optimization tries to move each node so as to improve the chosen criteria, considering the relative positions of the nodes and the traffic flows on the edges connected to each node.

Cai *et al.* compared their hybrid method with the simulated annealing proposed by Rivière [RIV 04], on the Chinese airspace. The simulated annealing approach only minimizes one of the two criteria chosen by the authors, so the comparison of the Pareto fronts is naturally advantageous to the multiobjective particle swarm optimization algorithm.

The results are also compared with the current routes network in China, showing significant improvements. The method proposed by Cai *et al.* is being integrated in the program used to modify the air route network in China.

2.2.3. *Defining 2D-corridors with a clustering method and a genetic algorithm*

In [XUE 09b], Xue proposes a method positioning a limited number of 2D-routes (or "corridors") to accommodate the biggest flows over the US territory. The aim is not to build a network for the whole traffic, but only for the big flows. How these corridors would be handled, concerning for example the entry and exit procedures, and how to solve conflicts at the crossing points of these corridors are not detailed in the publication. The work focuses on how to position these corridors, considering proximity criteria for the origin–destination flows.

There are many ways to specify an air traffic flow, for example by choosing an origin and a destination, or by considering the flow through a given sector, or through a specific sector boundary, or over a waypoint, etc. In his publication, Xue considers aircraft trajectories as great circles on the Earth's surface, and a flow is defined as a group of such great circles that are close to one from the others.

To cluster these great circles according to a proximity criterion, Xue transforms the direct trajectories from departure to arrival into a set of points in a dual space, using the Hough transform. In this dual space, each trajectory is represented by a couple (ρ, θ), where ρ is the shortest distance between the trajectory and a reference point, and θ is the angle between a reference direction and the perpendicular to the trajectory passing through the reference point. Xue then uses a basic *clustering* technique, usually applied in image processing, to aggregate points in the dual space. By placing a grid with step size $(\Delta\rho, \Delta\theta)$ over the set of points, he simply counts the number of points in each cell and determines the cells of highest density.

This method allows him to find groups of trajectories, geographically close to one another. In the dual representation of the biggest flows, the points in the cells of highest densities are replaced by a single corridor (a point in the dual space). As a first approximation, he takes the barycenter of the points (trajectories in the initial space).

One drawback of this representation in the dual space is that the arrival and departure points in the original space are lost during the transformation. We cannot directly measure the trajectory lengthening in the dual space for aircraft flying in the corridors computed by the method. The additional distance flown by the aircraft is an important cost criterion for airline operators.

A genetic algorithm [GOL 89, MIC 92] is then used to refine the approximate solution found by the earlier-mentioned method. This algorithm iterates on a population of individuals, following a Darwinian process of selection (according to a fitness criterion), crossover, and mutation. An individual is here a set of barycenters (representing corridors in the initial space). It is encoded as a collection of (ρ, θ) coordinates in the dual space. The initial population is built from the approximate solution found by the first method. The fitness criterion is the sum of trajectory lengthenings in the initial space, for all flights flying in the corridors.

With 200 elements in the population, 200 generations, a crossover probability of 0.8 and a mutation probability of 0.2, the proportion of flights flying in the corridors with no more than 5% trajectory lengthening goes from 31% in the initial solution to 44% for the best solution found by the genetic algorithm.

2.3. A network of separate 3D-tubes for the main traffic flows

In Chapters 7 and 8 of his PhD thesis [GIA 04a] (in French) and in other publications [GIA 04b, GIA 04c, GIA 05a, GIA 05b], Gianazza addresses a different kind of problem: instead of building 2D-routes or 2D-corridors as in section 2.2, he builds a network of separate 3D-tubes assigned to the main origin–destination traffic flows. Two strategies are tested. The first strategy is a sequential approach where an A^* algorithm is applied in turn to each origin–destination flow, in order to find the shortest 3D-tube separated from the other previously computed tubes. The second strategy is a global optimization approach, where all origin–destination flows are considered simultaneously, and where the aim is to minimize the overall deviation cost while satisfying separation constraints. A hybrid evolutionary algorithm (HEA), in which the mutation operator runs the A^* algorithm with a given probability, is used for that purpose.

Section 2.3.1 describes the simplified 3D-trajectory model used to test different algorithms on the 3D-tube separation problem. Sections 2.3.2 to 2.3.5 describe the different problem formulations, the algorithms, and their results on a toy problem, using the simplified 3D-trajectory model. A more realistic model is described in section 2.3.6, when applying the algorithms to real data.

2.3.1. *A simplified 3D-trajectory model*

In order to simplify the models and computations, 3D-trajectories are defined in a Euclidean space in which airports are at altitude $z = 0$. Latitudes and longitudes on the Earth's ellipsoid surface are converted into (x, y) coordinates, using a stereographic projection on a plane. As the real data used in this work come from French air traffic control centers, the point of contact of this plane with the Earth's surface is Paris. The z coordinate is the pressure altitude, in feet (ft). Isobar $1,013.25$ hPa is assumed to correspond to $z = 0$.

2.3.1.1. *3D-trajectories with lateral or vertical deviations*

In the simplified model, all aircraft are assumed to have the exact same performances, and to follow slopes at constant angle when climbing or descending. It is also assumed that all flights belonging to a same origin–destination flow request the same cruising flight level (requested flight level (RFL)), and that their preferred route is the direct route from origin to destination.

With this simplified model, we only need to assign one 3D-trajectory per origin–destination flow. Such a 3D-trajectory is just a sequence of line segments in a

Euclidean space. Figure 2.6 shows the most direct 3D-trajectory between two airports, with a climbing segment, originating at the departure airport, followed by a cruising segment at the RFL, and then a descent toward the destination airport.

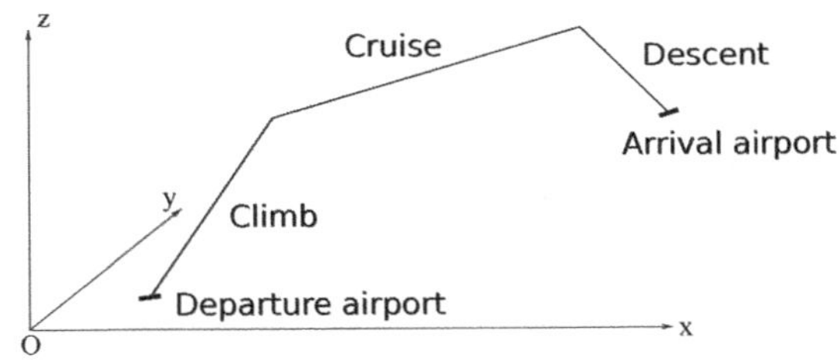

Figure 2.6. *A simplified model of 3D-trajectory*

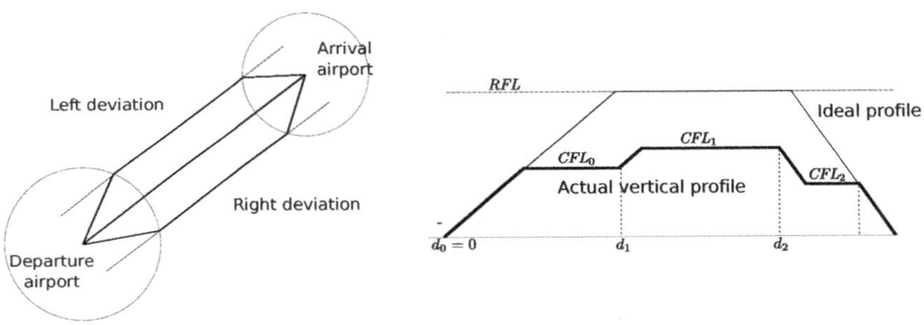

Figure 2.7. *Possible lateral (left) or vertical deviations (right)*

As the aim is to obtain separate 3D-trajectories, the computed trajectories might deviate laterally or vertically from the preferred ones. In the simplified model, three routes are possible: the direct route, a parallel route on the left or one on the right, as shown on the left part of Figure 2.7. The radius around airports and the lateral offset of the parallel routes are the two parameters defining the offset routes. Vertical deviations are defined by a sequence of intermediate flight levels, as shown on the right part of Figure 2.7. Each cleared[3] flight level (CFL) is taken between a minimum flight level and the RFL. The sequence of couples (d_j, CFL_j), where d_j is the distance flown along the route at which starts the climb or descent toward flight level CFL_j, characterizes the vertical flight profile.

2.3.1.2. *Deviation costs for the simplified model*

The cost associated to each trajectory i is directly related to the vertical and lateral deviations from the preferred route (i.e. direct route at RFL_i). The cost of a

3 The term "cleared flight level" comes from the air traffic control phraseology, where the term "clearance" was formerly used for the instructions given to pilots.

lateral deviation depends on the relative route lengthening $\frac{(l_i - lref_i)}{lref_i}$, where $lref_i$ is the length of the direct route and l_i is the length of the chosen route. The cost of a vertical deviation is based on areas divided by the route length for a purpose of equity between flights of different lengths.

The overall cost is a combination of the lateral and vertical costs and is defined as follows:

$$cost(i) = RFL_i - \frac{\text{Area}(profile_i)}{l_i} + K\frac{(l_i - lref_i)}{lref_i} \qquad [2.1]$$

In equation [2.1], K is a factor reflecting the relative preference toward lateral or vertical deviations. The term $\text{Area}(profile_i)$ is the surface between the ground ($z = 0$) and the chosen vertical profile.

2.3.1.3. *A simple criterion for 3D-trajectory separation*

Denoting δ_ℓ and δ_z as the lateral and vertical separation standards that must be maintained at all times between flying aircraft (see section 1.7), let $d(a, b)$ be the distance between the points a and b, defined as follows:

$$d(a, b) = \sqrt{\frac{(x_b - x_a)^2 + (y_b - y_a)^2}{\delta_\ell^2} + \frac{(z_b - z_a)^2}{\delta_z^2}} \qquad [2.2]$$

Considering two trajectories $\mathcal{T}_1$ and $\mathcal{T}_2$, each made up of a sequence of line segments, the definition of the separation criterion between these two trajectories is two-fold:

– two cruise segments $s1 \subset \mathcal{T}_1$ and $s2 \subset \mathcal{T}_2$ are separated if one of the two following conditions is satisfied: their vertical distance is at least δ_z or their lateral distance is at least δ_ℓ;

– two segments $s1 \subset \mathcal{T}_1$ and $s2 \subset \mathcal{T}_2$, of which at least one is a climb or descent segment, are separated if the smallest distance between the two segments, using the distance defined in equation [2.2], is greater than $\sqrt{2}$.

Note that, for the segments involving at least one climb or descent, this 3D-trajectory separation criterion is different from the one given in section 1.7.2, for the definition of a conflict between 4D-trajectories. Although it is not a necessary condition, the above separation criterion is a sufficient condition for all pairs of flights following $\mathcal{T}_1$ and $\mathcal{T}_2$ to be conflict-free.

In this simplified model, we have defined 3D-tube intersections through the notion of a distance threshold between 3D-trajectories. In the more realistic model presented later on in section 2.3.6, 3D-tube intersections will be detected by considering geometric volumes.

2.3.2. *Problem formulations and possible strategies*

2.3.2.1. *Sequential approach or global optimization*

The problem of finding N separated 3D-trajectories (or 3D-tubes) for N air traffic flows can be formulated and addressed in different ways.

One possible way to build separated 3D-trajectories is to consider the N flows as an ordered sequence, considering a criterion such as the number of flights per flow. In this "1 *versus* n" sequential approach, the $(n+1)$th trajectory is built so as to avoid the n previous 3D-trajectories. As a consequence, the flows with highest priority (e.g. the biggest ones) get the most direct 3D-trajectories. This "biggest first" policy might be considered a desirable objective, or not, depending on an arbitrary choice of equity policy.

Another possible approach is to formulate the construction of N separated trajectories as a global optimization problem, where the aim is to minimize the overall deviation costs while satisfying the separation constraints.

These two approaches are quite different in the sense that the "1 *versus* n" approach can be formulated as a sequence of N optimization problems, consisting each in finding a single optimal 3D-trajectory (or 3D-tube) separated from the preceding 3D-trajectories, whereas the second approach consists of a single global optimization problem.

2.3.2.2. *Problem difficulty and choice of algorithms*

The "1 *versus* n" problem is a standard path planning problem where the 3D-trajectories computed during the previous steps are considered as obstacles to avoid. It can be addressed by exact tree-search or graph-search methods such as the well-known A^* algorithm, which uses a "best-first" strategy to explore all possible paths from an initial state to a final state. This best-first strategy relies on a heuristic function estimating the cost of the path from the current state to a terminal state (here the destination). The complexity of the A^* algorithm depends on the state space and the quality of the chosen heuristic.

The global problem might be addressed by exact tree-search methods as well. However, the state space being explored would have to consider all possible combinations of trajectory deviations, considering N trajectories simultaneously. Except for small values of N, exploring a state space of such a size seems impractical for exact tree-search or graph-search methods such as the A^* algorithm. Using local optimization methods, such as Quasi-Newton methods or trust-region methods for constrained optimization, is also not an option. These iterative methods start from a randomly chosen point and make successive steps following descent directions, making use of the analytical expressions of the objective function and constraints and their derivatives, assuming they are available. In our global problem, the separation constraints split the admissible domain in several connected components, whose number increases exponentially with N. As it is not known in which connected component lies the global optimum, we would have to apply several times the chosen local optimization method, choosing at least one starting point in each component.

To better understand this connected components issue, let us consider the simplified model of 3D-trajectories shown in Figure 2.6. Two such intersecting 3D-trajectories can be separated either by deviating trajectory 1 below trajectory 2, or the opposite. As there is no way to move continuously from one solution to the other without violating the separation constraint, this defines two distinct sub-domains (called connected components) in the admissible domain. Now, considering N secant trajectories, this gives $2^{\frac{n(n-1)}{2}}$ connected components (i.e. more than 30 trillion connected components for 10 trajectories).

These considerations make metaheuristics a good option for tackling the global optimization problem. In [GIA 04a, GIA 04b, GIA 04c, GIA 05a, GIA 05b], the chosen metaheuristic is a hybrid evolutionary algorithm where the mutation operator embeds an A^* algorithm. Before describing this hybrid algorithm in section 2.3.4, let us present the A^* algorithm used alone in the sequential approach.

2.3.3. *An A^* algorithm for the "1 versus n" problem*

2.3.3.1. *General description of tree-search or graph-search methods*

The A^* algorithm belongs to the class of tree-search or graph-search methods which explore a state space represented by a tree or a graph. Starting from an initial state u_0– the tree root in the case of tree-search algorithms or a source node when using a graph representation – the objective of such problem-solving methods is to find a final state that is a solution to the problem being addressed. This final state is represented by a tree leaf, or by a sink node, depending on the chosen representation.

The general principle of these methods is quite simple: a frontier F, initially containing only u_0, is iteratively expanded until a solution state is obtained. At each iteration, a node u is chosen in the frontier F and removed from F. If u is not a solution state, it is developed by applying a set of production rules in order to obtain a set of successor states. These successor states are then inserted in the frontier F, and the process is repeated until a solution is found, or until the frontier F is empty.

The main difference between tree-search and graph-search methods is that in the case of a graph representation, we need to memorize the states that have already been developed, storing them in a set D. If a successor v of the current state u already belongs to D, there is no need to insert v in the frontier F, unless the path to v passing through u has a lower cost.

Different exploration strategies can be used – e.g. breadth-first, depth-first, or best-first for the tree-search methods – depending on how the current node u is chosen in the frontier F.

2.3.3.2. *The A^* algorithm*

The A^* algorithm uses a best-first strategy to find the path of minimum cost from an initial state u_0 (tree root or source node, depending on the chosen representation) to a final state (tree leaf or sink node). A heuristic function is used to estimate the cost of the path between the current state and a terminal state. The cost of the successive state transitions between u_0 and the state u is cumulated, and summed with the heuristic estimation $h(u)$. This sum $cost(u) + h(u)$ determines the priority of node u in F, which is implemented as a priority queue. The best element in F is then simply the one with the lowest cost estimate. This is the node which is taken first in F and developed.

A simple illustration of this algorithm is the path-finding problem in a road network. Let us assume u_0 is the departure town, and the objective is to find the shortest path to a destination town u_f. The set of terminal states is then simply $T = \{u_f\}$. In this problem, the cost $k(u_i, u_{i+1})$ of a transition between two successive states u_i and u_{i+1} (here two neighboring towns connected by a road) is simply the travel distance by road between u_i and u_{i+1}. The heuristic $h(u)$ of a node u can be chosen as the distance as the crow flies between u and the destination u_f. The cost of the path from u_0 to a node u is the sum $cost(u) = \sum_{\text{path}(u_0,u)} k(u_i, u_{i+1})$. The A^* algorithm picks up the node u in F for which the estimated path length $cost(u) + h(u)$ is the shortest. This node is developed by computing its successors $S = \{v_1, v_2, ..., v_k\}$. Each successor $v \in S$ is then added to the frontier F, with priority $cost(v) + h(v) = cost(u) + k(u, v) + h(v)$ if state v has never been encountered before. If it has been encountered before ($u \in D \cup F$), it is reinserted in F with its new priority only if $cost(u) + k(u, v)$, the cost of the path to v passing through u, is lower than the best cost of v found so far.

The formal description of the A^* algorithm is given in algorithm 1. The notations used in this algorithm are summarized in the following list:

u_0: initial state;

T: set of terminal nodes (solutions);

D: set of developed nodes;

F: set of nodes on the frontier. These are the generated nodes not developed yet;

$h(u)$: heuristic function estimating the cost of the path between the current state u and a terminal state belonging to T;

$cost(u)$: memorizes the best cost for the path from u_0 to u;

$f(u)$: estimate of the total cost of the path from u_0 to a terminal node, passing through u. This quantity $f(u) = cost(u) + h(u)$ is the sum of the cost of the path from u_0 to u and the heuristic $h(u)$ estimating the cost of the path from u to a terminal node;

$k(u, v)$: cost of a transition from state u to state v;

$parent(v)$: memorizes the parent of node v for which the path from u_0 to v is of lowest cost.

In addition to these notations, the three following functions implement the best-first strategy used by the A^* algorithm to explore the state space:

– EXPAND: function applying a set of production rules $\{p_1, p_2, ..., p_k\}$ to a state u, in order to obtain a set of successors $S = \{v_1, v_2, ..., v_k\}$. In the example of a road network, the successors of a town u are simply the neighboring towns linked to u by a road.

– BESTINFRONTIER: function returning the best node u in frontier F. This is the node for which the estimate $f(u) = cost(u) + h(u)$ of the total cost of a path passing through u is the lowest.

– ADDORREPLACE: add a node v to the frontier F, or replace its priority by the new estimate $f(v)$, if v was already in F.

ALGORITHM 1.–A^* algorithm

```
Require: Initial State u0
F ← {u0}
cost(u0) ← 0
while F ≠ ∅ do
    u ← BESTINFRONTIER(F)                    ▷ Take u ∈ F with the smallest value f(u)
    F ← F \ {u}                              ▷ Remove it from the frontier
    if u ∈ T then                            ▷ Case where u is a terminal node: return full path
        return PATH(u0, u)= u :: parent(u) :: parent(parent(u)) :: . . . :: u0
    else
        D ← D ∪ {v}                          ▷ Add node u to the set of developed nodes
        S ← EXPAND(u)                        ▷ Develop u (i.e. compute its successors)
        for all v ∈ S do
            if v ∉ D ∪ F or cost(v) > cost(u) + k(u, v) then
                cost(v) ← cost(u) + k(u, v)  ▷ Store the cost of path u0, . . . , u, v
                f(v) ← cost(v) + h(v)        ▷ Cost estimate f(v) giving the priority of v
                parent(v) ← u                ▷ Store u as the parent of v
                F ← ADDORREPLACE(v, f(v), F) ▷ Insert v in frontier F
            end if
        end for
    end if
end while
return FAILURE                   ▷ Case where the frontier is empty, and no solution was found
```

2.3.3.3. *State space representation for the simplified 3D-trajectory model*

For the sake of brevity and clarity, in this section and the following sections, we shall only present the state space and the cost and heuristic functions for the simplified model, knowing that they are quite similar in the case of the more realistic model.

The state representing a 3D-trajectory in construction is a collection of the following variables:

r: a discrete variable encoding the choice of the 2D-route.

l_c: the successive CFLs between the departure point and the end of the current trajectory segment. l_c is a list of couples (d_k, CFL_k), where d_k is the distance along route r at which begins a climb or descent toward flight level CFL_k.

$status$: the status at the current segment, represented as a categorical variable that can take one of the following values: *Start*, *Cruise*, *Climb/descent* or *End*.

$cdata$: additional data related to the current cruise segment, if any:

- if $status = Cruise$, the field $cdata$ contains a couple $(d_e, final)$ where d_e is the distance along route r at which it is planned to end the current cruise segment, and $final$ is a boolean. The cruise end can correspond either to the beginning of the final descent, in which case $final$ is set to $True$, or to the beginning of a new *climb/descent* segment that is not fully defined yet. In that case, the boolean $final$ is set to $False$;

- for any other value of $status$, the field $cdata$ should be empty.

To summarize, a state u is simply a tuple $(r, l_c, status, cdata)$. The initial state u_0 can be encoded by the tuple $(\_, [], Start, \_)$, where the underscore represents uninitialized variables and [] is an empty list.

The following rules are applied when computing the successors of state u:

– Initial state $u = u_0$.– There are as many successors to the initial state as the number of possible routes. With the simplified model, there are three parallel 2D-routes, and thus three successors to the initial state, one for each route. For each successor, the list l_c is initialized with $[(0, CFL_0)]$, where CFL_0 is the highest flight level for which the first climb segment intersects no other previous 3D-trajectory. It is at most equal to the RFL.

– Climb/descent segment $u = (r, l_c, Climb/descent, \_)$.– Assuming $l_c = [(d_0, CFL_0); \ldots; (d_j, CFL_j)]$, the successors of u correspond to two possible actions on the 3D-trajectory: change the current target flight level CFL_j, or freeze the cruising segment at flight level CFL_j. This gives us at most two successors:

- $v_1 = \big(r, [(d_0, CFL_0); \ldots; (d_j, CFL_j - \Delta FL)], Climb/descent, \_\big)$

- $v_2 = \big(r, [(d_0, CFL_0); \ldots; (d_j, CFL_j)], Cruise, (d_e, final)\big)$

The value of ΔFL in the expression of v_1 is set to 1,000 feet. The successor v_1 is discarded if the new climbing or descending segment intersects with other 3D-trajectories, or if $CFL_j - \Delta FL$ is below a minimum value FL_{min}. When computing v_2, the distance d_e is chosen as the longest possible distance for which the new cruise segment intersects no other trajectory. The largest possible value for d_e is when the cruise segment continues without intersecting other trajectories until the final descent toward the arrival airport begins. In this case, the boolean $final$ is set to $True$, and otherwise to $False$.

– Cruise segment $u = \big(r, l_c, Cruise, (d_e, final)\big)$.– If the current trajectory segment is a cruising segment, the successor states correspond to one of the three following possibilities: a shortening of the current cruise segment, the addition of a climb/descent segment or the addition of the final descent segment if $final = True$ and if this descent segment does not intersect with the other trajectories. Assuming $l_c = [(d_0, CFL_0); \ldots; (d_j, CFL_j)]$, this will give the three following successors:

- $v_1 = \big(r, l_c, Cruise, (d_e - \delta, False)\big)$

- $v_2 = \big(r, [(d_0, CFL_0); \ldots; (d_j, CFL_j); (d_e, CFL_{j+1})], Climb/descent, \_\big)$

- $v_3 = \big(r, [(d_0, CFL_0); \ldots; (d_j, CFL_j); (d_e, CFL_{arr})], End, \_\big)$

When computing v_1, the 2D-route is discretized and δ is chosen such that $d_e - \delta$ falls on the closest discretization point. For v_2, corresponding to the addition of a new climb/descent segment, the flight level CFL_{j+1} is chosen as the highest possible level, different from CFL_j and within $[FL_{min}, RFL]$, such that the climb or descent between levels CFL_j and CFL_{j+1} is free of any intersection with other trajectories. The successor v_3, which is a terminal state, is removed from the list of successors if the final descent to arrival intersects another trajectory.

– End segment.– This is a terminal state, with no successor.

Note that with these production rules, the algorithm always tries first to produce a vertical profile that is as close as possible to the ideal profile (cruise at RFL). The chosen value for any new CFL is by default the closest one to RFL for which the current 3D-trajectory (up to the current point) intersects with no other trajectory. This is why the CFL values are only decremented when computing the successors. The same applies to the length of the cruising segments: the longest possible length without intersection is chosen first, and the distances are decremented afterward, if required.

2.3.3.4. *Cost and heuristic for the simplified 3D-trajectory model*

The cost $k(u, v)$ of a transition from a parent state u to a successor v depends on the nature of u:

– if $u = u_0$ is the initial state, only the cost of route lengthening is taken into account:

$$k(u_0, v) = K \times \frac{l - lref}{lref} \qquad [2.3]$$

– if $u = (r, l_c, Cruise, (d_{j+1}, final))$ is a cruise segment ending at distance d_{j+1}, with $l_c = [(d_0, CFL_0); \ldots; (d_j, CFL_j)]$, and if the next state v is a climb/descent segment, the cost of the transition is the area between the actual vertical profile delimited by distances d_j and d_{j+1}[4], and the RFL, as shown in Figure 2.8;

– if u is the final descent segment and v is a terminal state (*End*), $k(u, v)$ is the surface between the final descent segment and RFL;

– In all other cases $k(u, v) = 0$.

The chosen heuristic function is computed by considering a vertical profile starting at the end of the current segment and joining the desired profile. Such a profile is illustrated in Figure 2.9.

Denoting $A(u, arr)$ the area shown in Figure 2.9, delimited by the end of the current segment u, the arrival point, the profile joining the ideal profile and flight level RFL, the heuristic function is expressed as follows, where d_{to_go} is the distance remaining to be covered to the destination:

$$h(u) = \frac{A(u, arr)}{d_{to\_go}} \qquad [2.4]$$

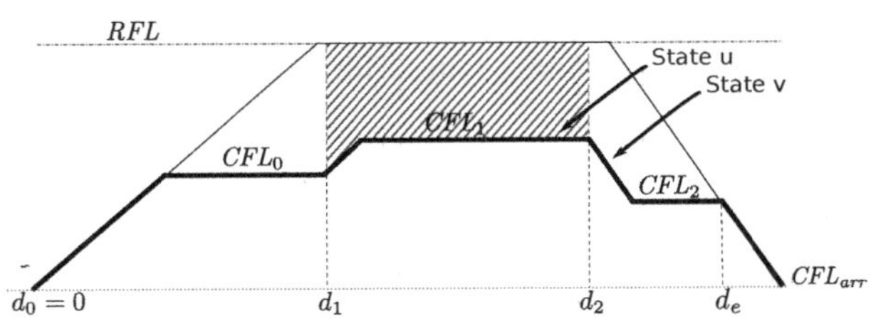

Figure 2.8. *Example of area used to compute the transition cost*

4 The same applies with d_j and d_e if $final = True$.

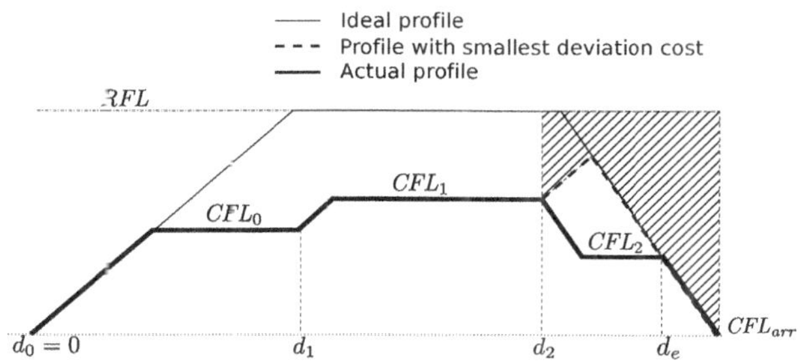

Figure 2.9. *Vertical profile with smallest deviation cost between d_3 and arrival, and area used to compute the heuristic*

By construction, this heuristic is a lower bound of the actual cost of any state transitions from the current state to a terminal state. Figure 2.9 shows an example of what these remaining transitions might be, with a descent toward flight level CFL_3, a cruise segment at CFL_3, and the final descent to the arrival airport. We can see that the actual cost of this intermediate level at CFL_3, which depends on the surface of the area above the actual profile, is higher than $h(u)$.

Note that by construction, the sum of the transition costs $\sum k(u, v)$ for the whole profile is equal to the deviation cost defined in section 2.3.1.2.

2.3.4. *A hybrid evolutionary algorithm for the global problem*

2.3.4.1. *General description of an evolutionary algorithm*

Evolutionary algorithms are population-based algorithms inspired from the Darwinian process of recombination, mutation and selection of the best fit individuals. Selection is based on a *fitness* criterion, which is used for example to select a pool of parents. These parents are recombined by pairs to produce offsprings. A mutation operator is also applied in order to introduce some variations in the population. After evaluating the new individuals, the fitness criterion is once again used to select individuals for the new population, choosing among recombined and mutated individuals and completing with individuals from the former population, if need be. This process is repeated until a stopping criterion is met or until a given number of iterations has been performed. The best individual in the resulting population is then returned. Alternatively, we can also return a set of best individuals, if we are looking for several possible solutions of good quality. These steps are summarized in algorithm 2.

ALGORITHM 2.–General scheme of an evolutionary algorithm.

Require: $popsize, P_m, P_c, maxiter$ ▷ Population size, mutation an crossover probabilities, maximum number of iterations

$k \leftarrow 0$
$pop \leftarrow$ INIT($popsize$)
Evaluate individuals in initial population
while $k < maxiter$ and not(STOP(pop, k)) **do**
  Select a pool of parents from *pop*
  Recombine pairs of parents, with probability P_c
  Mutate population individuals, with probability P_m
  Evaluate new candidates
  Select individuals for the next generation, and replace *pop* with the new population
  $k \leftarrow k + 1$
end while
return best individual(s) in *pop*

The genetic algorithms, introduced by Holland [HOL 75] and made popular by Goldberg [GOL 89] were among the first evolutionary algorithms proposed in the literature. In their canonical version, they use a binary encoding for the individuals, and recombination is done by taking bit sequences from the two parents. Mutating an individual consists of randomly changing one or several bits in its sequence.

Depending on the problem being addressed, individuals can also be encoded as vectors of real values. In this case, we can use for example an arithmetic crossover operator to recombine pairs of parents, and mutate an individual by adding a random noise to one or several components of its vector.

Although the general scheme of evolutionary algorithms is quite simple (see algorithm 2), their good performance depends on a number of refinements. For example, before selecting individuals on the basis of a chosen *fitness* criterion, we can apply *scaling* and *sharing* operators to the raw fitness values. These operations modify the fitness landscape and introduce a bias in the random selection process, generally giving a better chance to the poorly fit individuals so as to maintain a good diversity in the population. We can also adopt an elitist strategy, making sure that the best fit individuals actually appear in the new population[5]. For more details on these aspects of evolutionary algorithms, the reader can refer to [EIB 03], for example. Note that the performance of evolutionary algorithms also depends on the choice of the parameter values: $popsize, P_m, P_c, maxiter$ and possibly other parameters,

5 Without elitism, the best fit individuals are only given a higher chance to be selected. The selection is random, although biased toward good individuals, so there is a chance that the best individuals may not actually be selected in the next population. With elitism, a given number of places are reserved for them in the new population.

depending on the implemented refinements of EA. This parameter choice is problem dependent.

2.3.4.2. *Encoding individuals*

In the 3D-tube network problem, when applying a global minimization approach, the aim is to minimize the overall cost of all trajectory deviations while ensuring separation between all 3D-tubes. With the simplified model, this means ensuring a sufficient distance between 3D-trajectories, using distance d.

When using an evolutionary algorithm for this purpose, one individual of the population represents a whole network of 3D-tubes (or 3D-trajectories, with the simplified model). The population is made of $popsize$ different networks, each network comprising N 3D-tubes. Each 3D-tube is completely defined by a discrete variable r for the choice of the 2D-route, and by a list of couples (d_k, CFL_k), where d_k is the distance at which begins a climb or descent toward flight level CFL_k.

2.3.4.3. *Initial population*

The initial population comprises one specific individual: a network where every 3D-tube follows the most direct route with a cruise segment at the RFL. The other elements of the population are produced by randomly choosing values for r, d_k and CFL_k, for all values of k below a maximum number of segments. This number of segments is randomly chosen for each 3D-tube, within predefined bounds.

2.3.4.4. *Fitness criterion*

The fitness of an individual is related both to the deviation costs and number of separation constraint violations. A triangular matrix C is used to store some values used in the computation of the fitness. A diagonal element $C_{i,i}$ is the deviation cost for the 3D-tube $\mathcal{T}_i$. A non-diagonal element $C_{i,j}$, with $i \neq j$, is the number of intersections between 3D-tubes $\mathcal{T}_i$ and $\mathcal{T}_j$.

$$
\begin{aligned}
C_{i,i} &= cost(i) \\
C_{i,j} &= \sum_{(s_p,s_q)\in\mathcal{T}_i\times\mathcal{T}_j} \delta(s_p, s_q) \quad ,\forall i \neq j
\end{aligned}
\qquad [2.5]
$$

In equation [2.5], $cost(i)$ is the cost associated to 3D-tube $\mathcal{T}_i$, and $\delta(s_p, s_q)$ is equal to 1 when segments s_p and s_q intersect, and 0 otherwise.

When using the simplified 3D-trajectory model, $cost(i)$ is the cost defined in section 2.3.1.2, and δ is given by equation [2.6], where s_p and s_q are line segments and d is the distance defined in section 2.3.1.3.

$$
\delta(s_p, s_q) = \begin{array}{l} 1 \text{ si } d(s_p, s_q) \leq \sqrt{2} \\ 0 \text{ sinon.} \end{array}
\qquad [2.6]
$$

Denoting cv as the function returning the number of separation constraint violations, the number of constraint violations for the ith 3D-tube is given by equation [2.7]:

$$cv(i) = \sum_{j \in [1,N], j<i} C_{i,j} \qquad [2.7]$$

We have $cv(i) = 0$ when tube i intersects no other 3D-tube, and $cv(i) > 0$ otherwise. Consequently, the 3D-tubes are separated if and only if $\sum_{i \in [1,N]} cv(i) = 0$.

The fitness $\mathcal{F}$ of an individual (a network of 3D-tubes) is defined as follows by equation [2.8]:

$$\mathcal{F} = \begin{cases} 1 + \dfrac{N}{1 + \beta \sum_i C_{i,i}} & \text{if } \sum_i cv(i) = 0 \\ \dfrac{1}{\sum_i cv(i)} & \text{if } \sum_i cv(i) > 0 \end{cases} \qquad [2.8]$$

With this expression, we have $\mathcal{F} < 1$ when the 3D-tubes are not separated, and $\mathcal{F} > 1$ otherwise. In the latter case, the value of $\mathcal{F}$ increases when the deviations from the most direct 3D-tubes (or 3D-trajectories) decrease. In [GIA 04a, GIA 05a, GIA 05b], the parameter β is set to 1,000. This value was empirically found to give a good dispersion of the fitness values when there are no 3D-tube intersections[6].

2.3.4.5. *Parent selection*

Prior to the parent selection, the raw fitness values $\mathcal{F}$ of equation [2.8] are scaled, using a *sigma truncation scaling* [GOL 89]. The scaled fitness value is given by equation [2.9], where σ is the standard deviation of the raw fitness values, and $\mathcal{F}_{avg}$ is their average value, and where the coefficient c is set to 2.0:

$$\mathcal{F}' = \max\left(\mathcal{F} - (\mathcal{F}_{avg} - c\sigma), 0\right) \qquad [2.9]$$

A *clusterized sharing* operator [YIN 93] is then applied to the scaled fitness values. This niching method modifies the fitness landscape so as to form and maintain multiple different final solutions. Its primary objective is to avoid situations where, after a number of generations, the whole population ends up containing replicates of a single solution (usually a local optimum). The *clusterized sharing* method requires to define a distance Δ between individuals. Clusters of individuals are determined, using this distance criterion A method similar to the k-means method, but of $n \log n$ complexity,

6 With too small values of β, the fitness values are all close to 1 and the selection according to such fitness scores makes no clear distinction between individuals.

is used to compute the clusters, using two distance thresholds: Δ_{merge} for merging two clusters and Δ_{clust} for creating a new cluster. The clustering process starts with only one cluster containing one population element and considers each other elements in turn, following the two rules:

– if two clusters are at a distance less than Δ_{merge}, they are merged. The center of the new cluster is the barycenter of all points in the cluster;

– if an individual is at a distance greater than Δ_{clust} from all cluster barycenters, a new cluster is created, containing this individual. Otherwise, the individual is added to the closest cluster and new barycenter is computed.

Once the clusters are computed, each individual is weighed according to the distance to its cluster barycenter. Denoting e_i the ith element in the population, the weight m_i assigned to e_i is given by equation [2.10], where n_c is the number of elements in the cluster containing e_i, g_c is the barycenter of this cluster and $\Delta(e_i, g_c)$ is the distance between the element e_i and the center g_c.

$$m_i = n_c \left(1 - \left(\frac{\Delta(e_i, g_c)}{2\Delta_{clust}}\right)^{\alpha}\right) \qquad [2.10]$$

The general scheme of the sharing operator then consists of modifying the fitness values as expressed in equation [2.11]:

$$\mathcal{F}_i'' = \frac{\mathcal{F}_i'}{m_i} \qquad [2.11]$$

In practice, α is chosen equal to $+\infty$, and the fitness value after sharing is simply $\mathcal{F}_i'' = \frac{\mathcal{F}_i'}{n_c}$, where n_c is the number of elements in the cluster. The choice for the distance function Δ and the threshold values Δ_{merge} and Δ_{clust} is problem dependent. A reasonable choice of parameters is to take a ratio of $1/3$ for $\Delta_{merge}/\Delta_{clust}$.

For the 3D-tube network problem, it is not easy to define a distance between two individuals (i.e. two networks). However, we can still apply the *sharing* operator, using a function Δ representing the degree of similarity between two individuals (networks), even if this "similarity measure" Δ does not have all the mathematical properties of a distance. Here, this similarity measure takes into account the following factors, for each trajectory: difference in route lengths, distances between the starting points of climb/descent, difference between the CFLs, etc.

In order to preserve the diversity of the population, the *sharing* maintains a list of "protected elements." These protected elements are taken in different clusters and copied in the next population. If $\mathcal{F}''^k_{best}$ is the best fitness value at generation k, the best element of a cluster is protected if its fitness is $\mathcal{F}'' > sh \times \mathcal{F}''^k_{best}$, where sh is the sharing parameter. By construction, this is an elitist strategy, as it preserves one or several of the best elements. However, by taking these elements from different clusters, this method also ensures that the best elements preserved in the next generation are not all from the same region of the search space, near the best element.

Once the scaling and sharing operators have been applied to the initial fitness values, the random selection of the parents is made according to the well-known principle of *stochastic remainder without replacement* (see [EIB 03] for example), using the modified fitnesses.

2.3.4.6. *The crossover operator*

The specific crossover operator used for the 3D-tube network problem is inspired from a crossover operator introduced by Durand and Alliot [DUR 98]. This operator is particularly well suited to problems in high dimensions with partially separable objective functions (see [DUR 04] in French).

The principle of this adapted crossover operator is the following: in order to inherit "good genes" from the parents, we measure the contribution of each "gene" to the fitness of each individual. Let us assume that each element e of the population is encoded as a vector $(x_1, \ldots, x_N)$ of float numbers, and let us identify each variable x_k as a "gene" of the individual e. The contribution of gene k to the fitness of an individual $e = (x_1, \ldots, x_k, \ldots, x_N)$ is called *local fitness*, and denoted $f_k(e)$ or $f_k(x_1, \ldots, x_N)$. When using the adapted crossover, the offspring of two parents p_1 and p_2 is obtained as follows:

– if $f_k(p_1) > f_k(p_1) + \epsilon$ then the offspring inherits gene k (i.e. the value of variable x_k) from parent p_1;

– if $f_k(p_1) < f_k(p_1) - \epsilon$ then the offspring inherits gene k from parent p_2;

– if $|f_k(p1) - f_k(p2)| \leq \epsilon$ then a new value for variable x_k is randomly chosen, taking for example a random linear combination of the values of gene k in the two parents in the case of real-coded values (arithmetic crossover).

Note that taking $\epsilon = 0$ or ϵ small implies that, when producing two children o_1 and o_2 from two parents p_1 and p_2, both children inherit the same best genes from the two parents. This is an elitist crossover strategy that promotes the duplication of the good genes. However, it reduces the population diversity as both children share a large number of common genes. In order to increase the diversity, we can simply choose ϵ large enough, however the choice of ϵ is problem dependent.

A slightly modified version of the above crossover operator consists of randomly choosing, with a given probability, among two options. The first one is a random crossover operator applied to all genes of the two parents (here the standard arithmetic crossover operator). The second option is an elitist crossover strategy as described above, with a fixed value $\epsilon = 0$, and where the genes for which $f_k(p1) = f_k(p2)$ are left unchanged. If P_{es} denotes the probability to select the elitist crossover strategy, then $1 - P_{es}$ is the probability to choose the arithmetic crossover.

This modified version of the adapted crossover operator simply replaces the parameter ϵ by a more explicit parameter P_{es} setting the balance between an elitist crossover strategy or a more random strategy. The modified adapted crossover operator can be summarized as follows:

– with probability P_{es}, an elitist crossover strategy is chosen. Child o_1 inherits all genes from parent p_1 except those whose local fitness is strictly better in parent p_2. In such a case the gene is taken from p_2. Similarly, o_2 inherits all its genes from parent p_2, except those for which the local fitness is strictly better in parent p_1;

– with probability $1 - P_{es}$, a random strategy is chosen. Here, with real-encoded vectors, an arithmetic crossover is applied with a parameter α randomly chosen in $[-0.5, 2]$:

$$\begin{cases} o_1 = \alpha p_1 + (1 - \alpha)p_2 \\ o_2 = (1 - \alpha)p_1 + \alpha p_2 \end{cases}$$

In the 3D-tube network problem addressed in [GIA 04a, GIA 04b, GIA 04c, GIA 05a, GIA 05b], a "gene" is a 3D-tube, and an individual is a 3D-tube network made up of a number N of such genes. The local fitness f_k depends on how many 3D-tubes intersect with tube k. The probability P_{es} to choose the elitist crossover strategy is set to $1/3$, which makes $2/3$ chances to choose a random crossover strategy. One difficulty arises when applying the random strategy, though: a gene is not a single real-coded value here, but a collection of attributes such as the 2D-route choice variable r, the list of couples (d_k, CFL_k) for the successive CFLs, and possibly some entry flight levels (EFLs) and exit flight levels (XFLs) when a more realistic model is used (see section 2.3.6). Therefore, the adapted crossover operator that was described before for real-coded vectors cannot be applied as it is. In the 3D-tube network problem, the random arithmetic crossover that is applied when the random crossover strategy is chosen (with probability $1 - P_{es}$) is replaced by another random crossover where the offspring is first copied from the parents, and then some attribute values are exchanged between the corresponding genes of the two new individuals – this is the case for the distances d_j at which an climb/descent begins. Other attributes, such as the CFLs CFL_j, are replaced by a random linear combination of the attributes of the two parents. In one of the two children, this random crossover is applied to all attributes. In the other, it is applied only to one randomly selected attribute.

2.3.4.7. *The mutation operator, for simple test-cases*

The probability of mutation of any given individual in the population is P_m. Once selected for mutation, the individual is replaced by a new one with randomly modified characteristics.

For the 3D-tube network problem, a specific mutation operator has been designed. This is the mutation operator that the evolutionary algorithm is hybridized with the A^* algorithm presented in section 2.3.3.

When solving simple test-cases modeled with the simplified 3D-trajectories described in section 2.3.1, the chosen mutation operator follows the steps described hereafter to produce a new individual (3D-trajectory network):

– a 3D-trajectory i is selected among the N trajectories composing the individual selected for mutation. This selection is made as follows:

- a number m is randomly chosen in $[1, N/2]$,

- m 3D-trajectories are randomly drawn from the N ones in the network,

- if some of these m trajectories intersect, then the one with the most intersections is selected,

- if these m trajectories do not intersect, the one with the highest deviation cost is selected;

– the selected trajectory i is replaced by a new one, computed by the A^* algorithm. By construction, this new trajectory is the one with minimum deviation costs that avoids all other trajectories;

– if the A^* algorithm fails to find such a trajectory, some random noise is introduced in the selected trajectory i. This is done by introducing a random noise in one of the trajectory attributes: 2D-route choice, entry or exit levels (for more realistic models only) or cruising segments. Concerning the cruising segments, a random choice is made among the following options, with equiprobability: add a new cruising segment (d_j, CFL_j), remove an existing segment or modify an existing segment either by changing distance d_j of flight level CFL_j.

2.3.4.8. *The mutation operator for complex test-cases and real data*

Preliminary tests with the first hybrid mutation operator described above have shown good results, albeit with huge computation times (see [GIA 04a]). After investigating these results, it appeared that the A^* algorithm used in this mutation operator was not always able to find intersection-free trajectories, or to return failure to find such a trajectory, in a reasonable amount of time. The difficulty was increased by the fact that the 3D-trajectories in the initial population are randomly chosen, spanning the entire airspace.

A few other operators have been tried. Naturally, a non-hybrid method was tried first, actually even before designing the hybrid method. Pure random variations in the 3D-trajectories were found to give poor results. Another research path was to hybridize the evolutionary algorithm with another method, with the idea that 3D-trajectories or 3D-tubes could be locally improved by a simple iterative method that would replace the A^* algorithm in the hybrid mutation operator. The iterative method consisted in testing successive values for the distances d_j and flight levels CFL_j.

The best compromise that was found, in terms of result quality and computation time, is the following:

– select a 3D-tube at random, with a procedure depending on the value of $\mathcal{F}$:

- if $\mathcal{F} > 1$ (no intersection), make a random choice in $[1, N]$ with uniform probability,

- if $\mathcal{F} < 1$, choose among the two following options with probability 0.5 for either option: make a random choice in $[1, N]$ with uniform probability, or make a choice biased toward 3D-tubes with most intersections;

– modify the selected 3D-tube as follows:

- if the chosen 3D-tube intersect with no other tube, then with probability $1/3$ try to improve its deviation cost, using an *ad hoc* local search method iterating on the values of d_j and CFL_j,

- if the first option is not chosen, then choose among the following two options, with equiprobability:

– add a random noise to one of the attributes;

– apply the A^* algorithm.

In the last case, the A^* algorithm computes a new 3D-tube of minimum deviation cost, maintaining separation with other 3D-tubes in the network. This task may prove difficult, especially in the first iterations of the evolutionary algorithm where the 3D-tubes are mostly placed at random. To ease this task, when the current generation number is less than $maxiter/4$, the A^* algorithm tries to avoid only the 3D-tubes intersecting with the tube selected in the first step of the procedure. After $maxiter/4$ iterations of the evolutionary algorithm, the same strategy is maintained with probability 0.5, the alternative being to avoid all 3D-tubes in the network, not only the ones intersecting with the tube selected for change.

2.3.4.9. *Selecting individuals for the new population*

So far, we have detailed how the parents are selected from the current population, and how crossover and mutation is done. In the chosen evolutionary algorithm, the current population is wholly replaced at each iteration by a new population of constant size $popsize$. The procedure for the selection of the new population is the following, with P_c and P_m the crossover and mutation probabilities, respectively:

– draw, with replacement, $\frac{popsize \times P_c}{2}$ elements from the pool of parents, and then draw a second element for each such element. For each couple of parents, produce a pair of children, using the crossover operator;

– draw, with replacement, $popsize \times P_m$ elements in the pool of parents, and produce a mutated individual for each selected element;

– supplement the new population with:

- protected individuals from the current population (if elitist strategy, or clusterized sharing is applied),

- randomly drawn elements from the pool of parents.

2.3.5. *Results on a toy problem, with the simplified 3D-trajectory model*

2.3.5.1. *Description of the toy problem and test-cases*

Let us consider N airport-to-airport traffic flows whose departure and arrival airports lie on a circle or radius R. For $k \in [0, N-1]$, the origin O_k and destination D_k of the 3D-trajectories are given by equation [2.12]:

$$O_k = \begin{pmatrix} R\cos(\frac{2k\pi}{N}) \\ R\sin(\frac{2k\pi}{N}) \end{pmatrix} \qquad D_k = \begin{pmatrix} -R\cos(\frac{2k\pi+p}{N}) \\ -R\sin(\frac{2k\pi+p}{N}) \end{pmatrix} \qquad [2.12]$$

The values of R and p are chosen so as to ensure that the distance between origin and destination is large enough. In the following, two test-cases are considered: 10 trajectories on a circle of radius $R = 350$ nautical miles (NM), with $p = 3$, or 40 trajectories on circle of radius $R = 600$ NM, with $p = 5$.

In these test-cases, the climbs and descents are made at a rate of $2,000$ ft/min, with a speed of 250 knots (kts). The chosen parameters for the toy problems are the following :

– the step δ used to discretize the trajectories is chosen as $1/10\text{th}$ of the route length;

– the maximum number of cruising phases is three;

– the RFL is FL350 (i.e $35,000$ ft);

– the minimum flight level FL_{min} is FL145, except of the first and last cruising phases, when climb is interrupted at an intermediate level, or when the descent toward the arrival airport is anticipated. In such cases, aircraft can fly at a cruise level between FL60 and FL145, but the cruise segment should not be longer than 2δ;

– the chosen lateral separation standard is 6 NM, and the vertical separation standard is 999 ft (the actual value used in operation is $1,000$ ft).

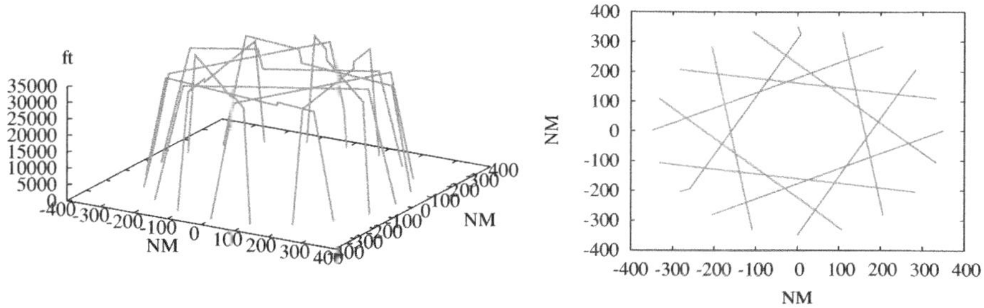

Figure 2.10. *Results of the A^* algorithm, for 10 trajectories ($R = 350$ NM, $p = 3$). For a color version of the figure, see www.iste.co.uk/durand/atm.zip*

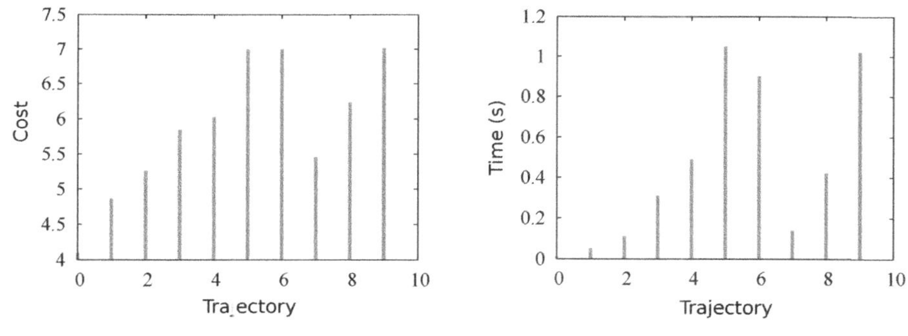

Figure 2.11. *Deviation costs and computation times for the A^*, for each 3D-trajectory ($N = 10$, $R = 350$ NM, $p = 3$). For a color version of the figure, see www.iste.co.uk/durand/atm.zip*

2.3.5.2. *Results of the A^* algorithm on the toy problem*

Figure 2.10 shows the 3D-trajectories computed by the A^* algorithm, on the test case with 10 trajectories. The deviation cost of each trajectory, as well as the computation times, are shown in Figure 2.11. In these figures, we can observe that the cost and the computation time regularly increase for the first six trajectories, and show no significant pattern for the next four ones. In this example, the computation time on a Pentium IV 3.2 GHz was 4.5 seconds, and the total cost for the 10 trajectories was 58.748. In order to compare these results with the ones obtained with the evolutionary algorithm, the fitness of the 3D-trajectory network found by the A^* was also computed. This fitness value is $\mathcal{F} = 1.1674$.

In order to illustrate the difficulties that can be encountered by the A^* algorithm, let us see the results for the more complex test-case, with 40 trajectories. The 3D-trajectories computed for this test-case are shown in Figure 2.12. The A^* algorithm found no solution for trajectories 21 and 26, so they are not drawn in Figure 2.12. The total computation time for the 40 trajectories, including the time for the two failures of the A^*, was 788.73 seconds, on the same machine as before. The cumulated deviation cost of the 38 computed trajectories is 222.060. The fitness value for the whole network is 0.0250.

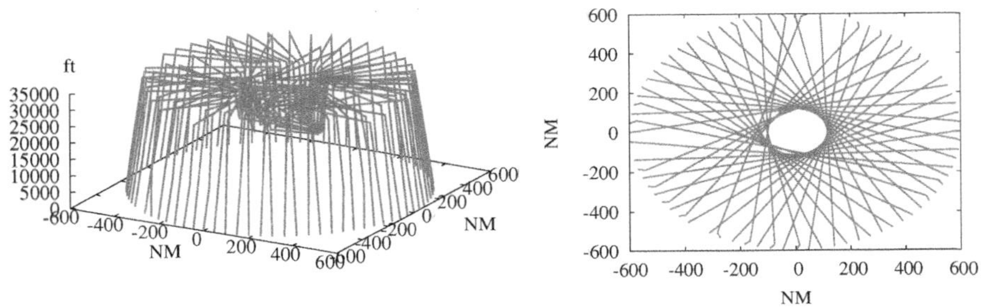

Figure 2.12. *Results of the A^* algorithm, for 40 trajectories ($R = 600$ NM, $p = 5$). For a color version of the figure, see www.iste.co.uk/durand/atm.zip*

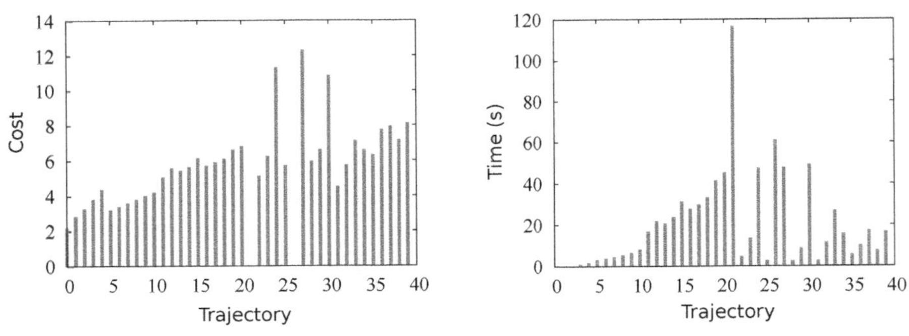

Figure 2.13. *Deviation costs and computation times for the A^*, for each 3D-trajectory ($N = 40$, $R = 600$ NM, $p = 5$). For a color version of the figure, see www.iste.co.uk/durand/atm.zip*

The costs and computation times for each trajectory are detailed in Figure 2.13. We can observe that the computation times increase regularly for the first 20 trajectories. Then, there is a peak of 116 seconds for trajectory 21, which is the time it took for the A^* algorithm to explore the search space and declare a failure to find a solution. For the remaining trajectories, there is no clear trend in the variations of the deviation cost and computation time.

The disparity in computation time does not come as a surprise: The effective complexity of the A^* algorithm depends both on the properties (admissibility, consistency) of the chosen heuristic function h and its adequation to the topology of the state space. We can have a linear complexity in the best cases, or an exponential complexity in the worst cases. In the 3D-trajectories problem, we see that the A^* behavior is relatively predictable when there are few obstacles to avoid (previous 3D-trajectories), and that things get more complicated when the search space is more constrained. With more obstacles, the A^* behavior can change significantly depending on how these obstacles are placed. It seems difficult to estimate a priori the time required by the A^* algorithm to solve a given problem. In some cases, it might be very fast to find a solution, or to come to the conclusion that there is no available path satisfying the constraints. In other cases, it might have to explore a huge number of states, taking much more time, before declaring a failure or returning a solution.

It is clear, however, that cases where the A^* algorithm spends a lot of time either to fail or to succeed in finding a solution are more likely to occur when the airspace is occupied by many other 3D-tubes.

2.3.5.3. *Results of the evolutionary algorithm on the toy problem*

In [GIA 05a], the two variants of the hybrid evolutionary algorithm described in section 2.3.4 are compared with more standard flavors of real-coded genetic algorithms. The methods compared are the following:

– GA: A standard genetic algorithm with multi point crossover, except that the genes encoding an individual are 3D-trajectories. Mutation is purely random in this variant: a 3D-trajectory is chosen at random, with uniform probability, and only one of the attributes of this 3D-trajectory is randomly modified;

– GA-ac: The same as GA, but with the adapted crossover operator described in section 2.3.4.6;

– GA-bm: The same as GA-ac, except that the selection of the 3D-trajectory, in the mutation operator, is biased toward trajectories with most constraint violations (as explained in section 2.3.4.7);

– HEA: the hybrid evolutionary algorithm with a mutation operator embedding an A^* algorithm (see section 2.3.4.7);

– HEA-real: the variant of the above hybrid EA with the mutation operator for more complex cases and real data (see section 2.3.4.8).

	# gen.	*popsize*	P_c	P_m	*sh*	Δ_{max}	time (s)	avg. $\mathcal{F}_{best}$
GA	1,000	350	0.6	0.05	0.3	70	1,702	1.199186
GA-ac	1,000	350	0.6	0.05	0.3	70	1,444	1.199669
GA-bm	1,000	350	0.6	0.05	0.3	70	1,723	1.198214
HEA	300	350	0.6	0.05	0.3	70	2,450	1.199227
HEA-real	300	350	0.6	0.1	0.3	70	906	1.199823

Table 2.1. *Comparison of several evolutionary algorithms, on the test-case with* 10 *trajectories*

Table 2.1 shows the results for the five flavors of evolutionary algorithm, on the test-case with 10 trajectories. As the non-hybrid algorithms are faster, in terms of computation time, and slower to converge toward good solutions, the maximum number of generations has been set to 1,000, instead of 300 for the hybrid algorithms. The other parameters are identical for all algorithms, except the probability of mutation in *HEA-real*, which was set to $P_m = 0.1$ so as to have approximately the same probability to call the A^* embedded in the mutation operator than with *HEA*. Parameter tuning is an important issue in evolutionary algorithms, as it impacts their performance significantly. The chosen values for the 3D-tubes problem were obtained by varying independently each parameter, considering a few parameter setting configurations (see [GIA 05a]). Note, however, that a more extensive and systematic study might have led to select different sets of parameters.

We see in the last column of Table 2.1 that the fitnesses obtained after the maximum number of generations reached are quite similar for all algorithms, at least on this relatively easy-to-solve test-case with 10 trajectories. Note that all evolutionary algorithms perform better than the stand-alone A^* algorithm applied in sequence to the 10 trajectories. Let us remind that, with this sequential approach, the fitness of the solution found by the A^* algorithm was $\mathcal{F} = 1.1674$, whereas all solutions found by the evolutionary algorithms have a fitness above 1.19. More than the performance of the algorithms themselves, it is certainly the chosen strategy that explains the difference in the results: the global optimization approach used in the evolutionary algorithm is more bound to give solutions of higher quality than the sequential application of the A^* algorithm, where the quality of the final solution depends on the order in which the trajectories are considered. In addition, the sequential approach does not account for the fact that small simultaneous deviations of several 3D-trajectories might be more efficient than giving priority to the biggest flows, in terms of deviation costs.

The final results of Table 2.1 do not allow us to compare the performances of the five evolutionary algorithms. Let us focus on what happens over the first generations. Figure 2.14 shows the evolution, over 150 generations, of the fitness of the best element in the population, with one run of each algorithm and the same parameter settings as before. In the first few generations, the hybrid evolutionary algorithm *HEA* described in section 2.3.4 and its variant *HEA-real* are clearly better than the other algorithms at finding intersection-free solutions with low deviation costs. Using the adapted crossover instead of the standard multipoint crossover does seem to improve the search for intersection-free solutions in the first few generations. However, after 20 generations, there is no clear difference with the other GA variants. Clearly, the hybrid algorithm *HEA* and its variant *HEA-real* perform better in improving the deviation costs. The reason is probably that optimal solutions of the 3D-tube network problem lie on the frontier of the feasible domain: for two conflicting 3D-tubes, the minimum deviation cost is achieved when they are separated by a distance δ_ℓ (the lateral separation standard) or δ_z (the vertical separation standard). Hybridizing with the A^* algorithm allows the mutation operator to better explore the frontier of the feasible domain, where the optimal solutions lie, to the expense of longer computation time.

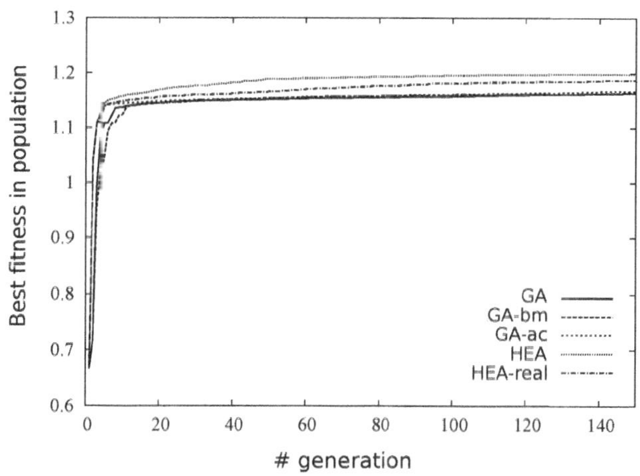

Figure 2.14. *Comparison of several variants of evolutionary algorithms, on the test-case with 10 trajectories*

The left-hand side of Figure 2.15 shows the evolution of the best and average fitness in the population across the generations, for the hybrid algorithm *HEA*, on the test-case with 10 3D-trajectories. The right-hand side shows the computation time (in seconds), as a function of the generation number.

Table 2.2 compares algorithms *HEA*, *HEA-real* and *GA-ac* on the more difficult test-case with 40 3D-trajectories. Considering the last two columns, we see that the genetic algorithm with the adapted crossover but without the mutation operator embedding the A^* algorithm could not find a solution after more than 7 hours of computation, even though the number of generations (2,000) and the population size (500) are higher than for the other algorithms. Let us recall that the sequential stand-alone A^* could not separate all 3D-trajectories either, on this more difficult test-case with 40 trajectories, and that the fitness of the 3D-trajectory network was 0.0250. The *HEA* finds the best solution, without any remaining intersections, but with the longest computation time. Its variant *HEA-real* finds a good solution in a much shorter time. The results in Table 2.2 are averaged over five runs, except for *HEA*, for which only one run was made.

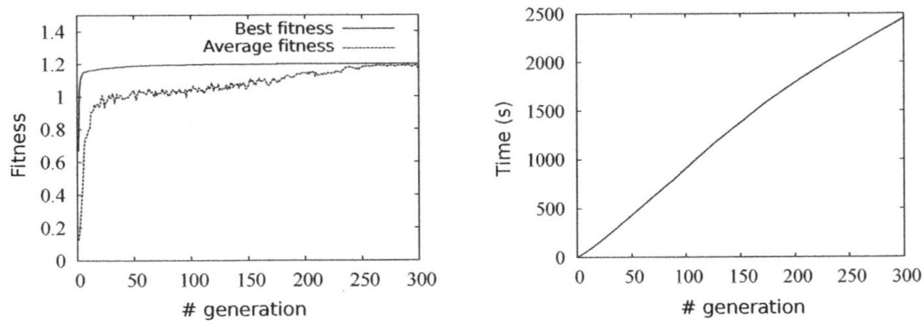

Figure 2.15. *Best and average fitness (left), and computation time (right), as a function of the generation number, for the HEA with* $popsize = 350$, $P_c = 0.6$, $P_m = 0.05$, $sh = 0.3$, $\Delta_{clust} = 70$, *on the test-case with* 10 *trajectories*

	# gen.	$popsize$	P_c	P_m	sh	Δ_{max}	time	avg. $\mathcal{F}_{best}$
GA-ac	2,000	500	0.6	0.05	0.3	70	7 h 49	0.097522
HEA	300	350	0.6	0.05	0.3	70	20 h 41	1.184649
HEA-real	300	350	0.6	0.05	0.3	70	3 h 42	1.153515

Table 2.2. *Comparison of three evolutionary algorithms, on the test-case with* 40 *trajectories*

Figure 2.16 shows the evolution of the best fitness (left) and computation time (right) over 300 generations, for the test-case with 40 trajectories, with a single run for each algorithm and the same parameter values as before. This figure confirms that the *HEA-real* variant of the hybrid algorithm is the best compromise between the quality of the final solution and the computation time. When increasing the mutation probability P_m to 0.1, this algorithm gives a solution with a best fitness of 1.1669, which can be improved to 1.1696 by applying the local method evoked in section 2.3.4.8 to the final solution found by *HEA-real*. With $P_m = 0.1$, the computation time is 6 hours and 25 minutes.

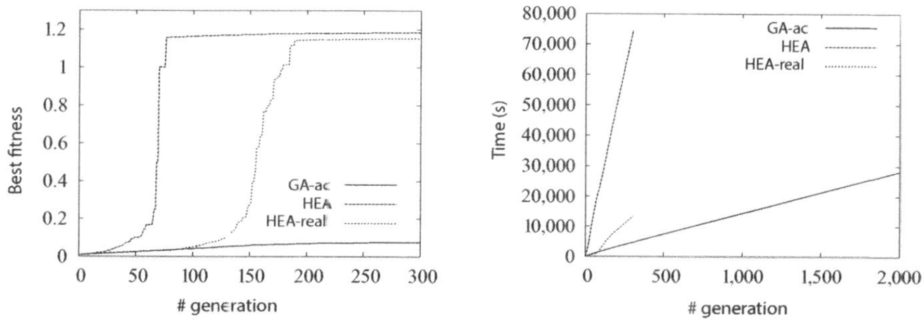

Figure 2.16. *Comparison of several variants of evolutionary algorithms, on the test-case with 40 trajectories*

2.3.6. *Application to real data, using a more realistic 3D-tube model*

In the toy problem considered in section 2.3.5, the whole flight was taken into account, from departure to arrival, assuming a single RFL per origin–destination flow. This simplified model was useful when comparing the performances of the proposed approaches on a few test-cases. However, it is not realistic enough for the purpose of assigning 3D-tubes to real traffic flows, for several reasons.

First of all, the simplified model does not take into account the variety of climb/descent performances of the actual aircraft. A second reason is that, in reality, we focus only on a portion of the whole airspace: we want to redesign the airways network at the national or continental scale, for example, not over the whole airspace over the Earth. Consequently, we must take into account the traffic entering or exiting the chosen area of interest, and add some attributes to the 3D-tube model, such as entry or exit flight levels when aircraft take off or land outside the area of interest. A third reason why a more realistic model is needed is that actual flights operating on a given origin–destination pair might not all request the same cruising flight level. The choice of the RFL depends on the aircraft type, the flown distance between departure (DEP) and arrival (ARR) airports and the cost policy of the airline operator.

Consequently, more realistic models are required for both the traffic flows and the 3D-tubes.

2.3.6.1. *Traffic flow model and computation*

A traffic flow in a given airspace is characterized by the following attributes: the point of origin O, which can be the departure airport or the entry point, on the border of the considered airspace, the point of destination D, which can be either the arrival airport or the exit point, the EFL (if any), the flight level requested for cruise RFL and the XFL (if any). In order to identify the main traffic flows, we must group flights according to the values taken by these attributes. As a result of this clustering process, there may be several sub flows with different values for EFL, RFL and RFL, for a same (O, D) pair.

Figure 2.17 shows the distribution of the RFLs, for several categories of flights based on the distance between origin and destination. These distributions are computed considering the 29,687 flights recorded over Europe on June 21, 2002[7]. A general trend can be observed for the observed flights: the farther they go, the higher they want to fly. We can observe several peaks per distance category. As an example, on that day flight levels FL280, FL330 and FL370 were the most requested levels for aircraft covering a distance of 450–500 NM.

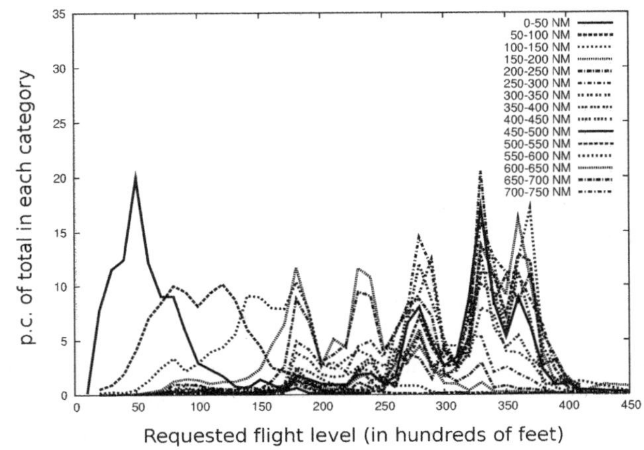

Figure 2.17. *Europe: distribution of the RFLs, for 15 categories of flights based on the distance between origin and destination*

In order to identify the main traffic flows according to the relevant attribute values, flights are first grouped by origin–destination pairs. For each pair (O, D), a variant of the k-means algorithm is used to find clusters of flights, according to a distance criterion based on the flight level values for EFL, XFL and RFL.

As a result of this clustering process, there can be several sub flows, corresponding to different values for the triple (EFL, RFL, XFL), for each O-D flow. The aim is to compute a 3D-tube for each of these sub flows.

2.3.6.2. *A more realistic 3D-tube model based on aircraft performances*

In real life, aircraft do not always follow line segments during climb or descent, and they might have very different performances, depending on the aircraft type.

7 Note that more recent data might give a very different distribution.

A more realistic model can be obtained by using the Eurocontrol BADA[8] performance model to compute the hull of the climb or descent profiles, for each traffic flow.

The BADA files provide performance data for each aircraft type, with various hypotheses. For example, some nominal, minimum or maximum climb rates corresponding to three hypotheses on the aircraft mass are provided, as well as a nominal descent rate corresponding to an idle thrust descent. Considering all the aircraft types in a given origin–destination flow, we can compute the hull of the vertical profiles corresponding to a given sequence of CFLs. As an example, Figure 2.18 shows the vertical profiles (left) and the upper and lower hulls (right) obtained for a same sequence of (d_j, CFL_j), for the variety of aircraft types belonging to a same flow (here A340, B742, B743, B744, B762, B763, B772, DC10, L101, MD11). These upper and lower hulls delimit the vertical uncertainty zone that replaces, in the more realistic model, the line segments that were used in the simplified model.

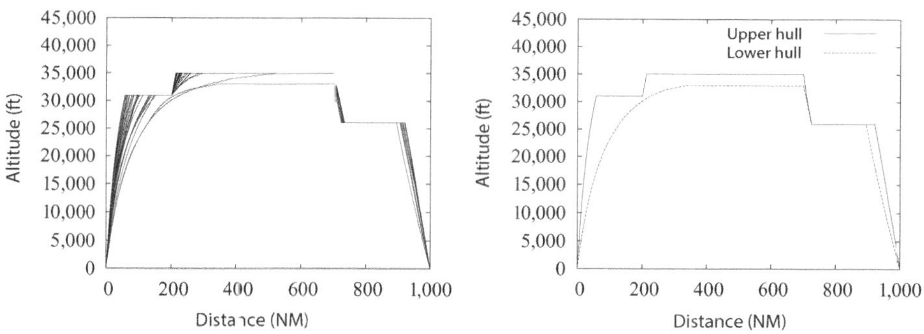

Figure 2.18. *Example of several different vertical profiles (left) and computed hull (right)*

2.3.6.3. *Attributes of the 3D-tubes*

As in the simplified model, given a 2D-route, the vertical profile of a 3D-tube can be fully computed from a list of couples (d_j, CFL_j) where d_j is the distance along the route at which starts a climb or descent toward flight level CFL_j. However, in a more realistic model, we might want to focus on a particular area of interest (e.g. the airspace of a given country). In such a case, some 3D-tubes might have their origin at the point where the 2D-route crosses the border of the area of interest. This might also be the case for the end of the 3D-tube. Except for very specific cases, traffic across such a border is usually delivered at a constant flight level. For such 3D-tubes, we need

8 BADA: Base of aircraft data.

to know the EFL and XFL at the border of the area of interest, and the lengths of the entry and exit cruise segments.

In the specific cases where the flights are climbing from a nearby airport when crossing the border, or descending toward such an airport, the EFLs and/or XFLs might be comprised within lower and upper bounds. However, we can avoid to complexify the model by including these nearby airports in the area of interest.

To summarize, in the more realistic model for the 3D-tubes, the attributes of a 3D-tube are the following:

r: A discrete variable encoding the choice of the 2D-route. When using real data, this variable can encode the choice among several paths from origin to destination, in the existing route network;

EFL: The entry flight level, if any, and the length of the constant level segment after entry;

len_E: The length of the cruise segment after entry;

l_c: The successive CFLs between the departure point and the end of the current trajectory segment. l_c is a list of couples (d_k, CFL_k), where d_k is the distance along route r at which begins a climb or descent toward flight level CFL_k;

XFL: The exit flight level, if any, and the length of the constant level segment before exit;

len_X: The length of the cruise segment before exit.

2.3.6.4. *Detection of 3D-tubes intersections*

In the simplified model, detecting if 3D-trajectories are separated or not using the distance defined in section 2.3.1.3 might not be realistic enough in some cases. A typical example is given in Figure 2.19, where a climbing trajectory levels off at a cruising flight level just below another trajectory. In such a case, the distance defined in equation [2.2] is such that a loss of 3D-trajectory separation will be detected, whereas it is not the case in fact, considering the conflict definition given in section 1.7. In addition, the distance between line segments of the simplified model cannot take into account the vertical uncertainties of the more realistic model described in section 2.3.6.2.

In order to avoid the false detection problem encountered when using the distance defined in equation [2.2], a 3D-tube can be defined as a geometric volume with a rectangular cross section of width δ_ℓ and height $h(d) + \delta_z$, where $h(d)$ is the height of the vertical uncertainty zone considered in section 2.3.6.2 at the distance d, along the route, where the cross section is computed. In other words, we simply add a buffer of size $\delta_z/2$ below and above the hull of the vertical profiles (see Figure 2.18), and another buffer of size $\delta_\ell/2$ right and left of the lateral trajectory.

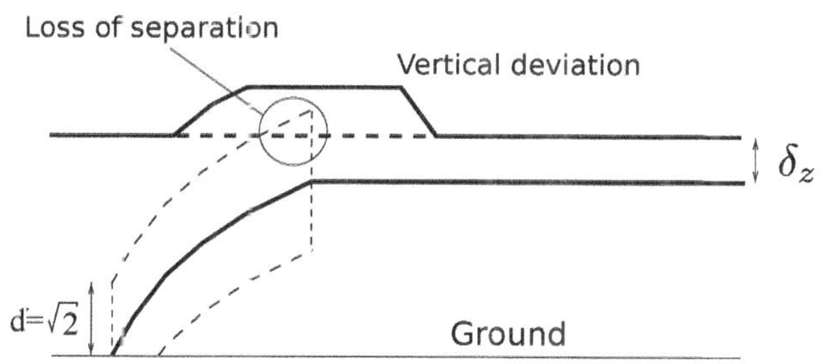

Figure 2.19. *Example of false detection of a loss of separation between two 3D-trajectories when using distance d defined in equation [2.2]*

With this model, two 3D-tubes $\mathcal{T}_1$ and $\mathcal{T}_2$ are secant if there exist $s_1 \subset \mathcal{T}_1$ and $s_2 \subset \mathcal{T}_2$ such that the 3D-tube segments s_1 and s_2 intersect. The algorithm used to detect intersections between such 3D-tubes is a little more complex (see [GIA 04a], in french) and more computation-intensive than that using the distance d.

2.3.6.5. *Adaptation of the algorithms*

Several considerations must be taken into account when applying the proposed algorithms to real traffic. Several *O-D* flows might share a same origin or a same destination point. A given *O-D* flow might contain several (EFL, RFL, XFL) sub flows. Each sub flow might be flown by different types of aircraft, with different climb/descent performances.

The last consideration has already been taken into account in the realistic model by computing the hull of the vertical profiles flown by various types of aircraft (see section 2.3.6.2). The first two considerations, however, require minor modifications in the detection of 3D-tube intersections.

The following exemption rules are added, when detecting intersections between 3D-tubes:

– an exemption radius is defined for each airport in the area of interest. The portions of the 3D-tubes starting or ending at a same airport and lying within this exemption radius are not considered as secant;

– several 3D-tubes assigned to sub flows that belong to a same origin–destination flow can share a common initial climb when the origin is a departure airport, and/or a common final descent when the destination is an arrival airport. In such cases, the portions of 3D-tubes corresponding to the overlapping initial climb segment, or final descent segments, are not considered as intersecting.

Concerning the 2D-route choice, the study on real data can be made more realistic by considering the actual route network. For every origin–destination pair, the recorded flight plan data may contain several routing options. These 2D-routes can be used instead of the parallel routes of the simplified model.

The A^* algorithm is slightly adapted to account for the new attributes used in the realistic model: EFL, XFL, lengths of the cruising segments at constant EFL or XFL. When necessary, the successors of a given state may comprise states with decremented values of EFL or XFL, or incremented values for the length of the segments at constant EFL or XFL (after entry or before exit).

The cost and heuristic functions presented in section 2.3.3.4 use the vertical profile of a 3D-trajectory made up of a succession of line segments. In the more realistic model, a 3D-tube is a geometric volume. There are as many nominal 3D-trajectories in each tube as there are of types of aircraft in the corresponding traffic flow (see Figure 2.18 in section 2.3.6.2). Actually, there are even more than one vertical profile per aircraft type because one must consider minimum and maximum performance profiles when computing the 2D-hull of the flight profiles.

To work around the difficulty posed by this multiplicity of 3D-trajectories within a 3D-tube, a single aircraft type is chosen. The same cost and heuristic functions as in section 2.3.3.4 are then applied, using the nominal vertical profiles corresponding to the chosen aircraft type. This strategy was deemed sufficient to evaluate the vertical deviations from the RFL. The geometric boundaries of the 3D-tubes are not used in the cost and heuristic functions. They are used only to detect the 3D-tube intersections.

2.3.6.6. *Results in the French airspace*

In this section, the A^* algorithm and the hybrid algorithm *HEA-real* are applied to a real problem instance in the French airspace. The route options and traffic flows are extracted from one day of traffic (June 21, 2002). Let us recall that in the sequential approach, the A^* algorithm is applied to each flow in turn, whereas in the global approach, the hybrid algorithm *HEA-real* is applied to a population of 3D-tube networks.

The algorithms are applied only to the main air traffic flows. The first step consists of selecting the O-D-EFL-XFL-RFL flows that contain at least a required number of flights (e.g. 20 flights per day). Prior to sequentially applying the A^* algorithm to the main traffic flows, these flows are sorted by lexicographic order, considering the following attributes: requested cruising flight level RFL, XFL and EFL, and number of flights in the flow. The evolutionary algorithm evolves a population of 400 elements, over 300 generations, with $P_c = 0.6$, $P_m = 0.1$, $sh = 0.3$, $\Delta_{clust} = 70$.

Table 2.3 gives the comparative results of the two algorithms, for the 72 flows comprising at least 20 flights with a RFLs above FL145. On this instance, the sequential A^* algorithm failed to find a solution for one of the flows, whereas the global approach with the HEA succeeded to do so, albeit in a very long computation time.

Note that, for this instance focusing on the French airspace, the selected 72 flows represent nearly 40% of the whole traffic on that day. Figure 2.20 shows an example of 3D-trajectory network over France. For the sake of clarity, only one nominal 3D-trajectory per 3D-tube was drawn, considering only one type of aircraft per flow.

	Sequential A^*	**HEA-real**
$\mathcal{F}$	0.083336	1.300095
Failures	1	0
Computation time (s)	106.95	66970.20
Deviation cost	(205.21511)	235.61843
% of overall traffic	39.30	39.60

Table 2.3. *Comparative results of the A^* and* HEA-real *algorithms on a real problem with 72 origin–destination flows comprising at least 20 flights per day, in France (2002, June 21)*

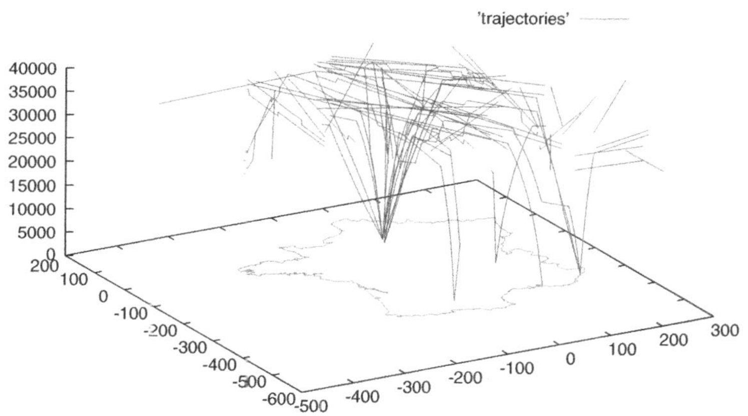

Figure 2.20. *Example of 3D-tube network found by the A^* algorithm, for flows of more than 20 flights in France, on June 21, 2002. For clarity, only one nominal 3D-trajectory per flow is represented. Horizontal distances are in nautical miles and vertical distances in feet. For a color version of the figure, see www.iste.co.uk/durand/atm.zip*

2.3.6.7. *Results in the European airspace*

The results on the European airspace are presented with two different methods for the detection of 3D-tube intersections:

DIST-A320: One 3D-trajectory per flow, assuming all aircraft are of the same type (Airbus A320). Intersections are detected using the distance d presented in section 2.3.1.3.

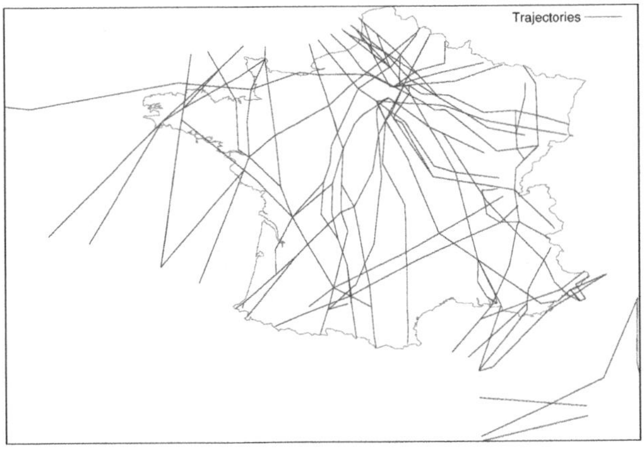

Figure 2.21. *Top view of the 3D-tubes found by the A* for flows of at least 20 flights, over France, with standard routes, on June 21, 2002. For a color version of the figure, see www.iste.co.uk/durand/atm.zip*

IZONES: All aircraft types are considered when computing the 3D-tube (see section 2.3.6.2), for the flights belonging to the considered flow. A geometric method is used to detect 3D-tube intersections.

Actually, only the second method is realistic enough to envision an operational application. The first method relies on the simplified model used for the toy problems, slightly adapted to take into account a more realistic vertical profile, using a single real aircraft type.

The traffic flows are extracted from the flight plan data, for the same day as in the French airspace instance. The algorithms try to assign separate 3D-tubes to the 65 flows comprising more than 20 flights. The 2D-route choice is made among the three parallel route options, as in the simplified model.

Tables 2.4 and 2.5 show the results with the sequential A^* algorithm and the hybrid evolutionary algorithm (*HEA-real*), respectively, for the flows of at least 20 flights on the considered day in Europe. With the DIST-A320 detection method, the A^* algorithm failed to find a solution for one of the 3D-trajectories, whereas the evolutionary algorithm found an intersection-free solution. When using the most realistic IZONES detection method, the A^* sequential method and the evolutionary algorithm both succeeded in finding solutions. The fitness value of the solution found by the A^* is slightly better, and the computation time[9] are much shorter than for the evolutionary algorithm.

9 Tests were run on a Pentium IV 2.8 GHz PC, at the time.

Detection method:	**DIST-A320**	**IZONES**
$\mathcal{F}$	0.010204	1.120674
Failures	2	0
Computation time (s)	139.35	506.06
Deviation cost	(566.08163)	545.95383
% of overall traffic	6.05	6.20

Table 2.4. *Results of the sequential A^* algorithm for flows in Europe with at least 20 flights, on June 21, 2002, with two different methods for the detection of intersections*

Detection method	**DIST-A320**	**IZONES**
$\mathcal{F}$	1.112151	1.119510
Failures	0	0
Computation time (s)	50309.76	204629.79
Deviation cost	587.52588	551.29116
% of overall traffic	6.20	6.20

Table 2.5. *Results of the* HEA-real *for flows in Europe with at least 20 flights, on June 21, 2002, with two different methods for the detection of intersections*

This good performance of the A^* sequential approach on this specific problem might be explained by the star-shaped topology of the network in the European airspace. This topology is illustrated in Figure 2.22, which shows the network found by the A^* sequential approach. There may be several origin–destination flows for which the 3D-tubes can be optimized independently from the others. This separation in subproblems allows the sequential A^* algorithm to find good solutions that might be close to a global optimum. In future works, we could also take advantage of this star-shaped topology in the evolutionary algorithm by identifying and addressing several independent sub problems in parallel. However, this approach is clearly not possible when focusing only on the French airspace, where the 3D-tubes associated to the main entry–exit flows are intertwined.

The total deviation cost, as shown in Tables 2.4 and 2.5, is higher with the DIST-A320 detection method than with the more realistic IZONES method based on the geometric intersection of 3D-tubes. This is most certainly due to the false detections induced by the use of distance d in the DIST-A320 method and exemplified in Figure 2.19 of section 2.3.6.4.

The last line, in Tables 2.4 and 2.5, gives the proportion of traffic that is contained in the main flows for which 3D-tubes are computed. In the European instance, the 65 main flows for which we define a network of separate 3D-tubes represent only about 6% of the total traffic. This comes in contrast with the French instance, where about 40% of the total traffic could be handled by 72 3D-tubes (see Table 2.3). The main reason for this difference lies in the nature of the origin and destination points. In the French instance, most of the origin and destination points are entry or exit points on the border of the airspace, and these points are taken from the actual route network. As a consequence, many flights share the same origin and destination points, even though they might not have the same departure and arrival airports, located outside the French airspace. In the European problem, most origin and destination points are airports located within the airspace of interest. Because airport-to-airport flows represent each a small part of the total traffic, the proportion of traffic in the 65 main flows is relatively small in the European instance.

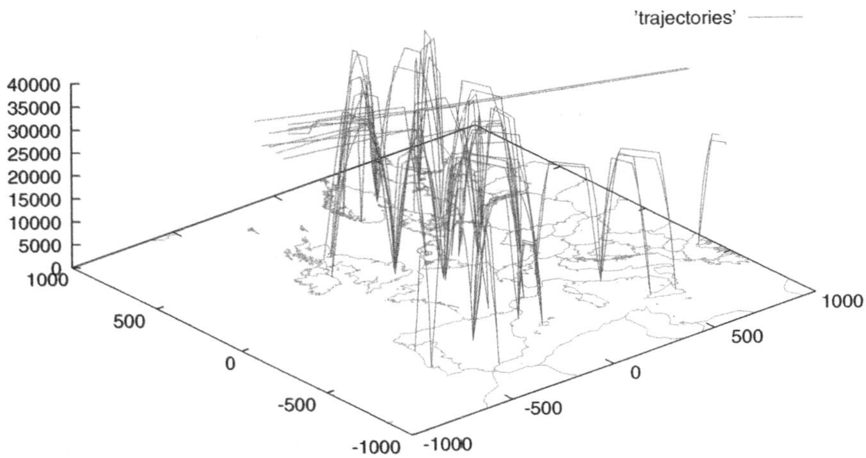

Figure 2.22. *Example of 3D-tube network found by the A^* algorithm, for flows of more than 20 flights in Europe, on June 21, 2002. For clarity, only one nominal 3D-trajectory per flow is represented. The stereographic projection is centered in Paris. Horizontal distances are in nautical miles and vertical distances in feet. For a color version of the figure, see www.iste.co.uk/durand/atm.zip*

In order to handle a significant amount of traffic on separated 3D-tubes, at the continental scale, we would have to cluster neighboring airports into large terminal areas (TMAs), before applying the proposed algorithms to the main TMA-to-TMA flows.

2.4. Conclusion on air route optimization

In this chapter, we have seen several very different approaches to the problem of optimizing the air route network. The proposed models for the air routes themselves can be classified in two general categories: 2D-routes where only a top view of the airways is considered or 3D-tubes where the airways are seen as geometric volumes in three dimensions.

Several approaches using the first category of models have been presented in section 2.2. In the works presented in section 2.2.1, the 2D-route network is modeled as a planar graph and it is completely redesigned, "from scratch," using clustering methods and computational geometry. In other works (see section 2.2.2), the positioning of the network nodes is optimized, starting from a regular grid, and using a metaheuristic (simulated annealing or a particle swarm optimization algorithm). In section 2.2.3, 2D-routes from origin to destination are modeled as great circles that can be represented by points in a dual space, using the Hough transform. A basic clustering method is used to identify clusters of routes, which are then replaced each by a single 2D-corridor. The solution is then refined by a genetic algorithm.

Approaches using the second category of models (3D-airways) are scarce in the literature. It is even more so for those addressing the difficult problem of separating these 3D-airways (or 3D-tubes) while minimizing the trajectory deviation costs. In section 2.3, we have presented the works of some of the authors where this problem is addressed using either a sequential A^* algorithm or a HEA. We have seen that, when the origin–destination flows are intertwined such as in the test-cases with the toy problem or the real instance in the French airspace, the sequential approach was more likely to fail in finding non-secant 3D-tubes than the global optimization approach with the evolutionary algorithm. The comparison is not so clear-cut for real instances where the traffic flows might be split in several independent or loosely dependent sub problems, such as in the European instance. Some work remains to be done to parallelize the evolutionary algorithm in order to apply it to the different sub problems. Hybridizing the evolutionary algorithm by embedding an A^* algorithm and a local search method has proved beneficial, when compared to non-hybrid variants of the evolutionary algorithm.

3

Airspace Management

In Chapter 2, we presented several approaches to building a route network or independent "tubes" for the principal flows. In section 2.2.1, the airspace partitioning into sectors was briefly modeled with Voronoï cells in which a density criterion can be calculated. This could be a way to build simultaneously a route network and an airspace partitioning into sectors.

In this section, we assume that the route network is defined, and we focus on three problems related to the definition and management of airspace sectors. In the first problem, we want to define the sector edges that minimize different criteria such as the workload due to the coordination of flights crossing sector boundaries or the workload related to trajectory monitoring and conflict resolution within the sector boundaries.

In the second problem, elementary sectors are defined, and we want to optimize functional airspace blocks (FABs)[1] in order to balance the traffic between blocks and limit the flows between the blocks.

In the third problem, we try to dynamically optimize the daily management of an airspace block: the problem is to group sectors in order to balance the controllers' workload, to avoid overloads and to respect different operational constraints.

In sections 3.1–3.3, we give examples of resolution using metaheuristics on these three problems.

1 A functional airspace block is a set of sectors on which several teams of controllers are qualified. Airspace blocks are independently managed by these different teams that relay to one another. Several sectors of the same airspace block can be merged and controlled by the same pair of controllers. However, two sectors from two different airspace blocks cannot be merged.

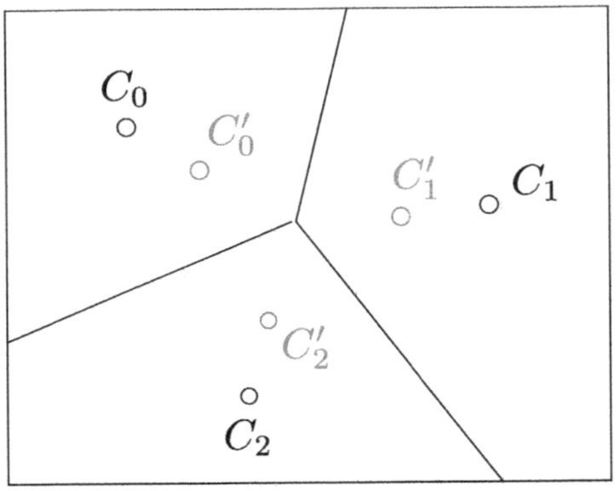

Figure 3.1. *Sector modeled by class centers*

3.1. Airspace sector design

The control sectors have evolved with the traffic increase but are still manually defined by human experts, mostly air traffic controllers. It is worth wondering if the airspace partition into sectors is optimal regarding the traffic evolution. The problem is difficult because the model must be able to consider various shapes of sectors, but remain simple enough to be solved. Delahaye [DEL 94, DEL 95a, DEL 95b] presented in his PhD report a simple model for sectors in the horizontal plane (he does not consider the vertical dimension).

n control sectors are characterized by n centers of a Voronoï diagram representing the limits of the sectors (see Figure 3.1).

The main advantage of this model is that a sector is defined by a single point. However, different sets of points can define the same Voronoï diagram. This is the case in the example in Figure 3.1, triplets (C_0, C_1, C_2) and $(C_0^{'}, C_1^{'}, C_2^{'})$ that define the same sector design. This is also the case for triplets (C_1, C_2, C_0), (C_2, C_0, C_1) and every permutation of triplet (C_0, C_1, C_2) that give the same result. Another issue of this model is that it only produces convex sectors, whereas real sectors are not always convex. Delahaye optimized the airspace sector design with a classical evolutionary algorithm as described in [GOL 89, HOL 75]:

– a vector of reals represents the coordinates of the class centers used to build the Voronoï diagram;

– the optimized criteria consider the coordination workload (number of aircraft flying from one sector to another), the monitoring workload (number of aircraft inside the sector) and the resolution workload (number of pairwise conflicts inside a sector). The objective function tries to balance these three criteria and respect constraints such as:

- the time spent by an aircraft in a sector should be longer than a minimum time,

- routes followed by aircraft should not cross too close to the border of the sector.

Giving an analytical expression to summarize all these criteria is not possible. Only a simulation can measure the quality of a sector design. Metaheuristics are a good option in such a case because the objective can be seen as a black box:

– the crossover operator identifies the closest class centers from both parents (which is a minimization problem) and applies a classical arithmetic crossover operation on these pairs;

– the mutation operator randomly moves one or several class centers in a defined neighborhood.

After his PhD, Delahaye proposed improved models in order to handle non-convex sectors [DEL 98]. He also added the vertical dimension to his model in order to make it more realistic [DEL 06, DEL 08]. Kicinger and Yousefi [KIC 09] also proposed an evolutionary algorithm combined with an elementary cell aggregation heuristic in order to partition the airspace into sectors. Xue [XUE 09a] introduced for the American airspace an approach using a Voronoï diagram optimized with an evolutionary algorithm. Zelinski [ZEL 09] compared three methods to define sectors, one based on traffic flow aggregation, another based on Voronoï diagrams optimized with evolutionary algorithms and the third method using integer linear programming. Experiments show the advantages and drawbacks of each method but none really outperforms the others.

3.2. Functional airspace block definition

In Europe, the airspace structure follows the country borders of the different states. Nowadays, more than 60 control centers cover the airspace of around 40 state members of the European Organization for the Safety of Air Navigation (Eurocontrol). In the context of the FABEC[2], the problem is to reorganize the control centers in order to simplify the global structure. Among the numerous criteria that Eurocontrol defined, three are quantifiable and can lead to a better balance of the center distribution:

– airspace blocks must minimize flows on their borders;

– important flows must take place inside the blocks;

– traffic must be balanced between different airspace blocks.

2 Functional Airspace Block Europe Central.

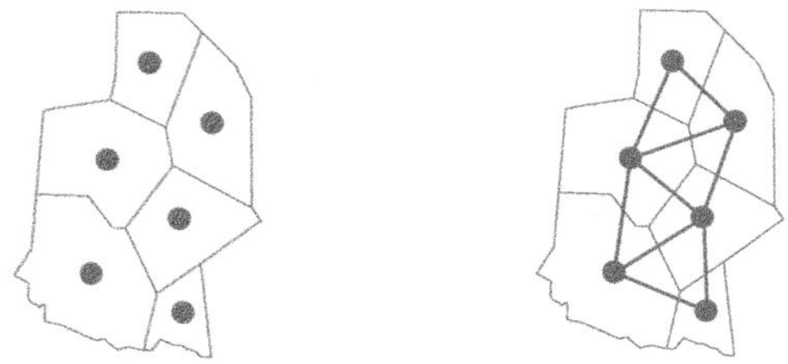

Figure 3.2. *Graph model for an airspace partition*

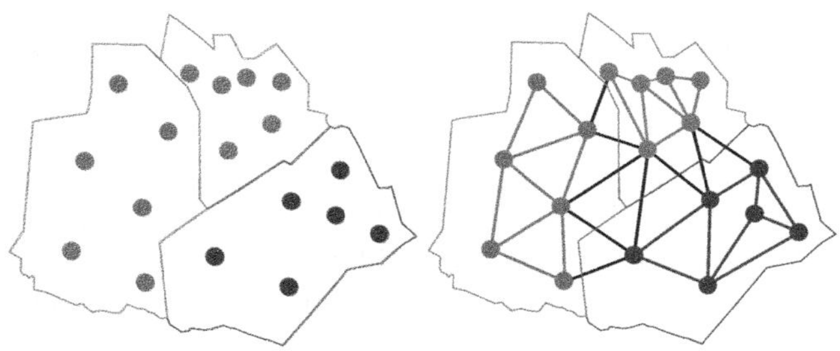

Figure 3.3. *Three functional blocks and corresponding sectors. For a color version of the figure, see www.iste.co.uk/durand/atm.zip*

In his PhD report, Bichot [BIC 07a] modeled the problem as a graph partitioning problem. The graph vertices are the sectors and the edges are the flows connecting sectors. The edge weights are the mean numbers of aircraft in the flows connecting sectors.

Figure 3.2 details the graph modeling a five-sector problem. Figure 3.3 represents a partition of the airspace into three functional blocks and the associated graph.

The minimization criterion chosen by Bichot is the normalized cut ratio criterion corresponding to the sum of the flows entering or exiting the functional blocks divided by the sum of the internal flows. He adds a balance constraint: the weight of a block must not exceed k times the mean weight of every block. After showing the problem is NP-complete [BIC 04], Bichot tested different classical algorithms on real recorded data (several months of European traffic), and compared them with two metaheuristics and also with an innovative metaheuristic called fusion–fission by analogy to nuclear reaction.

3.2.1. *Simulated annealing algorithm*

A simulated annealing algorithm uses a starting point. Bichot used a random configuration based on a percolation algorithm to build the starting point. He assumed that the graph is known, as well as the vertices and edges. The number of blocks is also fixed. Percolation simulates the movement of fluids through porous materials. Bichot defined as many sources of fluid as the desired number of functional blocks. Each source of fluid is a sector that is the kernel of the FAB to which all other sectors are progressively linked. A detailed explanation of the algorithm is given in [BIC 04]. With this starting point, Bichot used a standard simulated annealing algorithm: at every step a sector is randomly chosen in an FAB and linked to another airspace block. The algorithm is divided into two phases. During the first phase of the algorithm, the control temperature is still high and the chosen sector is linked to a block with a low cut ratio. During the second phase, the control temperature is lower, and the chosen sector is linked to a neighboring block. The temperature adjustment and the phase switching moment seem to be adjusted quite empirically.

3.2.2. *Ant colony algorithm*

In order to apply ant colony optimization to the FAB partitioning problem, Bichot introduced a model with one ant colony representing one block. Each block is the territory of one colony. The different colonies are competing to get sectors and deposit their pheromones. More concretely, a sector belongs to the colony that has the biggest amount of pheromones on it. After each ant movement, the value of the new state is calculated. If the ant movement decreases the criterion, the new partition is accepted, otherwise it is accepted with a probability following a rule similar to the simulated annealing method. This approach, like the previous one, requires us to adjust many parameters.

3.2.3. *A fusion–fission method*

Bichot introduced a heuristic called fusion–fission by analogy with nuclear fusion and fission [BIC 07a].

For the fusion, the idea is to merge two FABs sharing the most traffic (as shown in Figure 3.4). For the fission, the principle is to divide the biggest airspace block into two blocks (see Figure 3.5). Bichot refined his method by allowing some sectors to move from one block to another according to the cut ratio minimization criterion.

In [BIC 04], Bichot showed that this last approach seems more efficient and easier to apply than the simulated annealing and ant colony approaches. He also compared fusion–fission to classical graph partitioning methods.

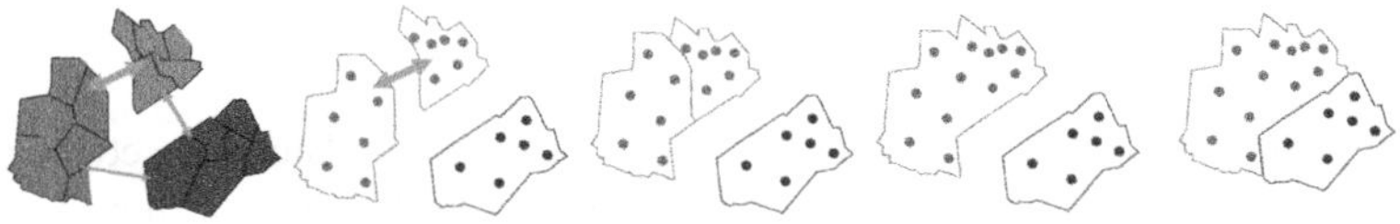

Figure 3.4. *Fusion of two blocks. For a color version of the figure, see www.iste.co.uk/durand/atm.zip*

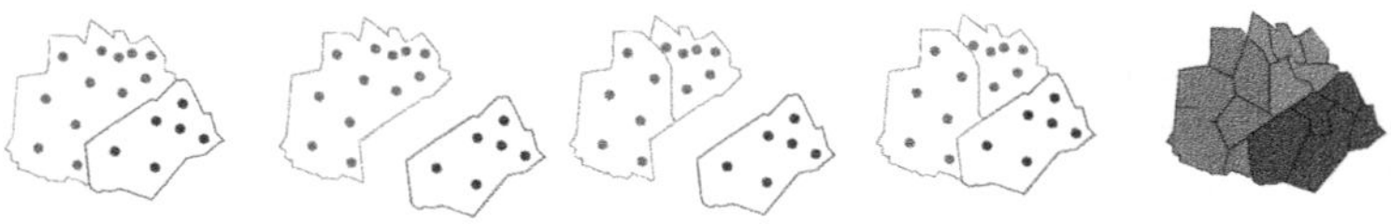

Figure 3.5. *Fission of the biggest functional airspace block. For a color version of the figure, see www.iste.co.uk/durand/atm.zip*

3.2.4. *Comparison of fusion–fission and classical graph partitioning methods*

In [BIC 07b], Bichot compared two classical graph partitioning algorithms (Scotch and Graclus) to the fusion–fission approach and showed that the latter is more efficient than Scotch and Graclus, but also much more time consuming. Table 3.1 compares the normalized cut criterion, the balance between block sizes and the maximum number of sectors per FAB for the three algorithms. It also gives the values of the criteria for the existing French airspace partition.

Algorithms	Ncut	Balance	Max number of sectors
Fusion–fission	1.09	1.14	26
Scotch	1.18	1.20	30
Graclus	1.28	1.52	38
Existing partition	1.64	1.50	31

Table 3.1. *French airspace partition*

Figures 3.6 and 3.7 show the existing and optimized functional blocks for two flight levels (16,000 and 36,000 ft). The optimized partition divides the French airspace into only five blocks instead of six for the existing partition. This result could be an argument in favor of a partition with more blocks in the lower airspace and fewer blocks in the higher airspace.

3.3. Prediction of air traffic control sector openings

We have seen in section 3.1 how to define the airspace sector boundaries, given the air routes and traffic flows. In section 3.2, we saw how to group these airspace sectors into functional blocks, each placed under the responsibility of an air traffic control (ATC) center. Operations such as sector design and FAB definition are in fact a strategic redesign of the whole airspace, which should take place well in advance of daily operations.

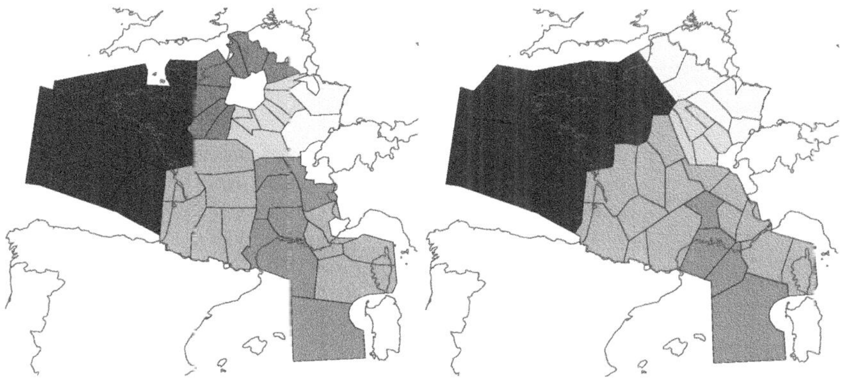

Figure 3.6. *Existing French functional airspace blocks (left: 16,000 ft; right: 36,000 ft). For a color version of the figure, see www.iste.co.uk/durand/atm.zip*

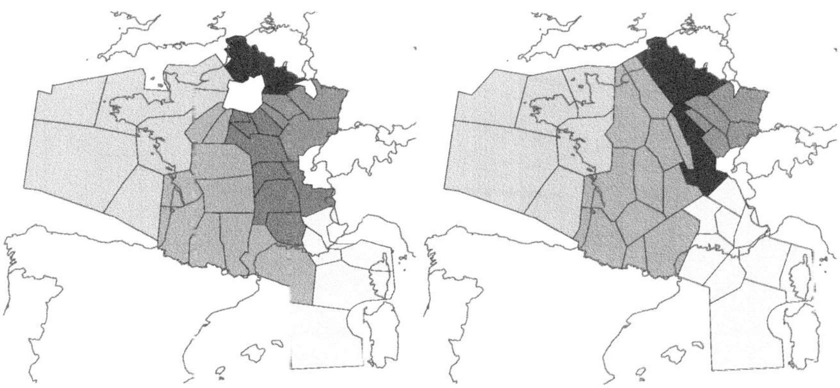

Figure 3.7. *Optimized French functional airspace blocks (left: 16,000 ft; right: 36,000 ft). For a color version of the figure, see www.iste.co.uk/durand/atm.zip*

In this section, we focus on real-time or pre-tactical operations, assuming that the airspace sector geometry is fixed and that sectors are already allocated to FABs, as a result of a strategic design of the airspace. We consider a set of airspace sectors belonging to an ATC center (or an FAB). In daily operations of a control room, airspace sectors are dynamically assigned to air traffic controllers' working positions.

Figures 3.8 and 3.9 illustrate the airspace partitioning into ATC sectors, on a toy example with five airspace sectors denoted by numbers and a list of acceptable groups denoted by letters.

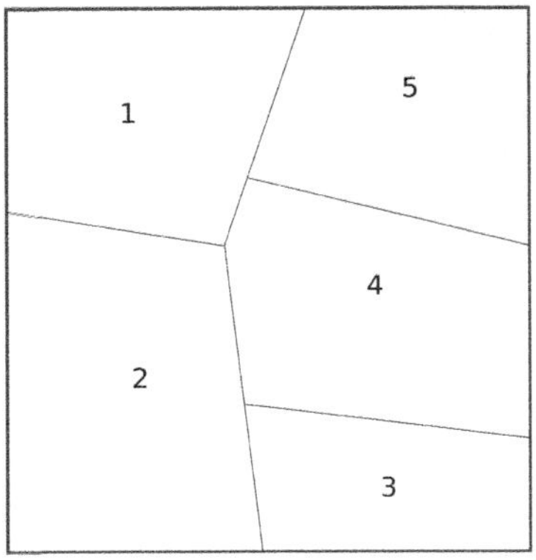

List of acceptable groups:
$a : \{2, 3\}$
$b : \{3, 4\}$
$c : \{4, 5\}$
$d : \{1, 5\}$
$e : \{1, 2, 3, 4, 5\}$
$s :$ *singleton*

Figure 3.8. *A toy example of airspace sectors belonging to the same functional block*

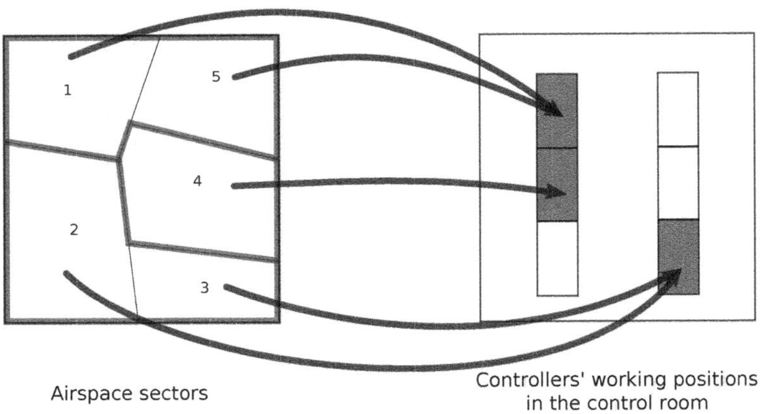

Figure 3.9. *Assignment of airspace sectors to controllers' working positions*

The airspace partitioning may change several times during the day, depending on the workload perceived by the controllers. Figure 3.10 shows a few other possible partitions that could be used instead of the partition presented in Figure 3.8. Some

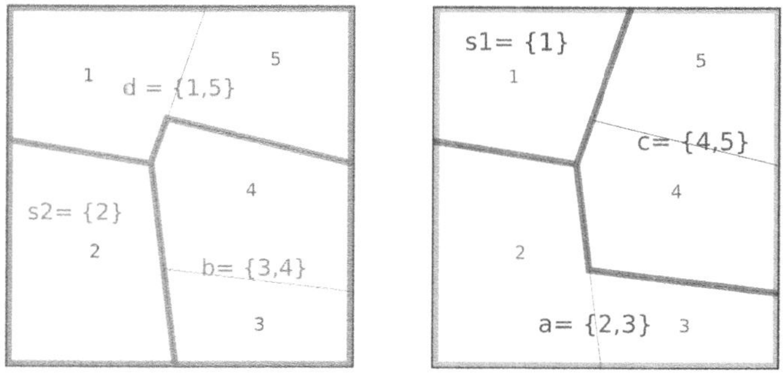

Figure 3.10. *Other possible partitions of the airspace*

operational constraints must also be considered: the duty roster, the maximum number of working positions that can be opened, the list of possible groups that can actually be operated as ATC sectors (already mentioned in Figure 3.9).

The primary objective of this dynamic partitioning of the set of elementary airspace sectors in ATC sectors is to avoid overloads, as these may threaten the overall safety of the flights controlled in the affected ATC sector. When an ATC sector becomes overloaded, some of its airspace sectors are transferred to another working position (a new one or one already open but underloaded), when this is possible. When such reassignments are not possible, one must enforce traffic regulation measures such as delaying departing flights or rerouting aircraft. Overloads must be anticipated with enough look-ahead time, so that regulation measures can be taken early enough. A secondary objective, which might sometimes come into contradiction with the primary objective of avoiding overloads, is to be as cost-efficient as possible by opening as few ATC sectors as possible and by avoiding underloads.

Currently, this reassignment of airspace sectors to controller working positions is quite efficient for the purpose of sharing the workload among ATC sectors, in real time. However, we are still lacking prediction tools that would allow control room managers and flow management operators to anticipate how workload and airspace partitioning could evolve in the next few hours. Such tools actually require two things: a reliable estimation of the future workload in any given ATC sector and an algorithm that can compute an optimal partition of the airspace in ATC sectors, according to the predicted workload.

3.3.1. *Problem difficulty and possible approaches*

The airspace optimal partitioning problem is highly combinatorial: the total number of candidate partitions is equal to the Bell number. However, considering operational constraints, such as restricting ourselves to the list of acceptable groups of airspace sectors, does reduce the number of sector combinations to explore.

For relatively small and sufficiently constrained problem instances, exact tree-search methods that exhaustively explore (or discard) all possible airspace partitions in ATC sectors might be tractable. For larger instances where the considered FAB is made up of a large number of airspace sectors, or for less constrained problems with a larger number of acceptable sector groups, such methods might be unsuccessful. In such cases, an optimal or nearly optimal partition can be searched using a metaheuristic.

3.3.2. *Using a genetic algorithm*

In [GIA 02a, GIA 02b], Gianazza and Alliot used a genetic algorithm [GOL 89, MIC 92] to build an optimal partition of the airspace in ATC sectors. This metaheuristic approach is compared with two tree-search methods (a *depth-first* branch and bound search and a *best-first* search) on airspace sectors belonging to the five French *en route* control centers.

In this approach, each element of the population is a sector configuration, that is a partition of the set of airspace sectors of the chosen control center. At each iteration, the genetic algorithm selects a pool of parents. Randomly chosen parents are then recombined, using crossing and mutation operators. The resulting offspring is added to the new population, which is completed by randomly picking individuals from the parents' pool. This completion is done so that the best fit individuals have a greater chance of being chosen. Several refinements exist for the selection, crossing and mutation operations, with for example the application of *scaling* and *sharing* operators to the raw fitness. A description of these refinements can be found in Chapter 3 of [EIB 03].

In [GIA 02a, GIA 02b], the mutation of an individual (a sector configuration) first picks at random one ATC sector and one of its neighbors. The volume of airspace made up of the two chosen ATC sectors is then repartitioned. This partial reconfiguration of the sectors is also random, with the constraint that the result should not contain more than three ATC sectors. The new ATC sectors then replace the two initial sectors in the mutated individual.

The crossover operator removes some ATC sectors in each of the two parents and tries to form a new partition from each amputated partition, using ATC sectors from the other parent. This usually does not result in a complete partition of the airspace.

A full partition is obtained by randomly choosing control sectors compatible with the incomplete partition.

The *fitness* criterion depends on the following factors, in decreasing order of priority: excessive overloads, number of working positions (i.e. number of ATC sectors in the configuration), excessive underloads and finally the small overloads or underloads. For any ATC sector, workload is assessed by considering the difference between the flow of incoming traffic and a threshold value called the sector *capacity*. The capacity values are those that were actually used in operations at the time. Once computed, the *raw fitness* criterion is modified using *clusterized sharing* and *sigma truncation* (see [GOL 89] or [EIB 03] p. 59), so as to leave a chance even to the least fit individuals to reproduce, thus allowing a better exploration of the search space. For the *sharing* operator, a difficulty arises in defining a distance criterion between partitions of the set of airspace sectors. A pseudo-distance between two partitions, similar to the Hamming distance, is specifically designed for this *sharing* operator. The only difference with the Hamming distance is that the sequence of symbols (ATC sectors) that are compared – counting the differences between the two partitions – may not have the same length.

An elitist strategy is applied in order to preserve the best individuals of the old population when building a new one. The new population is made up of the best fit elements from the previous population, the mutated individuals and the offspring resulting from the crossover operator. Both mutation and crossover operators are applied to individuals randomly chosen from a pool of parents, with probabilities P_c (crossover) and P_m (mutation). The population is then completed according to the *stochastic remainder without replacement* mechanism (see [EIB 03]), so as to attain the same fixed size as the previous population.

This approach using genetic algorithms is compared, on real instances, with two tree-search methods. Other authors have used constraint programming on a similar problem. We shall now briefly present these exact approaches that exhaustively explore the search space of possible airspace partitions.

3.3.3. *Tree-search methods, constraint programming*

Two tree-search strategies are presented in [GIA 02a, GIA 02b]. One is a *depth-first* search, illustrated in Figure 3.11, on our toy example with five airspace sectors. The other is a *best-first* search inspired from an A^*, which first develops the nodes having the best estimate of the total cost for the path from the root to a leaf of the tree.

In his PhD thesis [BAR 02b], Barnier successfully applied constraint programming methods to a similar problem of airspace partitioning (although not with the same capacity values). The partitioning problem is formalized as a *constraint satisfaction problem*. The resolution of this problem also relies on a tree-search method (*backtracking*) that iteratively reduces the domain of each variable.

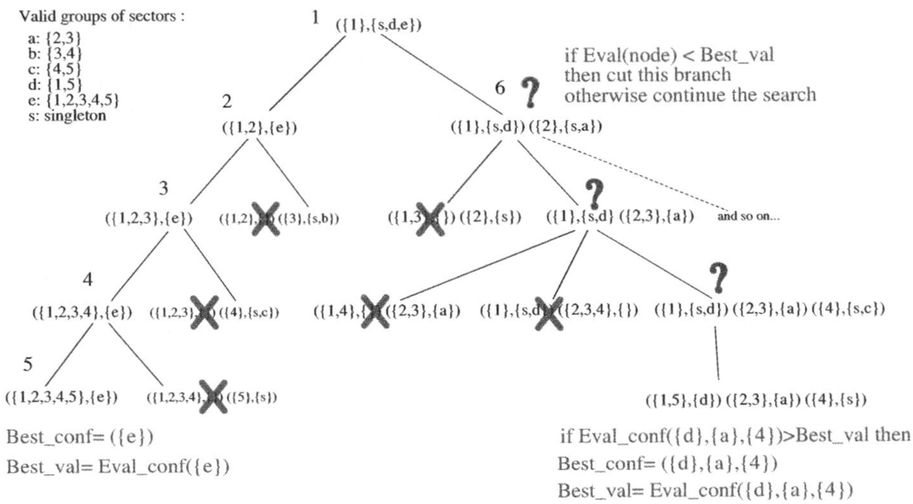

Figure 3.11. *Search for an optimal partition by a depth-first tree-search algorithm*

All these tree-search methods are tested on real instances, with the airspace sectors of the five French ATC centers. The results show that, on these real instances of relatively small size, when considering some operational constraints such as a list of restrictions concerning the valid groups of sectors, the global optimum can be reached in very short time (a few seconds at most, with a Pentium IV 1.8 GHz).

In [GIA 02a, GIA 02b], the *depth-first* and *best-first* strategies are compared with the genetic algorithm presented in section 3.3.2. With 220 elements in the population, evolving over 300 generations and with a crossover probability of 0.6 and a mutation probability of 0.2, the genetic algorithm finds the global optimum in nearly all cases. The computation times are however much longer (several minutes).

3.3.4. *A neural network for workload prediction*

In [BAR 02b, GIA 02a, GIA 02b], the chosen variables (input traffic flow) and the ATC sector capacities, which were those actually used in operations at the time, do not provide a reliable estimate of the air traffic controllers' workload. Further works [GIA 06a, GIA 06b, GIA 08] by Gianazza and Guittet aimed at selecting more relevant indicators, among the multitude of ATC complexity metrics proposed in the literature, to better explain the controller workload.

In these works, the chosen dependent variable assumed to represent the actual workload is related to the ATC sector status. Considering past sector openings, the following observations can be used to assess workload in any given sector:

– when the sector is "collapsed" (merged) with other sectors, to form a larger sector, we can assume that this is due to a low workload;

– when the sector is "opened" (i.e. actually operated on a controller working position), we can assume a normal workload;

– when the sector is "split" into several smaller sectors, this reflects an excessive workload in the initial sector.

The basic assumption is that this observed sector status ("collapsed," "opened" or "split") is statistically related to the actual workload perceived by the controllers.

A neural network is used to compute a triple (p_1, p_2, p_3) representing the probabilities for a sector to be in the above states. The network inputs are the ATC complexity indicators computed from aircraft trajectories and metrics on the sector geometry (sector volume). The neural network is first trained on a set of examples based on recorded traffic and historical data of sector openings from the five French ATC centers.

Training the neural network consists of adjusting the weights assigned to the network connections, so as to minimize the output error, when compared with the desired output in the examples. This requires the use of an optimization method operating in the weights' space. The first methods that were designed to train multi-layer perceptrons relied on the gradient of the error to iteratively search for the optimal weight vector. Starting from an initial point in the weights' space, every step consists of computing a new iterate from the current one, following a descent direction based on the error gradient. Under several conditions on the objective function, these descent methods converge to a local minimum. Such methods require the computation of the error gradient, which can be done efficiently using back-propagation of the error in the network (see [BIS 96]). More recently, several metaheuristics have also been proposed, either to optimize the network topology or to tune the weights: genetic algorithms [LEU 03], particle swarm optimization (PSO) [GUD 03], ant colonies [BLU 05], differential evolution (DE) [SLO 08], etc.

The results presented in [GIA 06a, GIA 06b, GIA 08] on ATC controllers' workload prediction are obtained using a quasi-Newton method (here BFGS[3]) to

3 BFGS is an optimization method discovered independently by Broyden, Fletcher, Goldfarb, and Shanno.

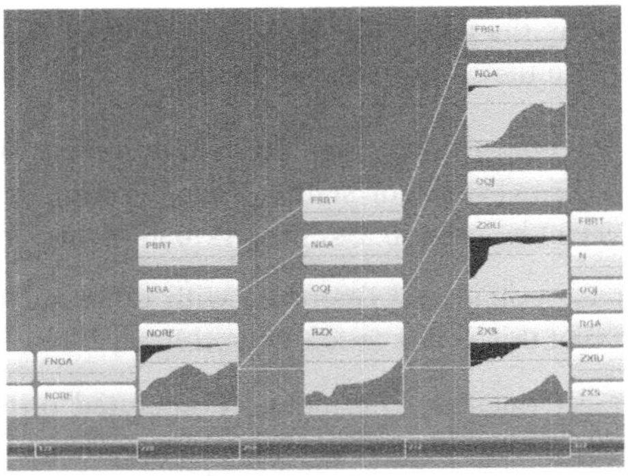

Figure 3.12. *Workload and airspace partitioning prediction*

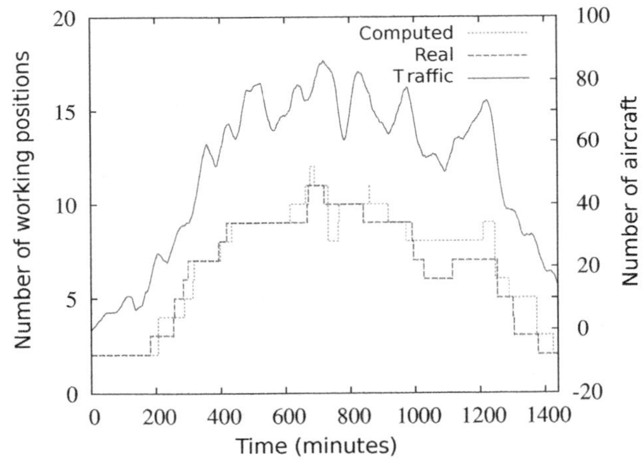

Figure 3.13. *Computed versus actual number of controller's working positions. For a color version of the figure, see www.iste.co.uk/durand/atm.zip*

train the network. Some preliminary results using PSO and DE show fairly similar results.

In [GIA 09, GIA 10], the *depth-first* tree-search algorithm that computes optimal airspace partitions (see section 3.3.3) is combined with the neural network for workload prediction, in order to provide realistic predictions of the ATC sector openings. This prediction of the workload and airspace partitioning is illustrated in Figure 3.12.

A first evaluation of this research approach was done by comparing the number of working positions computed by the algorithms with the number of positions that were actually open the same day. Figure 3.13 shows that the two dotted lines representing these quantities are quite close. The continuous line above the dotted lines is the total traffic in the ATC center and is given here only as an indication of the traffic evolution during the day.

3.3.5. *Conclusion on the prediction of sector openings*

We have seen that the difficulty of the airspace partitioning problem in ATC sectors assigned to controllers' working positions, which is in essence highly combinatorial, is reduced when considering operational constraints such as restricting the number of ways to group airspace sectors to the existing list of valid ATC sectors. We have also seen that a realistic prediction of ATC sector configurations requires a reliable workload prediction model.

Metaheuristics can be useful for both problems (airspace partitioning and workload prediction). For large instances that cannot be addressed by exact tree-search methods, metaheuristics are often the only option: they rely on a random walk in the search space, guided by a heuristic that introduces a bias toward good solutions. Metaheuristics can also be used to tune the weights of the neural network predicting the air traffic controller workload.

As a conclusion, it must be noted that in this specific example with real instances of airspace sectors and ATC sectors from the French airspace, metaheuristics are not the fastest and most efficient methods. For such instances of relatively small size, optimal partitions can be obtained in a short time, using exact tree-search methods.

However, exact methods can become impractical for larger instances with more airspace sectors or more ATC sectors. In such cases, using a metaheuristic can be a good alternative to find optimal or near-optimal partitions of ATC sectors.

4

Departure Slot Allocation

4.1. Introduction

Among the key concepts identified to meet Single European Sky Air Traffic Management Research (SESAR) performance objectives [COM 07], the planning of 4D-trajectories would allow en route capacity to increase, while preserving the current level of safety One of the goals of the Episode 3 project [GRA 06] was to estimate how strategic deconfliction schemes over the current air traffic flow management (ATFM) process could benefit from such regulations.

Currently, the Network Manager Operation Center (NMOC)[1] in Brussels is in charge of optimizing the traffic by, among other strategic or tactical measures, delaying departure slots for the flights involved in overloaded en route sectors. The purpose of this ground holding scheme is to respect the en route capacity constraints provided by each air traffic control center (ATCC) as a number of aircraft per hour, according to their daily schedule. Former studies such as [DAL 97] and [BAR 01b] aimed at improving this slot allocation over the greedy algorithm used at the NMOC. However, one of the limitations of this regulation model is that the definition of sector capacities (hourly rate of aircraft entering the sector) is poorly related to the complexity of the traffic with respect to the controller workload, as assessed by [GIA 06b].

In Allignol's PhD [ALL 11], instead of trying to satisfy en route capacity constraints, he proposed to directly solve the potential conflicts occurring between any two intersecting trajectories with departure time adjustments. A single delay would be associated with each flight such that all potential conflicts occurring above a given flight level (FL) would be avoided. This very fine grain model would of course generate much larger constraint sets than the macroscopic (at the sector level)

1 Previously called the Central Flow Management Unit.

capacitated sets, but would guarantee conflict-free trajectories all along the flight path, provided that aircraft were able to scrupulously follow their predicted route in the four dimensions.

Obviously, the latter hypothesis is far from being met nowadays, but the accuracy of flight management systems will be a crucial issue for future ATFM and air traffic control (ATC) systems, as advocated by [ALL 03]. Nevertheless, this approach could reduce air traffic complexity by "deconflicting" it in advance. The remaining conflicts due to deviation from the flight plan (or occurring in the lower airspace) would then be dynamically solved either by automated resolution systems as proposed in Chapter 6 or by more standard ATC procedures.

Several optimization paradigms were evaluated for this purpose by Allignol, namely metaheuristics, local search and constraint programming. We will focus here on the evolutionary algorithm approach.

In the following sections, we first introduce the context of the ground holding policies. Then we describe Allignol's model of a conflict-free slot allocation, starting by the conflict detection and details on the evolutionary algorithm. Next, results on instances of the French traffic are presented before concluding on remarks.

4.2. Context and related works

4.2.1. *Ground holding*

As aircraft obviously cannot be paused while airborne whenever the traffic complexity becomes too high to be safely handled by a controller, one of the simplest ways to leverage ATC workload is to postpone the takeoff of aircraft[2]. This kind of measure is however quite unpopular among airlines, as it can be very costly and may propagate in terms of missed connections and aircraft rotation (see [COO 04]), so the delays should be minimized as much as possible.

4.2.1.1. *Satisfying sector capacity constraints*

The aim of the NMOC regulations is to maintain the number of en route aircraft entering a given subset of sectors below some bound over given time periods (usually one hour), according to the constraints declared by experts in each ATCC for the day of traffic. The NMOC experts first identify the overloaded sectors and responsible flows with the PREDICT tool, then compute a slot allocation as ground delays for the involved flights with the CASA tool (see [CFM 00]).

2 Note that flights might be delayed for other reasons than en route capacity violation, such as bad weather or equipment failures.

CASA is able to consider many operational constraints and updates to optimize its allocation process, but the algorithm used has greedy properties and cannot guarantee to find a correct solution (which satisfies all the constraints) or an optimal solution. Constraint programming technology has been applied with good results to prove and optimize the allocation process with a relaxed model [DAL 97] or to smooth the resulting load profiles [BAR 01b] with a tighter model.

However, traffic complexity is very hard to define precisely, and sector capacities, expressed as a maximum number of aircraft entering the sector over a given time period, do not consider many other parameters relevant to the ATC performance. Observed actual capacities, as well as merging and splitting a subset of sectors, symptomatically present very different profiles than the predicted ones.

To overcome this issue, recent works such as [FLE 07] use a much more precise and complex workload constraint programming model to dynamically balance the traffic over the sectors of an ATCC in the upper airspace. Other works such as [BAR 02b] use constraint programming technology as well optimizing the ATCC opening schedules to match the predicted traffic more closely, or even attempting to redesign airspace sectors with better balancing such as [TRA 03].

4.2.1.2. *Solving the conflicts*

One of the key ATM operational concepts of the SESAR program that Episode 3 tried to validate is the design of conflict-free 4D-tubes within crowded airspace (whereas separation could be delegated to aircraft in less dense areas). So instead of only respecting sectors' capacities macroscopically, Allignol proposed to evaluate the cost of precisely solving all potential conflicts, only by ground holding, while minimizing the sum of allocated delays to maximize global performance. This large-scale optimization problem was based on a sliding forecast window principle.

This conflict-free model yields much larger problem instances than the capacitated models as all the conflicting trajectories' intervals above a given FL are considered as constraints. The resulting problem is intrinsically disjunctive as for each potential conflict between two flights i and j, either i must precede j or j precede i at each pair of points concerned (see section 6.17).

4.3. Conflict-free slot allocation

The ground holding model uses as input a set of temporal conflict constraints computed for each pair of flights that intersect in the three spatial dimensions. Section 4.3.1 describes the processing of flight plans to compute the conflict constraints and the modeling of deconfliction by ground holding.

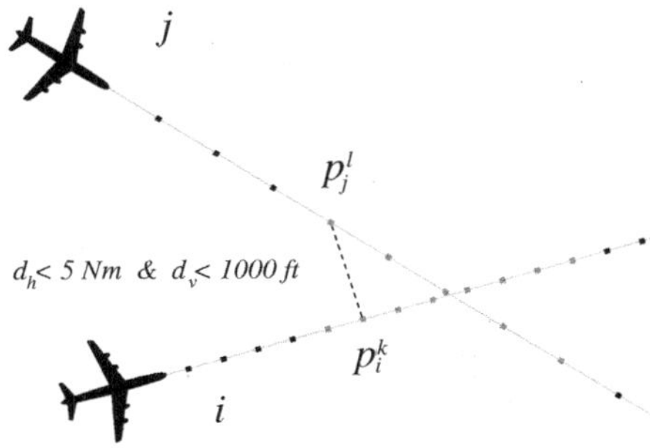

Figure 4.1. *Conflicting points detection*

4.3.1. *Conflict detection*

Data were provided by the Complete Air Traffic Simulator (CATS) developed at the French "*Direction des Services de la Navigation Aérienne*" simulator [ALL 97], which takes as input all filed flight plans concerning the French airspace for a given day of traffic and the relevant airspace configuration (sectors, waypoints, etc.), and outputs the corresponding 4D-trajectories. Trajectories were sampled with a 15 s time step, which is the largest interval to guarantee that at least two points of the trajectories of facing aircraft at the highest possible speed are closer than one separation norm, i.e. even the shortest conflicts are detected.

Trajectories are then probed pairwise for potential conflicts, considering the maximal allowed delay. The separation norm is thus tested for each pair of points of the two probed trajectories (up to $p = 900$ points per trajectory for up to $n = 9{,}500$ flights in $\mathcal{O}(n^2p^2)$) as illustrated in Figure 4.1 in the horizontal plane.

To reduce the complexity of this detection phase, trajectories are encapsulated into bounding boxes: each trajectory is split into segments (a segment being here defined as a constant heading portion of the trajectory), then each of these segments is encapsulated into a bounding box, such that every point of the segment is farther than half the separation norm from each side of the box, as illustrated in Figure 4.2 in the horizontal plane.

Consider two flights i and j with trajectories encapsulated in bounding boxes $(b_i^1, ..., b_i^n)$ and $(b_j^1, ..., b_j^m)$, respectively. If there is an intersection between boxes b_i^k and b_j^l, then the pairwise tests for conflicting points are only performed for points contained in b_i^k and b_j^l, thus saving a lot of useless tests for the rest of the trajectories. This filtering proved to reduce computing time for conflict detection dramatically.

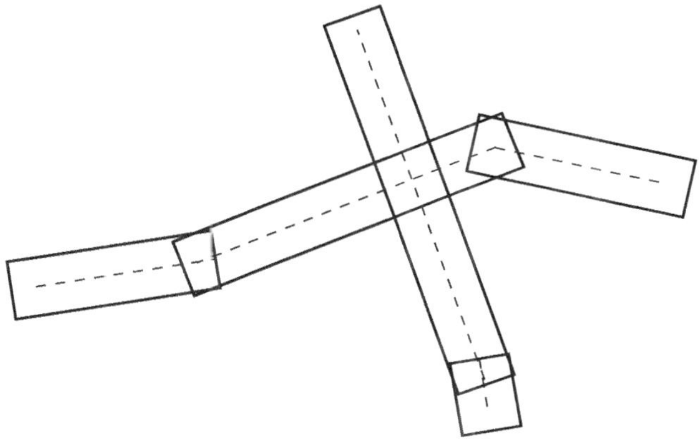

Figure 4.2. *Two intersecting trajectories and their associated bounding boxes. Conflicting point detection is only performed for points in the intersecting boxes*

Operationally, flights originating outside the European Organization for the Safety of Air Navigation (Eurocontrol) countries cannot be delayed, so their delay variable will be fixed to 0 in the constraint model, reducing the number of variables but tightening the constraints as well and offering fewer opportunities for optimization. Constraints corresponding to conflicts occurring between two such flights will of course be discarded as we cannot delay the flights to solve them. Such remaining conflicting cases would have to be taken care of by other ATC techniques beyond the scope of this study.

The FL of the detected conflicts can be filtered, for example to only consider conflicts occurring within the upper airspace (e.g. from FL290 and above). The minimal and maximal altitudes of each conflict are recorded during the detection stage and a conflict is discarded if it occurs entirely below or above the specified airspace slice.

Though the maximal allowed delay can be seen as a parameter of the resolution algorithm only, it also affects the conflict detection. Actually, when the maximal allowed delay is increased, the size of the problem grows as well, as more and more flights tend to be in potential conflict. Ultimately, if a 24-h delay would be allowed, the conflict detection could be done regardless of time, as any two geometrically conflicting trajectories would generate a constraint. So, whenever a particular instance could not be solved with a given maximal allowed delay δ_{max}, it has to be generated again with higher values of δ_{max}, which will later capture potential conflicts on the trajectory pairs.

4.3.2. *Sliding forecast time window*

In order to limit the size of the problem and to be reactive to uncertainties, the whole day is not treated at once, but only flights scheduled for takeoff during the next T_w minutes are considered. T_w represents the look-ahead time, also called *The forecast time window*. The situation is reconsidered every σ minutes (with $\sigma \ll T_w$), where σ is the time step used in the model to make the T_w time window *slide*. This approach ensures that the problem can be updated every σ minutes: if a flight needs to cancel or delay its departure for external reasons, it will be able to free its slot and be reconsidered later on. Flights that are already airborne at the current time are considered as constraints. This is also the case for flights scheduled in the next A minutes (see Figure 4.3) because an advance notice time is required to assign any delay to a flight. In practice, this advance notice time A can be longer or shorter than σ. In the numerical results, this value was set to 0 because it does not affect the quality of the solution.

Figure 4.3 gives an example of the evolution of a flight takeoff slot when the forecast time window slides. At the first step ($t = 0$), the aircraft is delayed to take

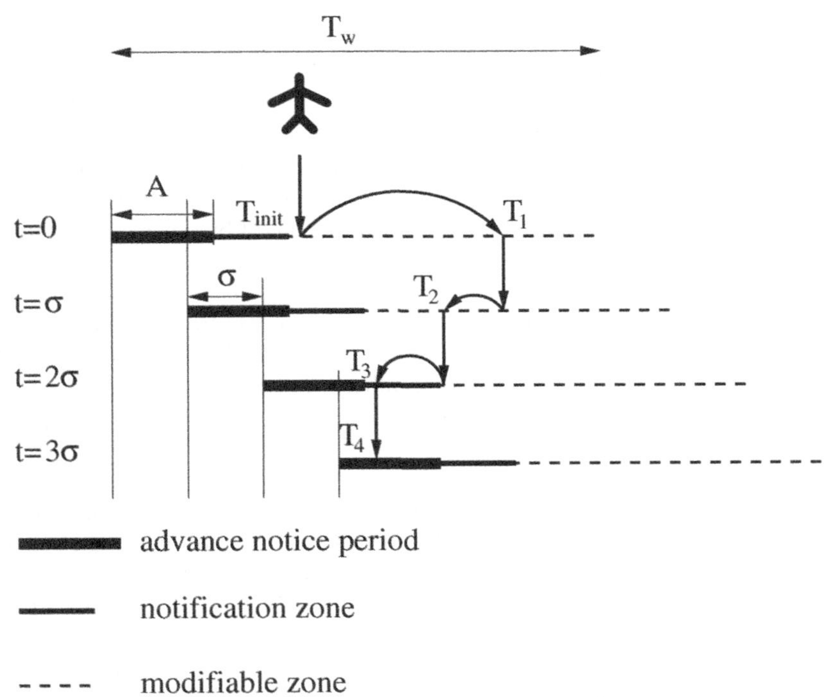

Figure 4.3. *Sliding forecast time window*

off at T_1. Because T_1 is far enough from the current time (more than $A + \sigma$ minutes ahead, in the dotted zone), the slot will still be modifiable when the current time is σ (second line). When the time window slides ($t = \sigma$), the delay might be reduced and a slot chosen at T_2 that is still modifiable. At $t = 2\sigma$, the delay can be reduced again and a slot chosen at T_3 that belongs to the notification zone. After this time (2σ), no modification is possible because at the next step ($t = 3\sigma$), the takeoff slot will be too close to the current time (less than the advance notice required).

The size of the forecast time window is an important parameter. If it is too big, the size of the problem will include a very large number of variables and the resolution might be difficult. If it is too small, the solutions found might be worse and the total delay induced over the day much higher. This will be debated in section 4.4.

4.3.3. *Evolutionary algorithm*

Classical evolutionary computation principles, such as described in the literature [GOL 89] and [MIC 92] were used for this approach. This section details the data structures, operators and parameters used in the evolutionary algorithm.

4.3.3.1. *Variables and data structures*

Given a flight i, the input data are noted:

– $\{p_i^k\}$ the chronologically ordered sequence of the 3D-points of its trajectory;

– t_i^k the time at which the flight will be at point p_i^k, should it not be delayed.

A set of decision variables for the problem is defined:

$$\Delta = \{\delta_i, \forall i \in [1, n]\}$$

where each $\delta_i \in [0, \delta_{\max}]$ represents the delay associated with each of the n flights.

We will also describe our model using the following auxiliary variables:

– $\theta_i^k = t_i^k + \delta_i$, the date at which flight i will be at point p_i^k if it is delayed by δ_i;

– $d_{ij} = \delta_j - \delta_i$.

A chromosome is defined by the n variables of Δ defined above.

4.3.3.2. *Constraints*

To compute the constraints of the model, the trajectories are probed pairwise for couples of conflicting points. For any geometrically conflicting points p_i^k and p_j^l such that the separation norm is violated (d_h being the distance in the horizontal plane and d_v in the vertical plane):

$$d_h(p_i^k, p_j^l) < 5\,\text{NM} \quad \text{and} \quad d_v(p_i^k, p_j^l) < 1000\,\text{ft}$$

we must temporally ensure that $\theta_i^k \neq \theta_j^l$, which can be rewritten with the difference variables d_{ij}:

$$d_{ij} \neq t_i^k - t_j^l$$

Starting at the first such point p_i^k that conflicts with a point of flight j, the whole continuous segment of trajectory j conflicting with p_i^k is considered:

$$\{p_j^l, \forall l \in [l_k, l_{k+r}]\}$$

for some r, and the separation constraint imposes that:

$$d_{ij} \notin \{t_i^k - t_j^l, \forall l \in [l_k, l_{k+r}]\}$$

$$d_{ij} \notin [lb^k, ub^k]$$

with lb^k and ub^k being, respectively, the lower and upper bound of the set of $t_i^k - t_j^l$.

If the next point p_i^{k+1} of the trajectory of flight i conflicts with a further segment of flight j, another forbidden segment $d_{ij} \notin [lb^{k+1}, ub^{k+1}]$ is obtained, taking part in the same potential conflict. The separation constraint imposes that:

$$d_{ij} \notin [\min(lb^k, lb^{k+1}), \max(lb^k, lb^{k+1})]$$

as the conflicting segments of flight j overlap.

So when considering all the successive points of flight i, starting at p_i^k, that conflict with overlapping segments of flight j, up to some last point p_i^{k+s}, with $\underline{lb}_1 = \min\{lb^{k+u}, u \in [0,s]\}$ and $\overline{ub}_1 = \max\{ub^{k+u}, u \in [0,s]\}$ being the overall lower and upper bounds of the corresponding forbidden intervals for d_{ij}, the first conflict between flights i and j can be defined: $d_{ij} \notin [\underline{lb}_1, \overline{ub}_1]$. Note that the maximal allowable delay $\delta_i \in [0, \delta_{\max}]$ is taken as a parameter of the problem instance, therefore the initial domain of $d_{ij} = \delta_j - \delta_i$ is the interval $[-\delta_{\max}, \delta_{\max}]$. Whenever $\overline{ub} < -\delta_{\max}$ or $\underline{lb} > \delta_{\max}$, the conflict is discarded.

A pair of flights may conflict several disjoint times over their entire trajectories, several such disjoint intervals may be forbidden for the difference of their delays. For two flights i and j conflicting q times over their entire trajectories, the union of forbidden intervals that represents the conflict is defined:

$$C_{ij} = \left[\underline{lb}^1, \overline{ub}^1\right] \cup \cdots \cup \left[\underline{lb}^q, \overline{ub}^q\right] \qquad [4.1]$$

and the following constraint is added:

$$d_{ij} \notin \mathcal{C}_{ij} \qquad [4.2]$$

For each pair of flights i and j, the Boolean variable c_{ij} is defined:

$$c_{ij} = \begin{cases} 1 \text{ if flights } i \text{ and } j \text{ are in conflict} \\ 0 \text{ otherwise} \end{cases}$$

which can be rewritten as:

$$c_{ij} = \begin{cases} 1 \text{ if } d_{ij} \in \mathcal{C}_{ij} \\ 0 \text{ otherwise} \end{cases}$$

4.3.3.3. *Fitness function*

The cost of a solution is simply the sum of the delays over the flights:

$$\text{cost} = \sum_{i=1}^{n} \delta_i$$

However, as solutions respecting the separation criteria cannot be built easily, these criteria need to be included in the fitness function.

The chosen fitness function is:

$$F = \frac{n - \sum_{i=1}^{n} \frac{\delta_i}{\delta_{\max}}}{1 + c}$$

where:

$$c = \sum_{i<j} c_{ij}$$

is the number of remaining conflicts.This function takes its values in $[0, n]$ and increases when the number of conflicts and the delays decrease.

A local fitness F_i for each flight i is also defined:

$$F_i = \frac{1 - \frac{\delta_i}{\delta_{\max}}}{1 + c_i} \qquad [4.3]$$

where:

$$c_i = \sum_{j \neq i} c_{ij}$$

represents the number of conflicts involving flight i. The local fitnesses are used in the crossover operator (see section 4.3.3.5).

4.3.3.4. *Mutation operator*

For each candidate to mutation, the delay of a flight being involved in many conflicts is modified. If every conflict is solved, a flight is randomly chosen and its parameters changed.

In practice, we say that flight i is *more constrained* than flight j if:

– $c_i > c_j$;

– or $c_i = c_j$ and $\delta_i > \delta_j$.

A number m is randomly chosen in the interval $[1, \frac{n}{2}]$, and m flights are randomly picked up in the population. Among these m flights, the most constrained one, w.r.t. the previous definition, is either locally optimized or randomly modified with a probability of 50%. We could be tempted to systematically locally optimize the delay of the worst flight, but this would make the algorithm become too deterministic and lead to premature convergence.

4.3.3.5. *Crossover operator*

The conflict resolution problem is partially separable, as defined in [DUR 98] and detailed in section 6.6.4.4. We use this property in order to increase the probability of producing children with a better fitness than their parents.

Considering a couple of parents a and b, local fitnesses F_i^a and F_i^b are computed for each flight i. If $F_i^a \ll F_i^b$ (resp. $F_i^b \ll F_i^a$), both children will have delay δ_i^a (resp. δ_i^b) for flight i. If $F_i^a \approx F_i^b$, children will randomly choose δ_i^a, δ_i^b or a combination of δ_i^a and δ_i^b.

The mutation and crossover operators are more deterministic during the first generations because there are many conflicts to solve and they focus on feasible solutions. When solutions with no conflict appear in the population, they become less deterministic.

4.3.3.6. *Sharing*

The problem is highly combinatorial and might have many local optima. In order to prevent a premature convergence of the algorithm, the sharing process introduced in [YIN 93] is used. The advantage of this sharing scheme lies in its $\mathcal{O}(p\log(p))$ complexity (instead of a $\mathcal{O}(p^2)$ complexity for classical sharing) if p is the size of the population. The distance used to compare two population elements a and b is:

$$D(a,b) = \frac{\sum_{i=1}^{n} |\delta_i^a - \delta_i^b|}{n}$$

4.3.3.7. *Parameters*

In the experiments, the following parameters were empirically chosen: the size of the population was set to 100, 20% of the population is crossed, 60% is mutated and the selection uses the stochastic remainder without replacement [GOL 89]. A sharing process is used, with the distance defined in section 4.3.3.6. In order to limit the execution time, the number of generations is limited to 500.

4.4. Results

This model has been implemented and produced the following results on various days of traffic over the French airspace in 2008, with up to 9,500 flights. About 10% of the flights are non-European flights, their delays were fixed to 0 as previously mentioned.

4.4.1. *Evolution of the problem size*

Simulations were performed using real flight plan data on the CATS simulator. Figure 4.4 shows the influence of the size T_w of the forecast time window on the problem size (i.e. number of flights that can be delayed) for a heavy day of traffic

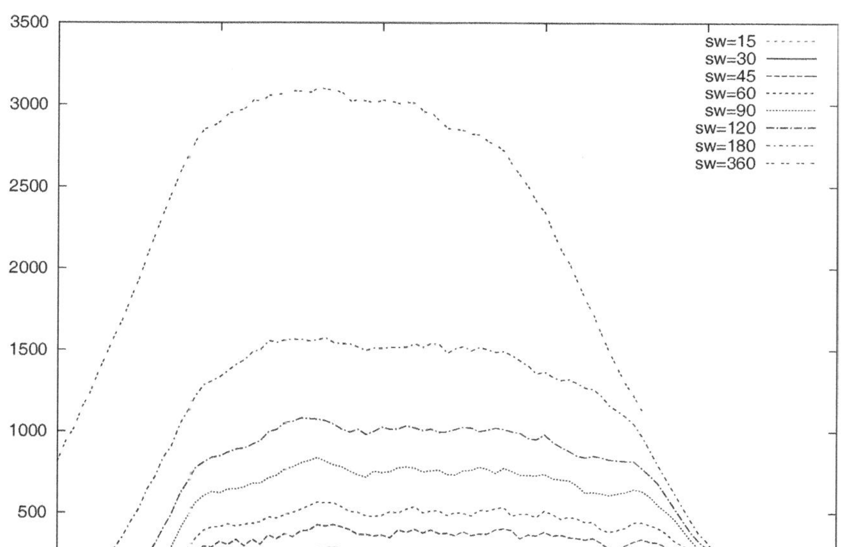

Figure 4.4. *Number of flights w.r.t. current time (hours) for different forecast time windows*

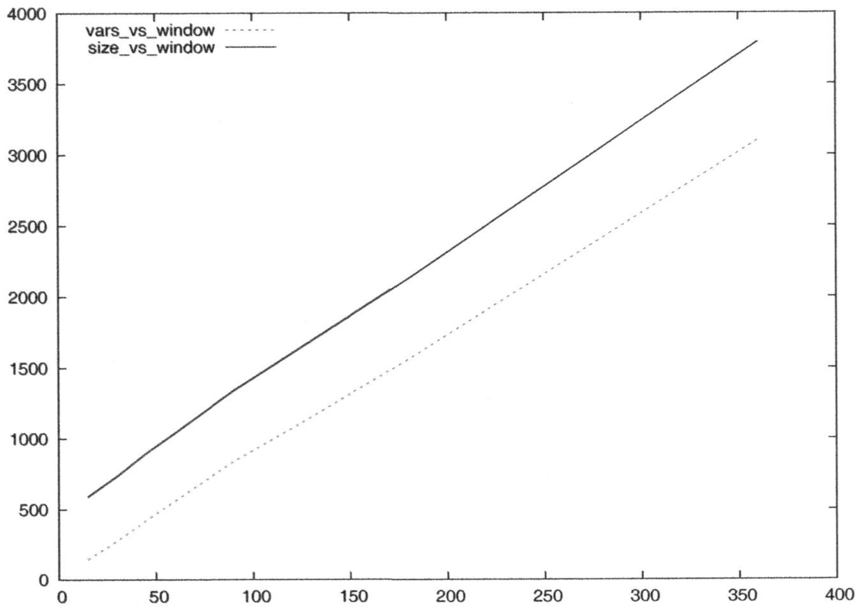

Figure 4.5. *Total number of flights (solid) and problem size (i.e. number of delayable aircraft, dotted) at 8 a.m. as a function of the forecast time window size* T_w

(October 10, 2008). The problem size increases until 5 a.m. and reaches a peak at 8 a.m. during rush hour. It decreases at the end of the day. Different time windows were tested, from 30 to 360 min. Figure 4.5 shows the size of the problem w.r.t. the size of the sliding forecast windows at 8 a.m. for that same day of traffic; it grows linearly with T_w.

Simulations also showed that it is not possible to separate the traffic into smaller problems that could be solved independently because the 3D-traffic clusters generally involve most of the current traffic, especially during peak hours.

4.4.2. *Numerical results*

The results presented here were obtained with $\sigma = 15$ min. Only conflicts occurring over FL290 were considered. With our evolutionary algorithm approach, all the conflicts could be solved by delaying less than a fifth of the aircraft.

Figure 4.6 shows the overall delay and mean delay per delayed flight for October 10, 2008. The mean delay is close to 7 min for $T_w = 30$ min but it increases with T_w.

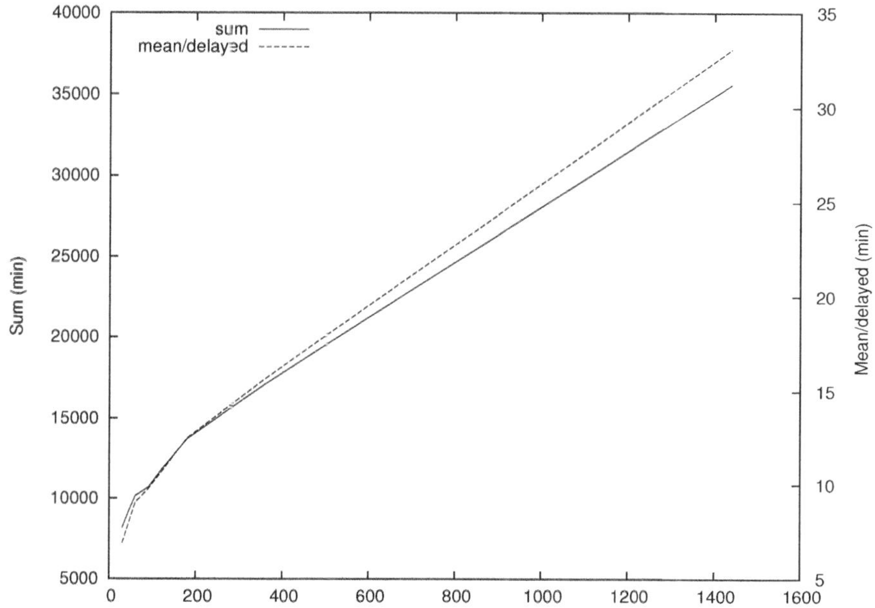

Figure 4.6. *Total amount of delay and mean delay per delayed flight w.r.t. forecast time window size T_w*

An explanation could be that when the size of the problem increases the evolutionary algorithm does not converge as easily.

The ratio of delayed flights decreases from 19% to 17% (1,184 to 1,076 flights delayed out of 8,693 flights) with T_w increasing from 30 to 1,440 min. As a consequence to this small variation in the ratio of delayed flights, the overall amount of delay has an evolution similar to the mean delay.

Figure 4.7 shows the computation times observed for various values of T_w (on an Intel Xeon 2.66-GHz processor). They are quite huge, at least for high values of T_w (>90 min). However, these computation times could be dramatically improved by the use of distributed computing techniques.

For most instances, a maximal delay around 90 min was obtained. However, in the worst cases, this conflict-free slot allocation could lead to huge maximal delay (up to 185 min in our worst case).

Results similar to those mentioned earlier were observed for various days of traffic over French airspace in 2008.

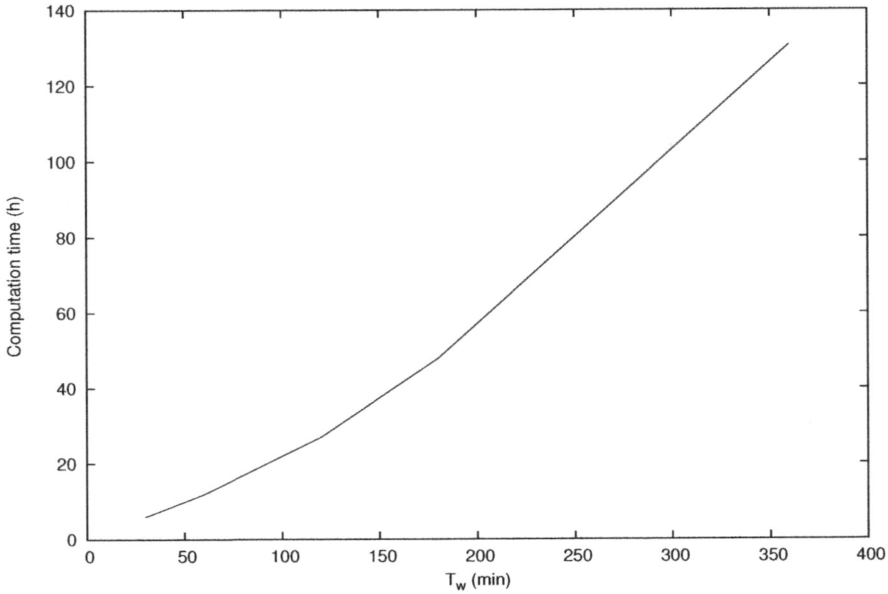

Figure 4.7. *Computation time (hours) w.r.t. forecast time window size* T_w

4.5. Concluding remarks

Results showed that every conflict could be solved by delaying less than 20% of the flights, with a mean delay per delayed flight of 7 min and a maximum delay of 87 min.

These first results had only addressed the resolution of conflicts within the French airspace. In a unified European ATC context, all conflicting traffic throughout the Eurocontrol countries should be considered. Such instances comprise up to 30,000 flights per day.

To be able to address such large instances as previously mentioned, while maintaining reasonable maximal delay figures, a ground holding algorithm with a prior FL allocation, possibly using constraint programming technology as described in [BAR 02a], was used by Allignol in his PhD [ALL 11].

This first step, computed to minimize horizontally conflicting flows by separating them vertically (trying as well to deviate as little as possible from requested FLs), "deconflicts" the traffic in a substantial amount before time slot allocation. The optimal cost then remains within much better bounds than with raw traffic.

A real-time resolution algorithm was implemented within a conflict solver described in section 6.6 with very good results. The regulation schemes could be assessed further by observing the workload of these algorithms when provided with the solutions and various kind of uncertainties, and whether the automatic resolution can cope with delays or if the resulting manœuvres will warp the plan entirely.

The results presented in this chapter were obtained with the assumption that aircraft were able to follow their 4D-trajectory precisely. In order to add robustness to the solutions, uncertainties were considered by Allignol. For example, uncertainties on takeoff times and on 4D-positions can be compensated by simply extending the conflicting intervals from definition 6.5 (see section 4.3.3.2) symmetrically by the same amount of time.

Other sources of uncertainty can be taken care of with the sliding forecast window described in section 4.3.2: every σ seconds, new information (e.g. flight cancellation and consequences of bad weather) could be integrated in the computation of takeoff times for better reactivity.

5

Airport Traffic Management

5.1. Introduction

5.1.1. *Airports' main challenges*

Airports are the meeting point of a multitude of actors, who have to manage the aircraft from their final descent to their next takeoff, as illustrated in Figure 5.1. Nowadays, all airports have to address many challenges concerning the environment (air and noise pollution reduction), security, safety and their capacity. In these perspectives, new concepts are studied to improve the efficiency and the predictability of their operations.

Coordination between the different actors is an important issue, which is addressed in the Airport Collaborative Decision Making (ACDM) project both in Europe and in the United States [EUR 12]. This project defines how and with what level of accuracy the information can be shared between the different airport stakeholders, leading toward more strategic and efficient decisions in real time. These improvements require new systems dedicated to aircraft traffic prediction and new decision support tools for the airport controllers:

– Arrival management (AMAN) systems predict and organize the arrival flow [EUR 10] from the approach sectors up to the airport: these systems help controllers to build optimized arrival schedules with flexible landing rates, ensuring automatic coordination between the approach sectors and the airport.

– Departure management (DMAN) systems [BUR 09, SIM 12, JAS 11] aim at providing accurate schedules for start-up and takeoff times: these schedules consider the runway capacity and favor departure delay at the gate (with engines off) rather than on the taxiways before the runway. To be efficient, these systems need to integrate all the constraints coming from the approach sectors, but also to estimate accurate taxi times for all the departures.

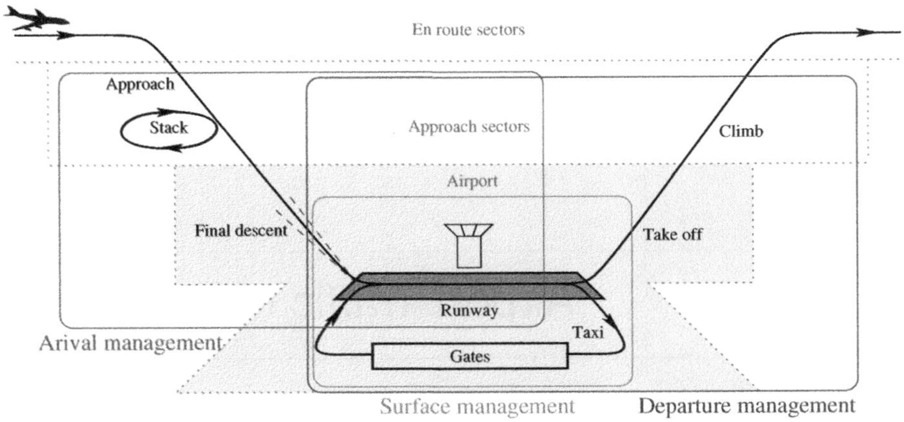

Figure 5.1. *Airport traffic management*

– Surface management (SMAN) systems aim at optimizing the use of the airport surface, under all weather conditions (including low visibility). The first step is to provide a reliable view of the ground traffic to the airport controllers and to deliver relevant alerts when some risks of dangerous events (as runway incursions) are detected. A lot of new features and improvements are expected in the surface routing and planning function, as described in the Advanced Surface Movement, Guidance and Control Systems (A-SMGCS) development program [EUR 11]. Some new technologies enabling these improvements are now available, such as reliable surface radar, automatic dependent surveillance in broadcast mode (ADS-B), differential global positioning system (D-GPS), data-link (automatic data communication between the controllers and the aircraft), airport lighting systems extended to the surface guidance. To be efficient, the SMAN systems need to be provided with a detailed description of the airport (runways, taxiways, gates, pushback procedures, etc.).

5.1.2. *Known difficulties*

Despite all the recent efforts described earlier, airport traffic predictability is still unsatisfying. Concerning the arrival flow, current AMAN systems are able to predict the landing times 30 minutes in advance with quite a good accuracy, but this is not the case for the start-up and takeoff schedules computed by the SMAN and DMAN systems.

The main difficulty concerns the numerous uncertainties that exist in the schedule of an aircraft on the ground (unlike what can be scheduled once the aircraft is flying):

– taxi times remain difficult to predict as congestion can appear in various areas (gates and taxiways intersections). The speed of taxiing aircraft is not even precisely specified (they are under the pilots' responsibility);

– the start-up time of a departure can also be affected by any kind of troubles during the turnaround process (aircraft preparation and fueling, passengers disembarking and boarding, baggage transport, etc.);

– the final takeoff time of an aircraft can still vary during taxi, according to the runway queue and the takeoff sequence decided by the airport controllers.

Estimation models based on statistical observations on a particular airport can be used to improve the accuracy of the schedule on average. However, they can hardly ensure an accurate prediction for a specific aircraft, as far as these uncertainties exist.

Other difficulties come from the complex interactions that exist between the different AMAN, DMAN and SMAN schedules of a single airport, and also between the different schedules of all the connected airports.

5.1.3. *Optimization problems in airport traffic management*

The availability of a lot of information in real time (concerning the airport current and future configurations, the flight's current positions, the traffic schedule, the meteorological predictions, etc.) and the possibility of using new technologies to guide and monitor aircraft more easily make it more and more promising to formulate and solve airport optimization problems, for the purpose of improving their capacities and traffic predictability.

In this chapter, three classical airport problems are first described: gate assignment, runway scheduling and surface routing and planning. These problems are highly combinatorial and the use of metaheuristics to solve them is common in the literature. In the last part, a global airport traffic optimization method (mixing the previous problems) is proposed and tested with fast time simulations on Roissy-CDG and Roma-Fiumicino airports.

5.2. Gate assignment

5.2.1. *Problem description*

Gate assignment appears to be a first important step in the daily airport planning process: it consists of deciding which gate will be used by which aircraft at which time. It can be considered in advance for some given fixed flights (static approach) but is also a real-time problem for airlines and airport services, when some changes have to be processed in the initial gate assignment schedule due to unexpected events (gate reassignment problem).

In any case, it involves a lot of operational and complex constraints, which can be different from one airport to another. Each gate is only compatible with a subset of aircraft types, and in some airports, some groups of gates can be configured differently to accept more or less aircraft of different sizes at the same time. Each gate also offers different facilities (remote from or fixed to a terminal, in or out of the international zone, with or without fueling or deicing services, etc.). These properties can be modeled as constraints or preferences for airlines. More generally, various objectives can be considered in the gate assignment problem, depending on the considered recipients:

– minimizing the passengers' transport times and walking distances (at the departure, during transit and at the arrival);

– minimizing the airline operating costs and the deviations to airline preferences (including baggage or freight transport, aircraft towing operations, gate facilities, fleet assignment, crew scheduling, etc.);

– minimizing the taxi times of aircraft, including the delay due to aircraft waiting for the availability of their gate, and minimizing the risk of such situations;

– maximizing the robustness of the solution, in case of deviations to the initial schedule, due to flight delay or equipment failures.

Thus, the gate assignment problem can be tackled with more or less realism. It can be considered as a mono-objective problem (by weighting together the different criteria) or as a multiobjective problem (providing multiple equivalent solutions to the airport operations). In the literature, the problem is most of the time expressed in the binary or integer programming formalism and some detailed comparative surveys can be found in [DOR 07] and [BOU 14].

5.2.2. *Resolution methods*

Some attempts to solve the gate assignment problem on actual airport flight data with exact methods (yielding and proving an optimal solution) can be found in the literature, using, for example, linear programming relaxation at Toronto International Airport [MAN 85] or branch and bound techniques at King Khalid International Airport [BOL 00] and at Chiang Kai-Shek Airport in a multiobjective formulation [YAN 01]. These kinds of attempts are promising but remain hardly applicable alone in a real-time environment because of their necessary computation time on large instances or because of their lack of practical relevance.

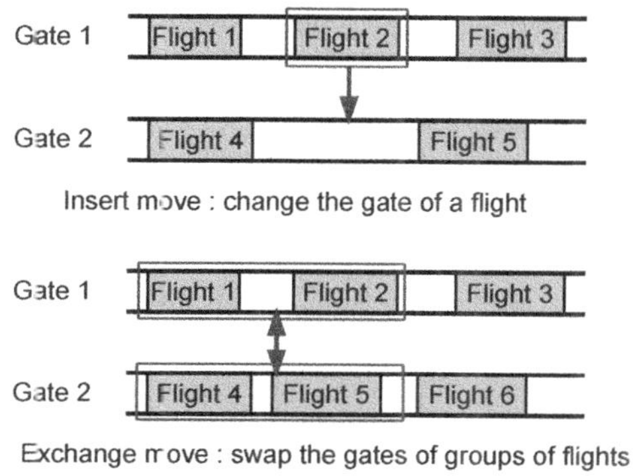

Figure 5.2. *Neighborhood moves for the gate assignment problem*

For these reasons, the gate assignment problem is also often solved using local methods (that do not ensure an optimal solution can be found). In [MAN 85] at Toronto International Airport, the authors observed that a heuristic method can find in a few seconds some near-optimal solutions (with only 3.9% higher walking distances per passengers, compared to the best solution found by their exact method). They also measured that the solutions found by the heuristic method can be used as an initial solution for their exact method, in order to significantly reduce its CPU time.

Metaheuristics are largely applied to the problem, as they can provide quickly some good solutions, and are easily adaptable to new constraints or new criteria, while maintaining a theoretical chance of finding the optimal solution.

In [GU 99], the authors tested the efficiency of a genetic algorithm to minimize the extra delay in the problem of gate reassignment, when the scheduled gate of an arriving aircraft is still occupied by a delayed departure. They obtained some solutions that appear at least as effective as those found by experienced gate managers.

Considering the static aircraft-gate assignment problem, with the objective of minimizing the dispersion of idle time periods [BOL 01], genetic algorithms are also used to find good alternative solutions to the single one provided by an exact method based on mathematical models. In [XU 01], the authors solved a more dynamic gate assignment problem with a tabu search, taking advantage of the special properties of different types of neighborhood moves (see Figure 5.2).

In [HU 07], the authors considered the gate assignment problem, with the objective of minimizing a balance between the aircraft waiting times on the aprons, the passenger walking distances and the baggage transport distances. They compared different possible encoding to solve the problem with a genetic algorithm, and they found out that a binary encoding, combined with a uniform crossover, makes the genetic algorithm more efficient.

Hybridization between different metaheuristics is also often used in the literature to improve the efficiency of the algorithms. In [CHE 12], on the same instances of the gate assignment problem at Incheon International Airport, a hybridization between a simulated annealing algorithm and a tabu search yielded better results than those obtained with the two metaheuristics alone.

When there are not enough gates for all the scheduled flights, the gate assignment problem is said to be over-constrained: in this case, a new objective is to minimize the number of flights that cannot be assigned a gate. In [DIN 05], the authors solved this problem with a new hybridization between a simulated annealing algorithm and a tabu search. They used the same kind of neighborhood operators as those described in [XU 01] to facilitate the use of heuristics and improve their results.

When a departure metering strategy is used at an airport (with a DMAN system), some departing aircraft are held at gate, which can create gate conflicts with some arriving aircraft. The initial gate assignment can try to minimize the probability of these conflicts, by maximizing the time gap between two consecutive flights at the same gate: in [KIM 14], using some actual flight data of New York-LaGuardia Airport, the authors used a tabu search with two neighborhood operators, in order to build a robust gate assignment, and measured a significant diminution of gate conflicts in their simulations.

5.3. Runway scheduling

5.3.1. *Problem description*

Airport runways are an important source of traffic congestion because of the important separations (in time and distance) that are required between each operation (takeoff or landing).

The main purpose of these separations is to free the following aircraft from the wake vortex turbulence of the previous aircraft. The wake vortex of an aircraft depends on its category (light, medium, heavy, super): the heavier an aircraft is, the stronger its vortex, but the less it is penalized by the vortex of the previous aircraft. The necessary wake vortex separation between two aircraft is generally expressed in time and depends on the category of the two aircraft: the separation time after an aircraft A depends not only on A but also on the following aircraft B, as illustrated in Figure 5.3. For this reason, the runway scheduling problem appears less symmetrical than many other scheduling problems, and the schedule of aircraft on the runways has a significant impact on the resulting delay.

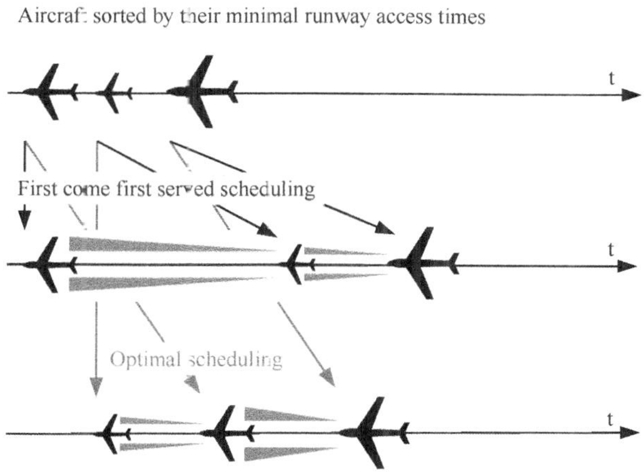

Figure 5.3. *Runway scheduling*

Additional separations can be considered by the airport controllers, in order to ensure a minimal distance between the aircraft in the approach sectors, before landing or after takeoff. In this case, the necessary separation depends on the speeds of the aircraft and on the standard terminal arrival route or standard instrument departure procedure used. These distance separations can be converted into times (considering the speeds of the aircraft) and mixed to the wake vortex separations (by keeping the most penalizing separation time between each pair of aircraft).

Some airports can also have crossing or parallel dependent runways, in which case some separations (that can still be expressed in time) have to be ensured between the operations of the different runways.

Depending on the airport configuration, a runway can be used either in mixed mode (used for takeoff and landing) or in segregated mode (with only one type of operation). In the literature, the runway scheduling problem is sometimes reduced to the airport landing problem or the airport takeoff problem, considering a runway used in the segregated mode.

In Europe, some specific constraints have to be added for the departure scheduling because the European Network Manager Operations Center can assign some calculated takeoff times (CTOT) to some flights that go through overloaded airspace. These constrained departures can only take off 5 min before or 10 min after their CTOT.

Respecting these different constraints, the main objective of the runway scheduling problem is to ensure a good level of performance for the airport operations:

– minimizing arrival and departure delay (which can be formulated as maximizing the runways throughput);

– maximizing the traffic predictability (which can be formulated as minimizing the deviations to an initial runway schedule and to the requested CTOT);

– maximizing the fairness among the different flights, to avoid the solutions where some particular flights are highly penalized compared to others.

5.3.2. *An example of problem formulation*

Considering a given set of dependent runways used either in segregated mode or in mixed mode, on which N aircraft are scheduled in a given time period (for takeoff or landing) and assuming that each aircraft is assigned a fixed runway by the airport controllers (as this is most often the case at big airports, due to approach constraints), the variables of the problem can be the takeoff and landing times that have to be scheduled for each aircraft:

$$(t_i)_{1 \leq i \leq N}$$

A lower bound L_i, a targeted value T_i and an optional upper bound U_i of t_i can be defined for each aircraft i ($1 \leq i \leq N$):

– for a departure constrained by a CTOT, T_i is the CTOT and L_i and U_i are given by the feasible takeoff slot around the CTOT, given the current position of the aircraft and its scheduled departure time for an aircraft at the gate;

– for other aircraft, L_i can be computed by considering the current position of the aircraft (in the air for an arrival or on the ground for a departure), U_i can be set to $+\infty$ or to L_i added to a maximal delay and T_i set to L_i or to the last scheduled takeoff or landing time. In a real case application, these values could be provided by the AMAN and DMAN systems, and the gap between L_i and U_i would be reduced to a few minutes for a landing aircraft, as far as the airport control is concerned.

As explained earlier, the separation rules can be modeled as a fixed minimal time s_{ij} between each pair of aircraft (i, j) when $t_i < t_j$ (even if the two aircraft are not scheduled on the same runway). With an additional fairness coefficient $\alpha \geq 1$, the problem can be formulated as follows:

Minimize: $\sum_{i=1}^{N} |t_i - T_i|^{\alpha}$

Subject to: $\begin{cases} L_i \leq t_i \leq U_i & (1 \leq i \leq N) \\ t_i + s_{ij} \leq t_j \text{ or } t_j + s_{ji} \leq t_i & (1 \leq i \neq j \leq N) \end{cases}$

5.3.3. *Resolution methods*

As described in a detailed survey [BEN 11], many runway scheduling problems can be formulated and solved with exact methods using dynamic programming or branch and bound algorithms. For more flexibility (or more realism) in the formulation of the constraints and the objectives of the problem, or to quickly obtain various good solutions on large instances, metaheuristics are also largely applied to the runway optimization problems.

The multiple runways aircraft landing problem consists of both assigning a runway to each aircraft and scheduling each aircraft on its runway. In [BEN 09], this problem was formulated as a job shop scheduling problem. The authors solved it with a hybrid method, in which ant colony optimization was used to generate the initial population of a genetic algorithm. They tested the efficiency of this hybridization on a collection of test data sets, involving up to 50 aircraft that have to be scheduled on 4 runways.

In [HU 09b], the authors also solved a multiple runways aircraft landing problem, with a genetic algorithm. They confirmed the efficiency of a specific encoding, based on a binary matrix, that specified the Boolean priority relationships between each pair of aircraft: this encoding can be associated with a uniform crossover (that makes each child inherit a specific part of the priority relationships of his parents) and provides better results than a more intuitive integer encoding, especially by avoiding some premature convergence toward local optima. Indeed, this kind of encoding can maintain some promising subsequences across several generations, while still favoring a good exploration of all the possible sequences. In [HU 09a], the authors again improved their results with a new *ripple spreading* genetic algorithm: in this model, each chromosome encodes an epicenter point in a two-dimensional artificial space, and a method to project each aircraft in this space (depending on its wake vortex category and its soonest landing time). The ripple spreading process is a simple algorithm that assigns a runway to each aircraft and defines the sequence on each runway, from the set of points in the artificial space (by sorting these points by increasing distance to the epicenter). Thus, each chromosome is reduced to five numbers $(x, y, \delta 1, \delta 2, \delta 3)$, where (x, y) are the coordinates of the epicenter and $(\delta 1, \delta 2, \delta 3)$ are the coefficients defining the projection in the artificial space. A big advantage of this method is that the size of the chromosomes no longer depends on the number of aircraft but only on the number of parameters used to characterize them.

The aircraft takeoff scheduling problem can appear more complex as it involves the whole departure process (with the need of predicting accurate start-up and taxi times). In [ALI 08] and [LEI 08], the authors considered the problem of the departure flow that have to be scheduled on a runway and that can use different routes to access this runway: each departure route is seen as a first-in-first-out queue (aircraft using the same route cannot change their order). The problem is to find the gate departure times and the takeoff times that minimize the time spent to offload the whole traffic (while maintaining the separation constraints between taxiing aircraft). The authors improved the convergence of a particle swarm optimization algorithm with an evolution function based on an oscillating equation of the second order (inherited from the control theory) [LEI 08] or by controlling the evolution with a simulated annealing method [ALI 08].

In [ATK 07], using an actual traffic sample at London Heathrow Airport, and with a quite realistic departure model (including the reordering possibilities offered by the runway access layouts), the authors combined a tabu search with different search methodologies and heuristics to minimize the departure delay and the deviations to the CTOT. In further work [ATK 08], the authors described how these techniques could provide decision support tools that would help the airport controllers in their real-time tasks.

In his PhD thesis [DEA 10], the author provided a formulation for the aircraft scheduling problem on a runway that can be used either in the segregated or in the mixed mode, and where some of the departures are constrained by a specific CTOT. This formulation is similar to that described in section 5.3.2, except that it is reduced to one independent runway with a neutral fairness coefficient $\alpha = 1$: the variables are the takeoff and landing times, and the minimization criterion is a balance between the deviations to the CTOT (of the constrained departures) and the delay (of the other flights). With this formulation, the author took advantage of some particular properties of the problem (symmetries, aircraft equivalences, and detection of sub-optimal scheduling as illustrated in Figure 5.4) and defined a branch and bound algorithm that finds and proves an optimal solution in a few seconds, for a large

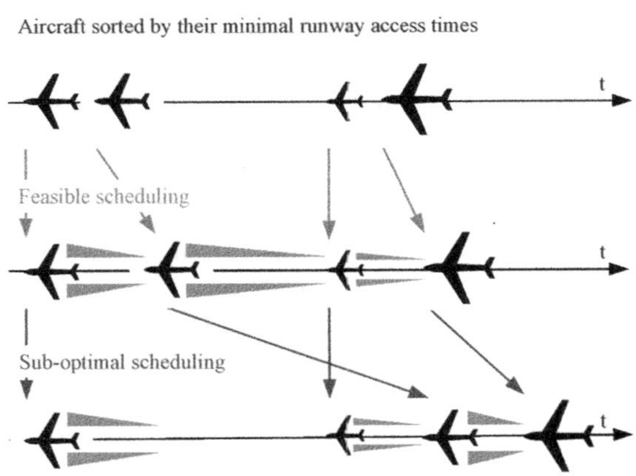

Figure 5.4. *Detection of suboptimal runway scheduling*

sample of problems involving more than 50 aircraft, extracted from actual data at Roissy-CDG Airport.

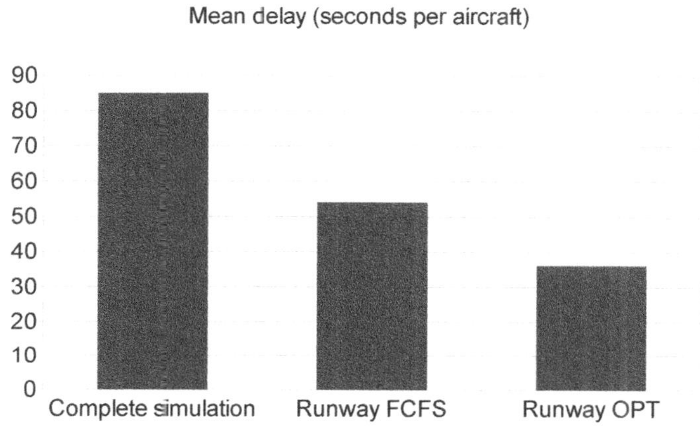

Figure 5.5. *Runway scheduling at Roissy-CDG Airport*

By applying this scheduling algorithm on shifting periods of a whole day of traffic at Roissy-CDG Airport [DEA 09], the authors found a feasible scheduling for all the operations on all the runways. As illustrated in Figure 5.5, the generated delay appears to be 20 s lower (in average per aircraft) than with a first-come-first-served (FCFS) runway scheduling and half less than that measured by a full simulation (including taxi conflict resolution) of the same traffic. These results show that the runways are not the only source of delay for big airports such as Roissy-CDG and that the traffic also needs optimization during taxiing.

5.4. Surface routing

5.4.1. *Problem description*

In the airport surface routing problem, the goal is to assign a strategic taxi route to each aircraft and to plan when each aircraft should move along this route, in order to maximize the efficiency and predictability of the airport surface operations. This process has to be integrated with the other planning systems of the airport (AMAN, DMAN), in order to match (or update) the runway schedules, using some coordination mechanisms that have to be defined.

As mentioned in section 5.1.2, a first issue of the surface routing problem is due to the numerous uncertainties that affect the prediction of the aircraft ground operations, especially concerning the departure times and the taxi speeds.

A second issue is to formulate the constraints of the problem, as they involve all the airport circulation rules (pushback and gate entry procedures, one-way taxiways, avoidance of runways and gates areas, runway crossing procedures, etc.). Much information on ground procedures can be found in the airport controllers' operational handbook, but some information describes some standard procedures that are not mandatory, and not always applied by the controllers themselves. For instance, some taxi routes between gates and runways are exhaustively described, as they ensure the dispatch of traffic efficiently during heavy periods but are not appropriate for light periods, during which the use of shorter routes is far more favorable. Moreover, the separations that have to be maintained between aircraft on the ground are not precisely defined (except as a collision avoidance principle).

For all these reasons, the problem of surface routing can be formulated with more or less precision, considering some maximum throughput on each taxiway portion, or trying to solve the different conflicts between taxiing aircraft.

The possible objectives of the problem can be formulated more concretely:

– minimize the taxi times (as fuel burn, gas emissions and noise);

– minimize the deviations to the runways schedules;

– minimize the variability of taxi times;

– minimize the risk of congestion, by minimizing the number of conflicts between taxiing aircraft.

5.4.2. *Related work*

In [ROL 08], the authors provided a mixed integer linear programming (MILP) formulation for the surface routing problem: the binary variables describe when each aircraft will travel each portion of taxiway and the constraints ensure that each aircraft will be assigned a feasible route, with holding positions that solve all the conflicts with other aircraft. The objective function to minimize is a weighted combination of the total taxi time and the total holding time. In [ROL 09], the authors applied this work on the daily traffic of Amsterdam Airport Schiphol, using the ILOG, CPLEX solver. In [LEE 14], the author also proposed an MILP model to minimize both runway delay and taxi times at Detroit Metropolitan Airport, and compared this approach to another sequential approach, in which runway scheduling is coordinated with taxiways scheduling.

Metaheuristics can also by applied to the surface routing problem, in order to deal with some more detailed and more flexible problem formulations. Considering the routing problem on the airport of Madrid-Barajas [GAR 05], the authors combined a deterministic flow management algorithm with a genetic algorithm to assign a route and a beginning time to each flight (a landing time for an arrival and a start-up time for a departure), in order to find solutions with minimum delay: the genetic algorithm is applied to a quite realistic representation of the problem, while the proposed flow-management algorithm optimizes a simplified one. An integration scheme is defined to combine the solutions of each algorithm. This hybridization yields some significant improvements of the solutions found by the genetic algorithm in medium traffic situations (during heavy periods, the simplified flow-management algorithm does not help the genetic algorithm to find better solutions).

In [GOT 04], the author developed a first work applied on Roissy-CDG Airport [PES 01]:

– a detailed description of the airport layout (gates, runways and taxiways) is used to model the airport as an oriented graph connecting the gates to the runways (and conversely), and some path enumeration algorithms are defined to compute a set of alternative routes for each aircraft;

– aircraft trajectories are predicted with a given uncertainty on their speeds (see Figure 5.6), and the conflicts are detected considering all the possible positions of each aircraft: the minimal separation rules are defined in distance between taxiing aircraft and in time between landing or takeoff operations.

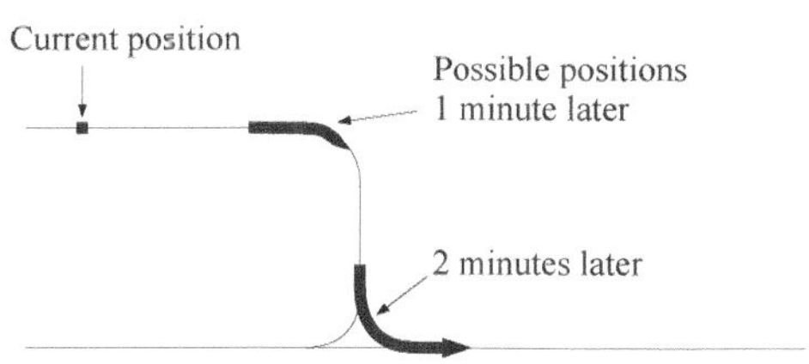

Figure 5.6. *Trajectory prediction under speed uncertainties*

The routing problem is then formulated as the choice of a route and of some holding positions for each aircraft, in such a way that the minimal separations are ensured between each pair of aircraft at each time step. The objective function to minimize is a combination between the total delay (due to routes lengthening and holding times) and the deviations to the CTOT. To solve this combinatorial problem, the author compared a sequential deterministic method, a genetic algorithm and a hybridization between the two:

– the sequential method consists of simplifying the problem, by first fixing priority levels, so that aircraft are sorted according to a total order. Each aircraft is assigned a trajectory (a route and some holding positions) in the given order: the nth aircraft has to avoid the $n-1$ previous aircraft, once their trajectories are fixed. In this way, the problem is split into a succession of best path searches with obstacle avoidance, which can be performed very quickly by an A^* or a branch and bound algorithm;

– the genetic algorithm deals with the whole problem: each chromosome describes a route and some holding positions and holding duration for each aircraft (see Figure 5.7). With this kind of encoding (per aircraft), some partial fitness (one per aircraft) can be used to highlight the parts of the chromosomes that are the least promising, in order to speed up the convergence of the algorithm;

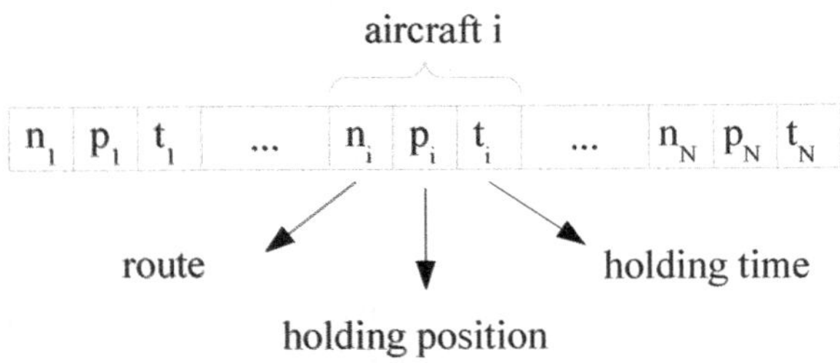

Figure 5.7. *GA encoding for the routing problem*

– the hybrid method is based on a genetic algorithm, in which each chromosome describes a route and a rank for each aircraft (see Figure 5.8). A branch and bound algorithm is used to evaluate each chromosome, considering the aircraft one after the other (by increasing rank, on their specified route) in order to find a conflict-free trajectory for each of them.

Measured by simulation of some actual traffic at Roissy-CDG Airport, the hybrid genetic algorithm appears the most efficient, as it significantly reduces the mean delay during heavy periods (see Figure 5.9), applying all the CTOT with a better scheduling (more than 80% happen at less than 1 min around the specified time).

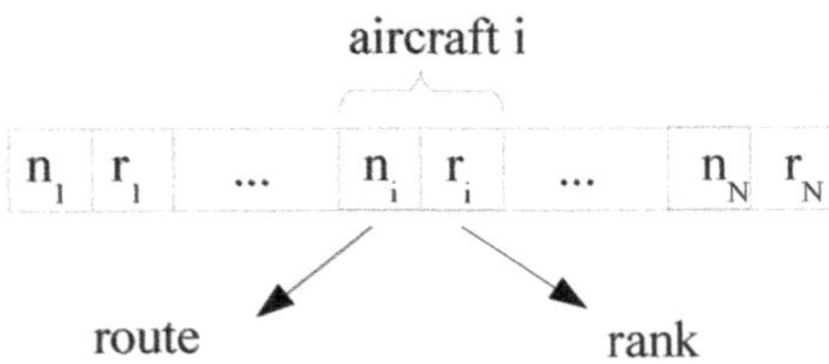

Figure 5.8. *Hybrid GA encoding for the routing problem*

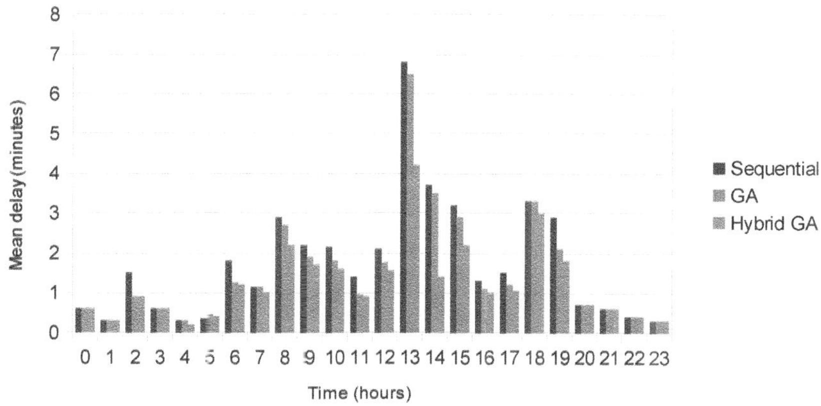

Figure 5.9. *Taxi delay minimization at Roissy-CDG Airport. For a color version of the figure, see www.iste.co.uk/durand/atm.zip*

5.5. Global airport traffic optimization

5.5.1. *Problem description*

In [DEA 09], the authors noticed that the granularity and the magnitude of the traffic prediction is not the same in the different airport optimization problems:

– The gate assignment or reassignment problem (that is part of the SMAN system) can be considered from one day to a few minutes before the actual traffic situation.

– The runway scheduling problem (for the AMAN and DMAN systems) can be considered between 1 h and 30 min before the actual landing or takeoff of the aircraft.

– The conflicts resolution problem (for the SMAN system) can only be considered a few minutes before the actual traffic situation, as far as the uncertainties on departure times and taxi speeds are not reduced.

The authors also pointed out the obvious dependency problems that concern the different predictive systems: the delay of an arriving aircraft can affect the start-up time of its following departure, and the decisions made while handling taxiing aircraft can quickly result in situations where the runway schedules should be updated (as the start-up and landing times should be, when a runway is used in the mixed mode).

As a consequence, a coordination scheme must be defined to ensure consistency and strategic updates in the different airport predictive systems.

5.5.2. *Coordination scheme between the different predictive systems*

In this section, an iterative process is proposed and tested to coordinate the different predictive systems of an airport (see Figure 5.10):

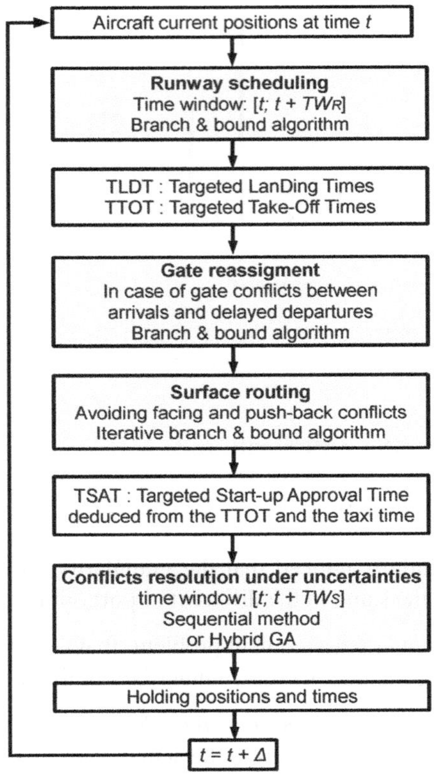

Figure 5.10. *Global airport traffic optimization*

– for each traffic situation (every $\Delta = 1$ min), the runway schedules are computed, considering a runway time window $TW_R = 30$ min. These schedules can be built with an FCFS strategy or with an optimal branch and bound algorithm, as described in [DEA 09]. The results of this first step are the targeted landing times (TLDT) and the targeted takeoff times (TTOT);

– according to the runways schedules, a gate reassignment can be performed when necessary: in the proposed simulations, this happens only when the gate of an arriving aircraft is not available in time, due to a delayed departure. In these situations, a gate reassignment is performed for the incoming flights in the same terminal, by a branch and bound algorithm that minimizes the total delay;

– routes are then assigned (or reassigned) to the aircraft that are active in the TW_R time window, considering the main conflicts that can be detected: in the proposed simulations, these are defined as the facing conflicts (routes that use the same taxiway in the opposite direction at the same time) and the pushback conflicts (routes that go through the pushback position of an aircraft, which can be blocking during several minutes). This route assignment is also performed by a branch and bound algorithm, considering the aircraft one after the other, sorted by their predicted gate time (ending time for an arrival or start-up time for a departure);

– for each departure that is still at the gate, a targeted start-up approval time (TSAT) is updated, deduced from its route and its TTOT (DMAN process);

– the conflicts between aircraft are solved in a limited time window $TW_S = 5$ min, considering uncertainties on start-up times and on taxi speeds: a minimal distance is required between all the possible positions of the aircraft and some minimal time separations are required between each runway operation. This conflict resolution can be performed by the sequential method or the hybrid genetic algorithm described in section 5.4, except that they are limited to one route per aircraft and that the criterion to minimize measures the deviations to the TLTD and TTOT (rather than the delay).

5.5.3. *Simulation results*

The proposed global optimization scheme is tested in fast time simulations, on a sample of actual traffic at Roissy-CDG and Roma-Fiumicino airports, whose features are quite different:

– at Roissy-CDG Airport (see Figure 5.11), the four runways are considered independent, and are used in the segregated mode (two external runways for landing and two internal runways for takeoff), so that landed aircraft have to cross the departure runway to join their gate (which creates a lot of conflicts with departures). The large size of the airport provides various routing possibilities but results in higher taxi times, and congestion appears frequently around the gates and at certain intersections of taxiways;

– at Roma-Fiumicino Airport (see Figure 5.12), the eastern arrival runway crosses the middle departure runway (so that the operations on the two runways have to be separated in time). The airport is smaller but a lot of gate areas have a single dead end access, resulting in large holding times for aircraft when leaving or reaching the gate.

Four scenarios are compared:

– FCFS sequential: first-come-first-served runway scheduling, and the sequential method used to solve the surface conflicts;

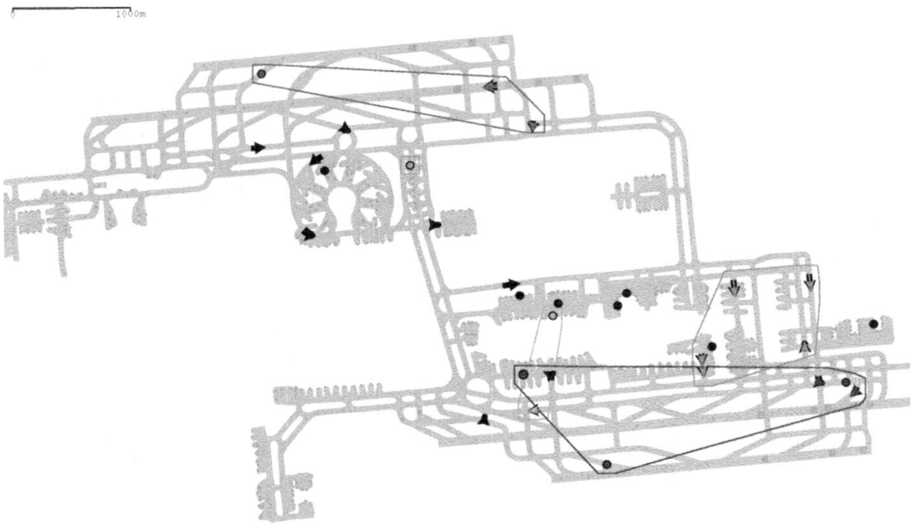

Figure 5.11. *Fast time simulations at Roissy-CDG Airport*

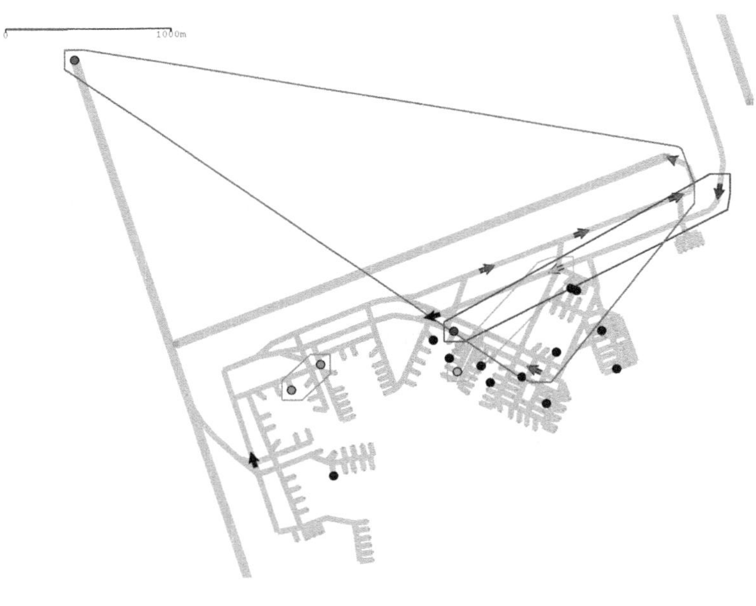

Figure 5.12. *Fast time simulations at Roma-Fiumicino Airport*

– FCFS hybrid GA: first-come-first-served runway scheduling, and the hybrid genetic algorithm used to solve the surface conflicts;

– OPT sequential: optimal runway scheduling, and the sequential method used to solve the surface conflicts;

– OPT hybrid GA: optimal runway scheduling, and the hybrid genetic algorithm used to solve the surface conflicts.

All the simulations are carried out with the same general parameters:

– uncertainty on departure times: $\delta_D = 1$ min;

– speed uncertainty: $\delta_S = 30\%$;

– prediction time window for runway scheduling: $TW_R = 30$ min;

– prediction time window for surface conflicts resolution: $TW_S = 5$ min;

– shifting period: $\Delta = 1$ min.

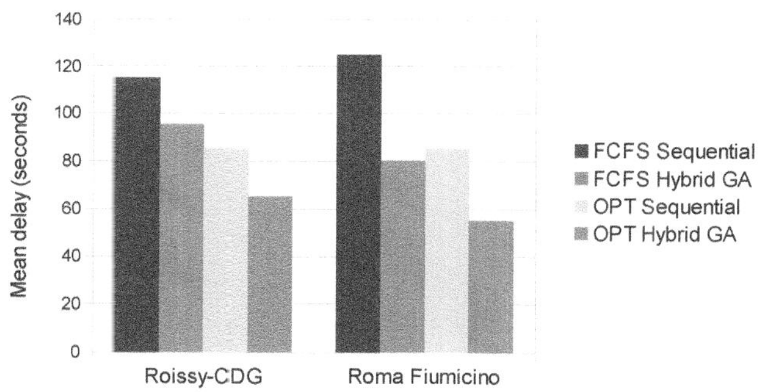

Figure 5.13. *Aircraft mean delay. For a color version of the figure, see www.iste.co.uk/durand/atm.zip*

Figure 5.13 shows the mean aircraft delay obtained for each scenario: at both Roissy-CDG and Roma-Fiumicino airports, the optimal runway scheduling and the solutions found by the hybrid genetic algorithm yield a significant delay reduction (about 30 s over less than 2 min on average). These results confirm that the FCFS principle is not an appropriate runway scheduling, not only because it is not optimized, but also because it does not consider the impact of the surface conflicts. Similarly, the sequential conflict resolution method is less efficient because the priority between aircraft is fixed (according to the runways schedules), instead of being adjusted with each new traffic situation.

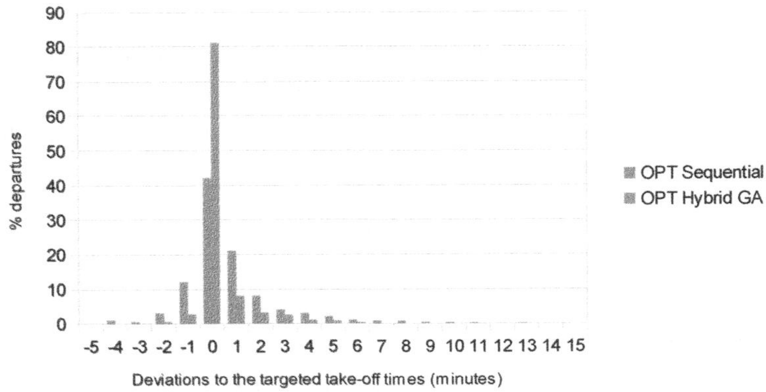

Figure 5.14. *Traffic predictability at Roissy-CDG Airport. For a color version of the figure, see www.iste.co.uk/durand/atm.zip*

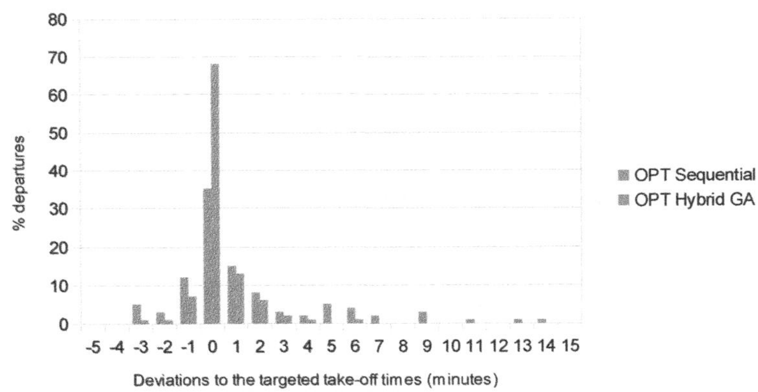

Figure 5.15. *Traffic predictability at Roma-Fiumicino Airport. For a color version of the figure, see www.iste.co.uk/durand/atm.zip*

In terms of traffic predictability, Figures 5.14 and 5.15 show the distribution of the differences between the TTOT (computed 30 min earlier) and the final takeoff times, in the scenarios involving an optimal runway scheduling. The solutions found by the hybrid genetic algorithm are more compliant with the runway schedule, with more than 80% departures (at Roissy-CDG) and near 70% departures (at Roma-Fiumicino) that takeoff at less than 30 s around the targeted time.

This explains why the sequential conflict resolution method generates more delay: the targeted optimal runway schedules are not achieved as well.

5.6. Conclusion

Airport traffic management is the source of many optimization problems that have to be solved in real time. These problems are combinatorial and can be formulated with more or less realism and applicability. Even if some exact resolution methods can be used to solve some of these problems' formulations, the use of metaheuristics is also very common, as they can yield various good solutions very quickly and are less dependent on the problem formulation. As seen in many examples in this chapter, metaheuritics can also provide better solutions than deterministic methods, when these can only be applied on a simplification of the initial problem.

In section 5.5, a global optimization scheme for airport traffic optimization is put forward, involving gate reassignment, runway scheduling, surface routing and conflicts resolution. Different optimization methods can be considered at each step of this process, and the proposed hybrid genetic algorithm has shown to find the most efficient solutions to the conflicting ground situations, as these solutions enable us to properly maintain the targeted optimal runway schedule, despite all the uncertainties that were considered.

6

Conflict Detection and Resolution

6.1. Introduction

Tactical air traffic controllers do not have many support tools to make decisions. Unlike pilots, who can rely on highly automated systems, controllers cannot count on automated tools to help their task. Their main tool is a two-dimensional (2D) representation of the traffic with some indications of the aircraft altitude, speeds and followed routes. In France, they can activate vectors showing the future position of the aircraft in 3, 6 or 9 minutes and can see the positions of the aircraft during the last minute. They are trained to deal with high densities of traffic and are responsible for separating aircraft.

The literature on air traffic conflict detection and resolution was very poor before the beginning of the 1990s. The first attempts to automate the controller's task started in the late 1980s and showed that the problem was challenging. AERA[1] [NIE 89a, NIE 89b] in the United States and ARC2000 [KRE 89, FRO 93, MEC 94] in Europe failed in improving the controller's task. AERA only focused on pairwise conflict resolution problems and did not deal with the combinatorial aspects of multiple aircraft conflicts. ARC2000 imagined building 4D trajectories and sequentially solving the conflicts, which means that the trajectory of the last aircraft would have to avoid the trajectories of all the previous aircraft. Beside not being able to deal with high densities of traffic, none of these projects dealt with the transition phase, where controllers might still be in charge of the traffic but would be helped by decision support tools. Poor consideration was given to uncertainties in the trajectory prediction and execution.

In the mid-1990s, different approaches were investigated to tackle the problem. They can be classified into three categories:

1 Automated en route air traffic control.

– autonomous approaches in which every aircraft is responsible for solving encountered conflicts. This approach is often called "free-flight" concept;

– iterative approaches in which aircraft are sorted with priorities. Aircraft with priority 1 chooses its trajectory first, aircraft with priority n chooses a trajectory that avoids conflicts with every aircraft with priorities $k < n$;

– global centralized approaches in which the whole problem is considered at once and globally solved. These approaches are the most challenging because the problem is very combinatorial. Metaheuristics are mainly used for this approach.

Different models were used, some of them are very simple and consider aircraft as moving points in the space. Some are more realistic and consider various uncertainty aspects:

– even with the GPS (global positioning system) capabilities, the aircraft's current position is not perfectly known, especially on the ground, because aircraft do not transmit their positions every second. However, the current position uncertainty does not evolve with time;

– trajectory prediction uncertainties are more difficult to deal with. Aircraft are assigned routes and can follow them on the 2D horizontal plane with a good accuracy. Uncertainty on the aircraft trajectory prediction is however quite big in the vertical dimension when aircraft are climbing or descending. Air traffic controllers generally manage this uncertainty by assigning intermediate flight levels to climbing or descending aircraft, making sure that they cannot be "too early" on a flight level that would still be occupied by other aircraft. In the horizontal plane, aircraft correct the cross wind but generally not the headwind or tailwind. Thus, the trajectory prediction is affected by the longitudinal component of the wind;

– air traffic controllers communicate with pilots using Very High Frequency radio. The given maneuver orders are generally not executed instantly and uncertainty remains. For example if a heading change is proposed, the pilot may execute it instantly or 10, 20, 30 seconds later. As long as pilots manually control the aircraft trajectory (even through an automated pilot), this uncertainty will remain.

Other uncertainties must be noticed in other phases of the flight, such as the takeoff times, which are hard to predict with a good accuracy: a passenger or a luggage can be missing, the taxi time is hard to control. When lining up for takeoff, pilots might take more or less time before brake release.

We will try to focus on these uncertainty aspects in the literature review. This will help the reader understand why metaheuristics are some of the most efficient approaches to tackle the conflict resolution in a realistic environment. Indeed, a lot of research consider the underlying problem with very little consideration to usability of the solution found. They very often model aircraft by points moving at constant speed in perfect conditions. We will show in section 6.8 how the model can be separated from the resolution tool in order to test exact methods such as constraint programing (CP) algorithm while keeping the model as flexible as possible.

6.2. Conflict resolution complexity

Two aircraft are in conflict if their horizontal separation distance is less than the horizontal separation standard (generally 5 NM) and their vertical separation is less than the vertical separation standard (1000 ft). Two aircraft are potentially in conflict when a loss of separation is detected within a prediction time window T_w.

The relation "is potentially in conflict with" defines an equivalence relation among the aircraft population. The equivalence classes are called clusters of aircraft in conflict. Figure 6.1 gives an example of cluster involving seven aircraft and seven conflicts. Even if aircraft A, D and H are not potentially in conflict, they belong to the same cluster.

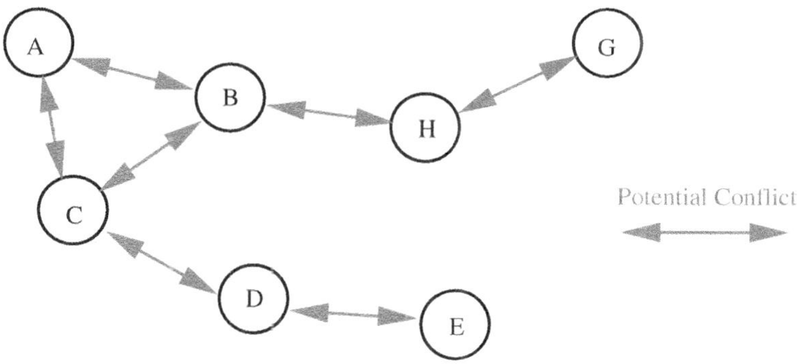

Figure 6.1. *An example of cluster involving seven aircraft*

In [DUR 03], we analyzed the structures of the clusters using graphic sequences and showed how the number of possible different structures of cluster increases with the size of the cluster. Figure 6.2 gives the different cluster structures for two, three, four and five aircraft.

Table 6.1 gives the number of possible and observed cluster structures (graphic sequences) in function of the number of the cluster size (number of aircraft) on a simulation of a real traffic day (May 21, 1999) in the French airspace using the real route network. The prediction time window T_w used is 8 min and uncertainties on the horizontal speed (5%) and on the vertical speed (15%) are used to detect conflicts

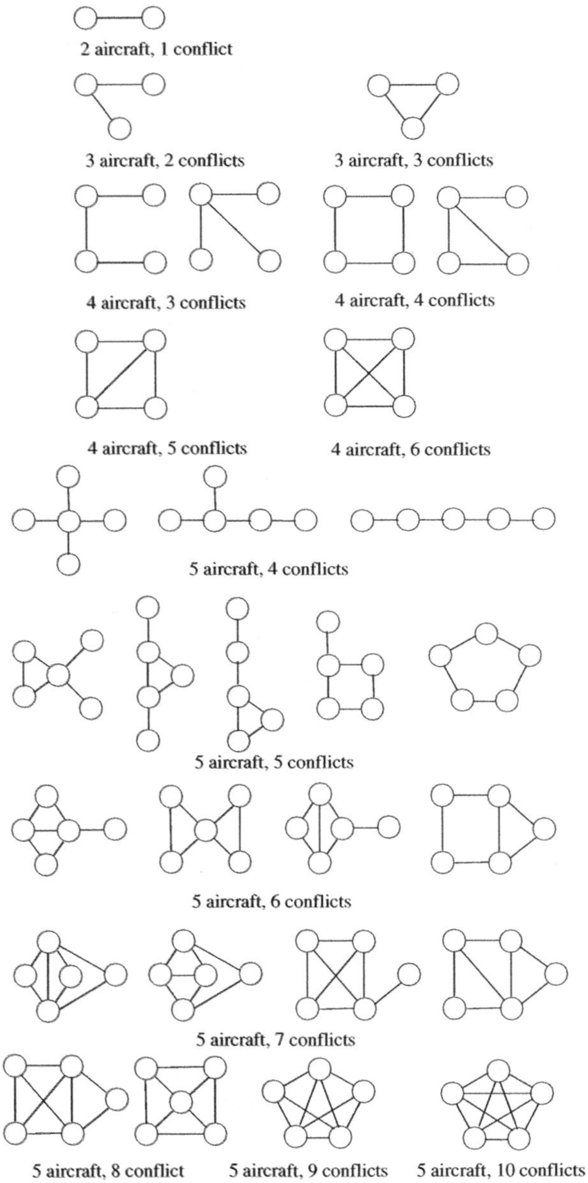

Figure 6.2. *Different cluster structures for two, three, four and five aircraft.*

(see section 6.6.2). Table 6.2 also gives the number of clusters of each size and the ratio in the total simulation. Because the traffic demand was not regulated and no specific sequencing was done for landing, the size of the clusters can reach 21 aircraft. The purpose of the air traffic management (ATM) described in Chapter 1 is to prevent air traffic controllers from having to deal with complex situations involving more than three or four aircraft. The exponentially increasing number of cluster structures may explain why human brains are not able to handle so many different situations.

Cluster	Graphic sequences			Clusters	
Size	Possible	Observed	Ratio	No.	Ratio
2	**1**	1	100.00	18,119	66.78
3	**2**	2	100.00	4,952	18.25
4	**6**	6	100.00	1,883	6.94
5	**20**	19	95.00	905	3.34
6	**68**	53	77.94	479	1.77
7	**236**	98	41.53	270	1.00
8	**863**	119	13.79	198	0.73
9	**3,137**	92	2.93	112	0.41
10	**11,636**	52	0.45	55	0.20
11	**43,306**	56	0.13	59	0.22
12	**162,728**	36	0.02	37	0.14
13	**614,142**	27	0.00	27	0.10
14	**2,330,454**	10	0.00	10	0.04
15	**8,875,656**	8	0.00	8	0.03
16	**33,924,699**	9	0.00	9	0.03
17	**130,038,017**	4	0.00	4	0.01
18	**499,753,560**	3	0.00	3	0.01
21	**28,723,877,046**	1	0.00	1	0.00

Table 6.1. *Cluster structures - standard routes - 5 and 15% of uncertainty -* $T_w = 8$ *mn -* $\delta = 2$ *mn - May 21, 1999 - French traffic*

Conflict resolution is a complex problem. In the horizontal plane, with two aircraft A and B, there are two different ways to solve a conflict. A may avoid or be avoided by B "by the left" or "by the right". Durand [DUR 96a] showed in his PhD thesis that the set of solutions is divided into two connected components when considering the horizontal plane and non-looping trajectories. When n aircraft are involved in a cluster, the number of aircraft pairs is $\frac{n(n-1)}{2}$ and the number of connected components is $2^{\frac{n(n-1)}{2}}$. Table 6.2 gives the number of aircraft pairs and connected components for different problem sizes.

No. of aircraft	Aircraft pairs	Connected components
2	1	2
3	3	8
4	6	64
5	10	1,024
6	15	32,768
7	21	2,097,152
8	28	268,435,456
9	36	68,719,476,736
10	45	35,184,372,088,832

Table 6.2. *Number of aircraft pairs and connected components in the horizontal plane for different size of problems*

We can note that for only four aircraft, the number of connected components is already 64, which means that there are already 64 ways to combine non-looping trajectories of the four aircraft in the horizontal plane. In each connected component, a locally optimal solution can be found.

What makes the conflict resolution complex? First, the number of cluster structures increases exponentially with the number of aircraft. Second, the number of connected components of the set of solutions increases exponentially with the number of aircraft. These two aspects make the conflict resolution very complex and thus challenging.

This explains why the air traffic control system is organized to prevent controllers from complex situations. Even if they have to handle many aircraft at a time, clusters generally do not involve more than two or three aircraft.

In [HOE 03], the authors pretended that the complexity is reduced if every aircraft deals with its conflicts instead of centralizing the problem on the ground. For an n aircraft cluster, the number of aircraft pairs is $\frac{n(n-1)}{2}$ but each aircraft only sees $(n-1)$ possible intruders. This simple statement has been abusively used to pretend that the problem complexity could be reduced by delegating the resolution to the pilot. This is not true because coordinating the pilots actions then becomes complex without using reactive techniques that are not effective in a dense environment.

6.3. Free-flight approaches

In the 1990s, the airlines pushed research toward systems that could delegate the conflict resolution task to the pilots. Different facts motivated such approaches. First, in low-density areas, such approaches could reduce the cost of control. Second, it could simplify procedures in areas not covered by air traffic control. Finally, if an efficient algorithm was found for high-density areas, it could allow a different organization of the traffic in which sectors would not necessarily exist anymore, aircraft could fly direct routes from origin to destination.

Today, aircraft are equipped with TCAS[2], which triggers an alarm when another aircraft is getting too close. The TCAS advice must be followed by the pilots on both aircraft. It is a coordinated vertical maneuver that separates both aircraft. It only works for two aircraft. It is not supposed to operate in normal conditions when air traffic controllers do their job correctly. It relies on the fact that there is very little chance that the traffic control fails, and when that is the case, there is very little chance that more than two aircraft are involved at the same time.

6.3.1. *Reactive techniques*

To build effective methods that can handle more than two aircraft in the horizontal plane, different methods have been tried. Zeghal [ZEG 98] introduced sliding forces to solve conflict. Kosecka *et al.* [KOS 98] used potential or vortex fields. In 1999, Eby and Kelly [EBY 99] proposed a model based on an analogy to electrical particles repulsion for the free-flight problem. The main drawback of Zeghal, Kosecka and Eby's approaches is that they use continuous maneuvers and do not consider uncertainties on future aircraft positions. The trajectories computed would be difficult to explain to pilots who are still responsible for making decisions on board.

6.3.2. *Iterative approach*

In 2008, Archibald *et al.* [ARC 08] used a collaborative game theory approach to coordinate maneuvers between aircraft. The paper assumed that aircraft are ranked in a unique way and that rank ordering of conflicting aircraft are consistent from the point of view of all participants.

In 2001, we proposed [GRA 01a, GRA 01b] a token allocation strategy combined with an A^* algorithm to solve conflicts with more realistic maneuvers considering current practices and different levels of uncertainties. A complete ranking of aircraft is necessary. At each resolution step, aircraft detect conflicts in a neighboring zone. We build a global resolution order from the priority order with the following strategy:

– first each aircraft receives a token from every conflicting aircraft that has a higher priority in its detection zone. Aircraft that are not in conflict never receive any token. In the example of Figure 6.3, with a priority order ($A > C > B$), aircraft B receives two tokens, whereas with a priority order ($A > B > C$), aircraft B receives a token from aircraft A, aircraft C receives a token from aircraft B;

2 Traffic collision alert system.

– then, each conflicting aircraft with no token solves conflicts with every aircraft in its detection zone that has no token. It does not take into account aircraft that have one or more tokens;

– when this trajectory has been computed, the aircraft broadcasts its new trajectory. All aircraft that have received a token from this aircraft take this new trajectory into account, and cancel the token received from this aircraft;

– second and third steps are repeated until no token remains.

With this strategy, aircraft in different detection zones may simultaneously choose their trajectories, saving time for the whole process to end. This is the case for priority order $A > C > B$ for which aircraft A and C are token free at the same time.

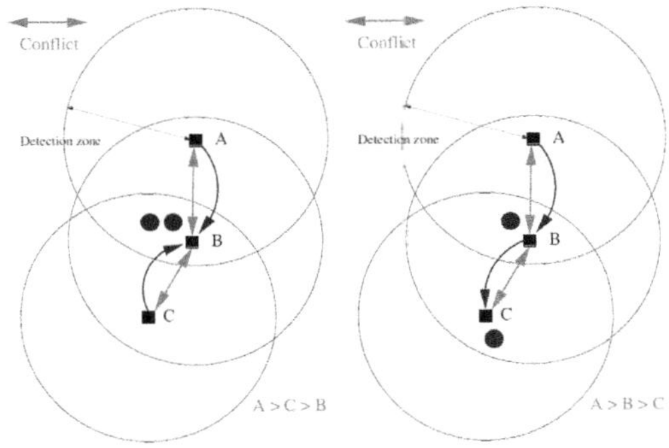

Figure 6.3. *Three aircraft configurations. Left: priority order = A>C>B. Right: priority order = A>B>C*

Simulations using real traffic data above flight level 320 showed that this modeling could work for low densities if trajectories could be predicted with a good accuracy. Archambault and Durand [ARC 04] showed that finding a good priority order for this modeling is very challenging.

6.3.3. *An example of reactive approach: neural network trained by evolutionary algorithms*

In 1996, we proposed another approach using neural network (NN) to solve conflicts in the horizontal plane [DUR 96c].

6.3.3.1. *Problem modeling*

The problem we wanted to solve was the following: an aircraft flying at a constant speed detects another aircraft flying at the same altitude (more or less 1,000 ft) in a 20

NM diameter disk. We want to build an NN that modifies the heading of this aircraft when there is a conflict (respecting operational constraint of 45° maximum per 15 s). The other aircraft is supposed to have the same embarked system so that it also detects the first aircraft and reacts using the same NN with different inputs.

The system was supposed to use an embarked radar to detect other aircraft. Consequently, all the inputs of the NN had to be given by the radar information.

In our problem, it seems clear that if no conflict occurs, no NN is needed to solve it. Consequently, at each time step, we first check if both aircraft can reach their destination without heading change and without generating conflicts. In such a case, we do not modify aircraft headings. If we detect a conflict in less than 20 min, we compute a new heading for both aircraft with the NN.

6.3.3.2. *The inputs*

Seven inputs were used by the NN (see Figure 6.4):

– the heading to the destination α and its absolute value $|\alpha|$ (in degrees);

– the distance to the other aircraft λ and its gradient $\frac{d\lambda}{dt}$;

– the bearing of the other aircraft γ (in degrees);

– the converging angle of the trajectories β;

– a bias set to 1.

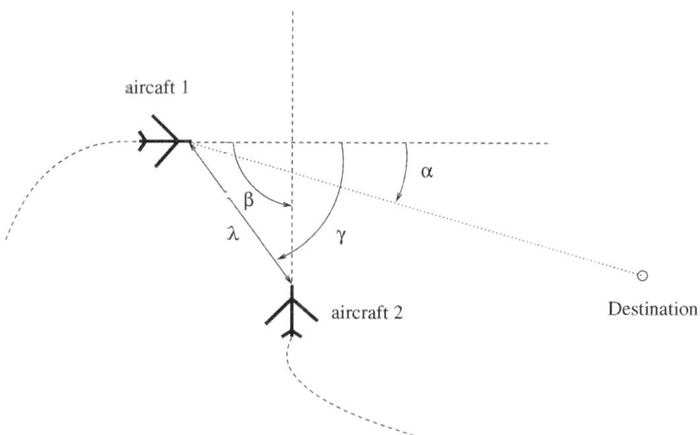

Figure 6.4. *The neural network inputs of aircraft 1*

6.3.3.3. *The neural network structure*

The NN structure was as simple as possible. We chose a three-layer network (see Figure 6.5), which returned a heading change of 45° maximum (for a time step of 15 s). We used the following activation function:

$$act(s) = \frac{1}{1 + e^{-s}}$$

In Figure 6.5, the first layer takes the six inputs described earlier along with the bias. The second layer holds 13 units whereas the third layer holds the output unit.

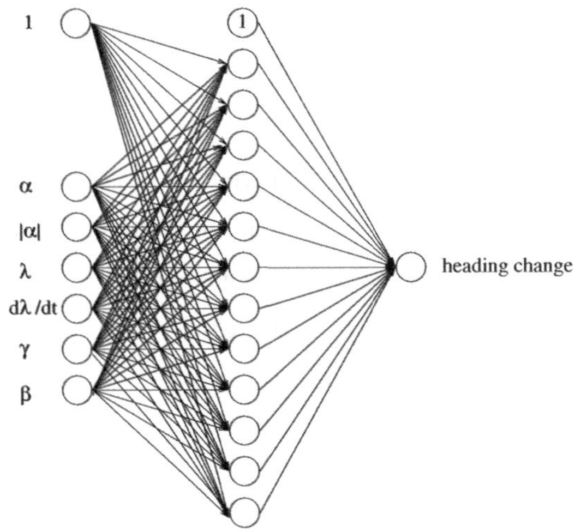

Figure 6.5. *The neural network structure*

6.3.3.4. *Learning the neural network weights*

Classical back-propagation of gradient could not be used in our case because conflict-free trajectories were not known in every configuration. We decided to use unsupervised learning with genetic algorithm and compared results of the network with optimal trajectories computed by the large and nonlinearly constrained extended Lagrangian optimization techniques software named LANCELOT [CON 92].

6.3.3.5. *Evolutionary algorithm used*

We used classical evolutionary algorithms (EAs) described in the literature [GOL 89, MIC 92]. Each NN was coded by a matrix of real numbers that contained the weights of the NN. "Stochastic remainder without replacement selection" was used: First, the fitness f_i of the n elements of the population is computed, and the average $a = \sum f_i/n$ of all the fitness is computed. Then each element is reproduced p times in the new population, with $p = truncate(n \times f_i/a)$. The population is finally completed using probabilities proportional to $f_i - p\,a/n$ for each element.

Arithmetic crossover was used: two parents are recombined by choosing randomly $\alpha \in [-0.5, 1.5]$ and creating child 1 (resp. child 2) as the barycenter of some randomly chosen weights of $(parent_1, \alpha)$ (resp. $(parent_1, 1-\alpha)$) and $(parent_2, 1-\alpha)$ (resp. $(parent_2, \alpha)$). In the experiments, the crossover probability used was 60%.

For the mutation operator, we chose to add a Gaussian noise to one of the weights of the NN. The mutation probability used was 15%.

In the experiments, the population size was 500 and the number of generations was 500.

6.3.3.6. *Computing the fitness*

One of the main issues was to know how to compute the *fitness* of a chromosome. The constrained problem to solve takes the following criteria into account:

– aircraft trajectories must be conflict free;

– delay due to deviation must be as low as possible.

To compute the fitness, a panel of different conflict configurations was created. The fitness was computed as follows:

$$F = \frac{1}{D} e^{-V}$$

where D is the average delay due to deviations and V is the average number of conflict violations.

6.3.3.7. *The learning examples*

To learn the weights of the NNs, 12 configurations were created. In each configuration, at $t = 0$ aircraft are 20 NM distant.

In four configurations (see Figure 6.6), aircraft have the same speed and converge with different angles (20°, 60°, 120°, 150°). In four other configurations, aircraft have different speed, their headings are calculated to generate a conflict (one aircraft speed is 500 knots (kts) and that of the other aircraft is 300, 350, 400 and 450 kts).

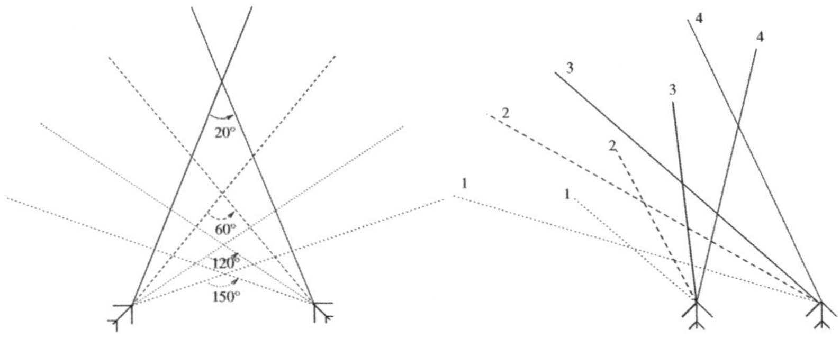

Figure 6.6. *Four configurations at the same speed and four configurations at the different speeds*

In two configurations, aircraft have opposite headings and the same speed. In two other configurations, aircraft have the same heading but different speeds (see Figure 6.7).

Figure 6.7. *Two configurations of facing aircraft and two configurations of parallel aircraft*

Because of symmetries, these 12 configurations summarize all the situations that can happen. We call "positive configuration" (see Figure 6.8) a configuration in which the angle between the slowest and the fastest aircraft is positive. When a "negative configuration" occurs, the symmetrical positive configuration is used in the NN to calculate the deviation. Therefore, some of the inputs and the outputs are given the opposite sign.

6.3.3.8. *Numerical results*

Figures 6.9–6.13 compare the results obtained with the NN to optimal solution calculated with a gradient method (when the work was done, LANCELOT was one of the most efficient softwares to compute optimal trajectories on this problem, but it was still very slow). Results showed that solutions found with the NN are less optimal, but the loss of optimality is not significant (the delay induced by the NN was never more than four times the minimal delay, which is generally very small).

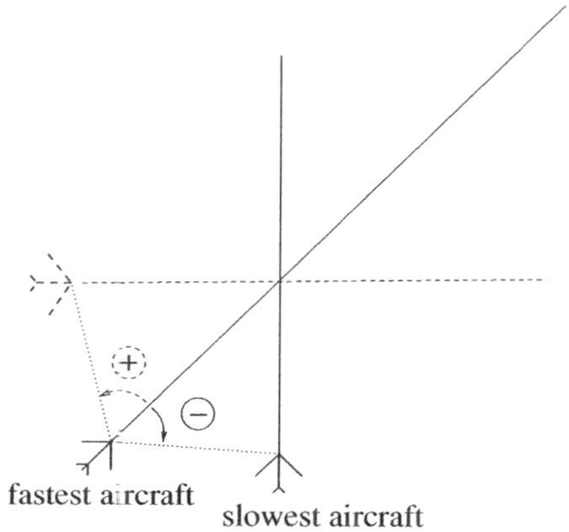

Figure 6.8. *Symmetrical configurations*

The configurations used to compare the NN to optimal solutions are not learned configurations. This shows the capacity of the NN to generalize to non-learned situations. For each solution, the mean lengthening of the trajectories is given in percentage:

– Figure 6.9 gives an example of conflict at 90° in which aircraft have the same speed. NN (1.08%) and optimal solution (0.26%) are similar.

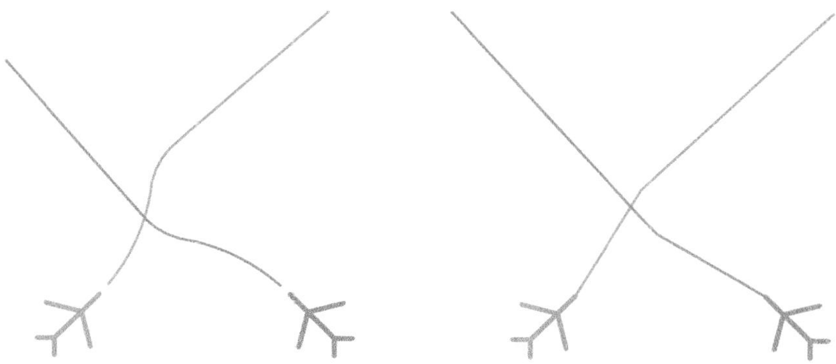

Figure 6.9. *Neural network solution (left), optimal solution (right)*

– Figure 6.10 gives an example of conflict at 15° in which aircraft have the same speed. Such a conflict is particularly difficult to solve. Solutions are different, but for such a difficult conflict, the NN (2.30%) gives a solution that is robust and quite as good as the optimal solution (2.23%). This conflict is the most difficult conflict to solve (in the five examples presented). It is interesting to see that the difference of lengthenings is the smallest.

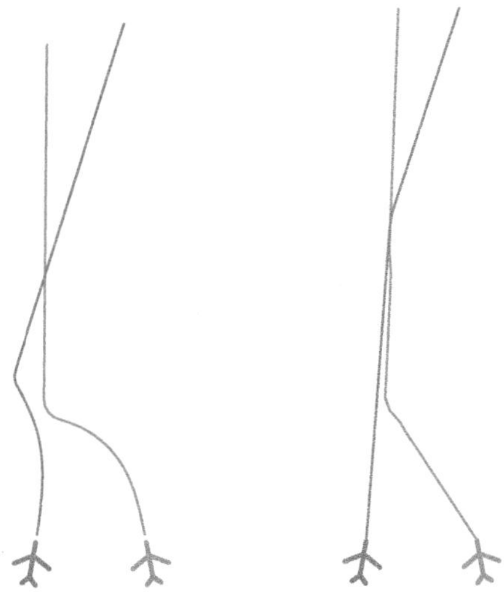

Figure 6.10. *Neural network solution (left), optimal solution (right)*

– Figure 6.11 gives an example of aircraft at different speeds (400 and 500 kts) with crossing at a small angle (30°). The NN solution (1.32%) appears very similar to the optimal solution (0.28%) even if its lengthening is worse.

Figure 6.11. *Neural network solution (left), optimal solution (right)*

– Figure 6.12 gives an example of aircraft crossing on the same route. This problem is easy to solve and solutions are similar. The NN solution (1.18%) is robust but worse than the optimal solution (0.25%).

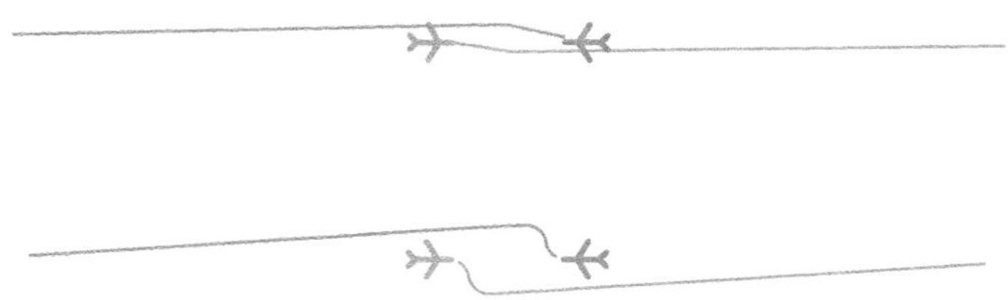

Figure 6.12. *Neural network solution (down), optimal solution (up)*

– Figure 6.13 gives an example of aircraft flying on parallel routes at different speeds. This problem is easy to solve. Solutions are similar. The NN solution (1.02%) is robust but worse than the optimal solution (0.21%).

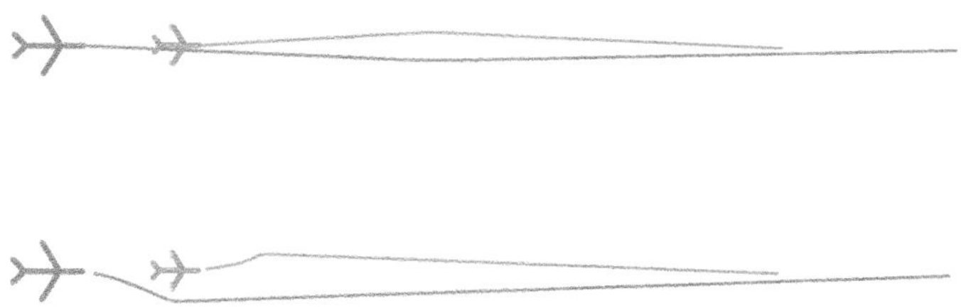

Figure 6.13. *Neural network solution (down), optimal solution (up)*

These five examples show that the principal advantage of the NN is to be very robust. It does not give optimal solutions. However, it gives very good solutions for difficult conflicts. Tests conducted on non-learned situations gave as good results as tests conducted on learned situations. It is however hard to extend this research to conflicts involving more than two aircraft: building a learning set of example becomes very challenging.

6.3.4. *A limit to autonomous approaches: the speed constraint*

Geometrical approaches have also been widely studied [HWA 07, LEN 10, SNA 10, VAN 11] in robotics. They give very good results when the speed is not constrained or when the speed can be modified in a small range. In [DUR 15], we adapted the algorithm described by Van den Berg *et al.* [VAN 11] and checked through different simulations its behavior when the longitudinal speed of aircraft is constrained.

Figure 6.14 gives examples of simulations with 10 and 100 leveled aircraft flying in a 500 × 500 NM^2. Figure 6.15 gives the percentage of failures (cases for which the algorithm failed to find a conflict-free trajectory) for different levels of speed constraint $s_{\text{lon}} \in [0., 1.]$. When s_{lon} is fixed, aircraft speeds can take values in

$[(1 - s_{\text{lon}})n_s, (1 + s_{\text{lon}})n_s]$, where n_s is the nominal speed of the aircraft. When $s_{\text{lon}} = 0$, the longitudinal speed of the aircraft cannot be modified and results show that the algorithm cannot always handle low densities whereas when $s_{\text{lon}} = 0.3$, 80% of the most dense cases can be completely solved. These results argue in favor of centralized approaches for air traffic, at least when the traffic is dense.

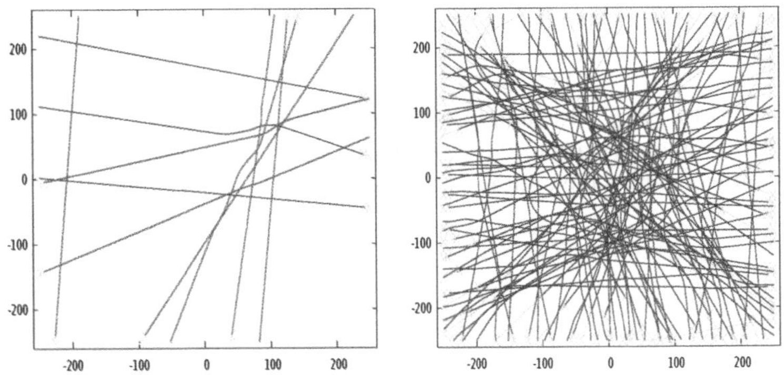

Figure 6.14. *Scenario examples with 10 and 100 aircraft*

6.4. Iterative approaches

Iterative approaches reduce the problem complexity by offering a degraded resolution. The principle is to order aircraft (finding the best order is a problem itself) and decide the aircraft trajectories one by one following the chosen order. The first aircraft will not alter its trajectory, a trajectory is chosen for the second aircraft to avoid the first aircraft, a trajectory is chosen for aircraft n to avoid the $(n - 1)$ previous aircraft. This approach was tried by the Eurocontrol Experimental Center in the ARC2000[3] project [KRE 89], but was also modeled in [CHI 97, HU 02]. Such an approach makes the problem easy to solve but finding an appropriate ranking, as we have discussed before, is very challenging [ARC 04].

6.5. Global approaches

In the 1990s, very few research was conducted on conflict resolution using a global approach. After the failure of *AERA* [NIE 89a, NIE 89b] in the United States, pragmatic approaches were tried. Erzberger *et al.* [ERZ 97] introduced a very complete aircraft detection tool taking into account uncertainties on trajectories. The

3 Automatic radar control for the 21st Century.

tool was able to provide the controller with a conflict probe giving the severity of future conflicts. However, the conflict resolution tool was provided only for a pairwise conflict.

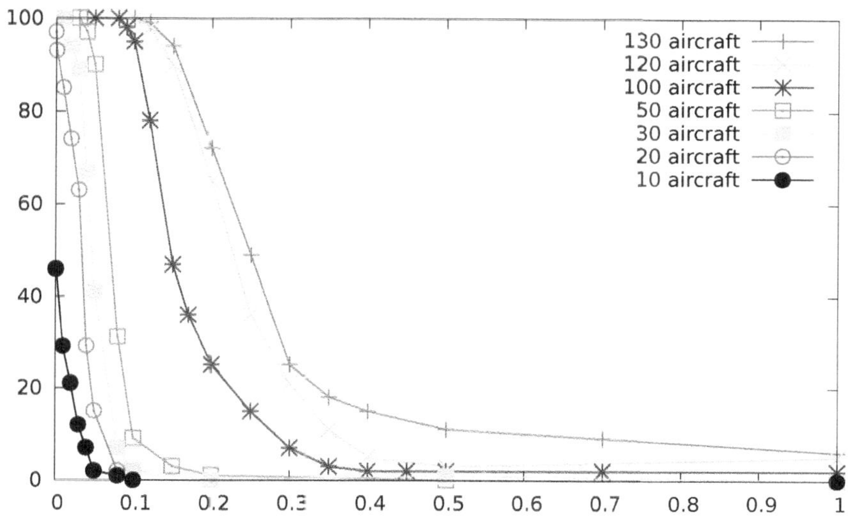

Figure 6.15. *Total number of failures for different densities of aircraft as a function of the speed range* $s_{\rm lon} \in [0., 1.]$

In the late 1990s, mathematical formulations of the problem were proposed. Oh *et al.* [OH 97] and then Frazzoli *et al.* [FRA 01] introduced a semidefinite programming approach to the conflict resolution problem. The approach is very powerful and is able to tackle the multi-aircraft problem. However, the solution found is only locally optimal and the model requires to use constant speeds and perfect trajectory prediction. Pallottino *et al.* [PAL 01, PAL 02] developed a mathematical model using mixed integer linear programming that could be solved by CPLEX and ensured the global optimality of the solution. Christodoulou and Kontogeorgou [CHR 08] extended the model in 3D in 2006, the use of constant speed during climbing phases was also required. Gariel and Feron [GAR 09] refined the horizontal model in 2009.

We decided to address the problem using simulation instead of a mathematical formulation for different reasons:

– first, aircraft do not fly at constant speeds, especially during the climbing and descending phases. Even during the cruise, they experience evolutive head or tail winds. It is hard to model the trajectory prediction with mathematical equations;

– second, building solutions robust to uncertainties is essential in a safety context. Therefore, a realistic model needs to take into account all kinds of uncertainties, related to the trajectory prediction, but also to the presence of human pilots. In a transition context in which controllers would still be in charge of the traffic but automated tools could help them in their task, the problem modeling must also take into account the controller uncertainties;

– third, variables of the problem can be discrete or real, many constraints can be added in a simulation, which is not always the case when using a mathematical formulation. Generally, simulations are much more flexible than mathematical formulations.

In section 6.2, we explained why the conflict resolution is highly combinatorial and can not be globally solved with local optimization methods.

6.6. A global approach using evolutionary computation

We proposed to use an EA to solve multiple aircraft conflicts with simple maneuvers (similar to those used by air traffic controllers) and showed that we were able to solve every conflict on existing traffic data [DUR 96b, DUR 97]. Our model took into account uncertainties in the trajectory prediction and could handle any other kind of predictor.

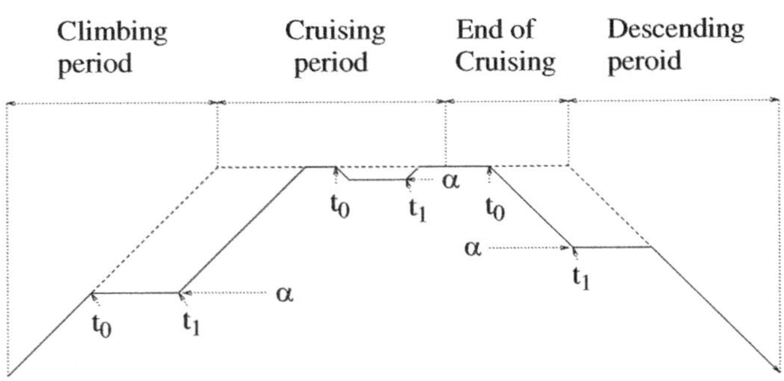

Figure 6.16. *Vertical maneuver modeling*

6.6.1. *Maneuver modeling*

The first model we built took into account the following operational constraints in the vertical plane (see Figure 6.16):

– a climbing aircraft can only interrupt its climb at a fixed level and resume its climb later. Most controllers "clear" aircraft at intermediate levels;

– when an aircraft has reach its en route preferred flight level, it can only be asked to descend one flight level and resume its original level after a while. Long-haul flight are not always able to climb. They can always descend;

– when an aircraft is close to its top of descent (e.g. 50 NM), it can be asked to anticipate its descent and finish cruising at a lower level.

In the horizontal plane, pilots are generally familiar with simple heading changes of 10°, 20° or 30° right or left of their current heading (see Figure 6.17).

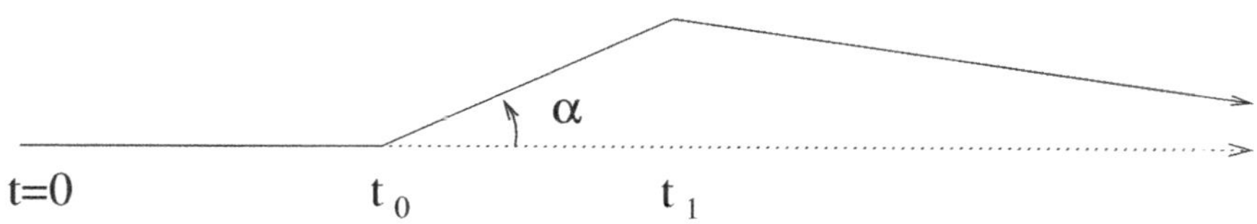

Figure 6.17. *Horizontal maneuver modeling*

A maneuver will be determined by three variables:

– the maneuver starting time t_0;

– the turning point time t_1;

– the deviation angle α for a horizontal maneuver or a flight level α for a vertical maneuver depending on the flight phase.

The first two variables t_0 and t_1 are time steps, and the last variable α is qualitative.

We also decided to give at most one maneuver at a time for each aircraft, and not to change the maneuver type once it is started. This means that the pilot will be given a vertical or a horizontal maneuver and that once the maneuver is started, only its duration can be changed.

6.6.2. *Uncertainty modeling*

A traffic simulator was used to predict trajectories taking into account the previous maneuvers. It considers uncertainties on aircraft future positions. With the progress of ground positioning, the main uncertainties remaining are due to head and tail winds in the horizontal plane and the aircraft climbing rate in the vertical plane. Flight management systems (FMS) are able to predict the aircraft future position with a good accuracy but a ground system cannot be as precise. In Figure 6.18, we show how the uncertainty can be modeled. At $t = 0$, the aircraft is represented by a point at its current position. Because the aircraft speed along its track is not well known, the point becomes a segment, increasing in size. At time step $t = 4$, the new heading transforms the segment in a parallelogram, and at time step $t = 7$, the parallelogram becomes an hexagon. In the vertical plane, a low and high climbing rate is defined and the aircraft position in modeled by a cylinder increasing in size when the aircraft climbs, or descends. When the aircraft is leveled, the cylinder is flat. If a maneuver interrupts a climbing phase at $t = 2$ and resumes its climb at $t = 6$, the uncertainty evolves as shown in Figure 6.19.

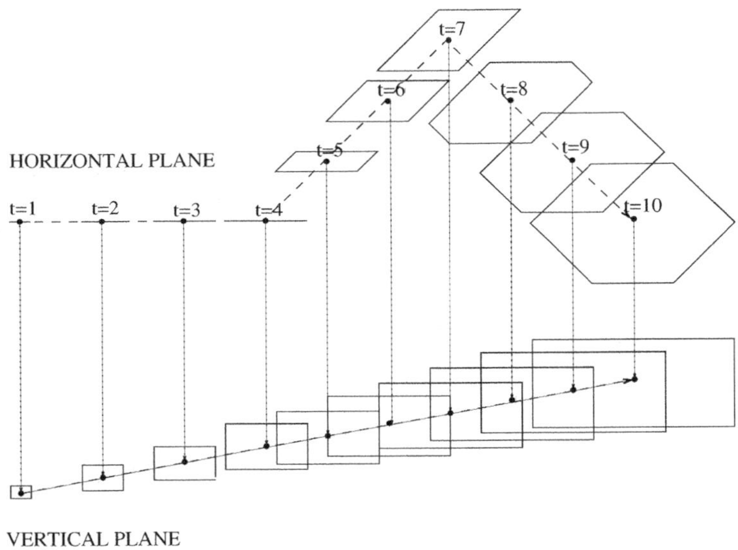

Figure 6.18. *Uncertainty modeling*

6.6.3. *Real-time management*

The resolution is computed during a prediction time window T_w (10 to 20 min) and the situation is updated every δ minutes (2 or 3 min in practice). Figure 6.20 details the real-time modeling. Three periods are defined in the time window. The first period, which lasts δ minutes, is called the locked period. No trajectory modification can be done during this period. Indeed, aircraft fly during the time necessary for the detection, the resolution of possible conflicts and the transmission of maneuvers to the deck. Their trajectories cannot be modified during this locked period.

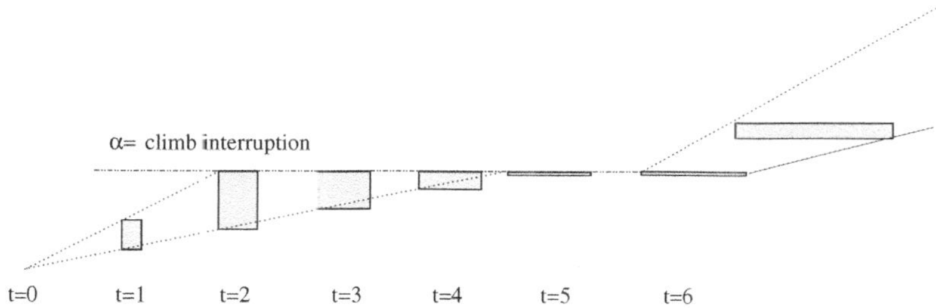

Figure 6.19. *Vertical uncertainty modeling*

The next δ minute period is called the notification period, because the maneuvers given for this period will not be modifiable during the next iteration. Consequently, any maneuver that happens during this period should be notified to the pilot.

The last period is the modifiable period. These maneuvers will be reconsidered during the next iteration. Because of uncertainty, some conflicts can disappear without maneuvering any aircraft.

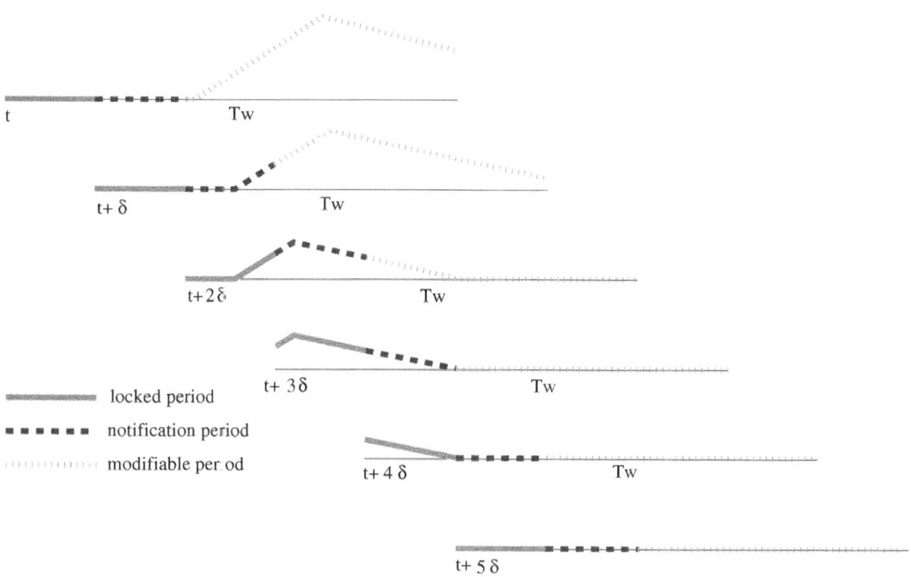

Figure 6.20. *Modeling in real time*

6.6.4. *Evolutionary algorithm implementation*

For each cluster of n aircraft in conflict during the next T_w minutes, we look for a combination of n maneuvers, one maneuver per aircraft. The optimization criteria should:

– ensure all aircraft separations;

– minimize delays;

– minimize the number of maneuvers and the number of aircraft undergoing maneuvers;

– minimize the duration of maneuvers so that the aircraft are freed as soon as possible.

A solution is represented by a vector of tuples $(t_{0_i}, t_{1_i}, \alpha_i)$, with $i \in [1, n]$.

6.6.4.1. *General description*

The EA implemented is a simple algorithm as described in [GOL 89].

An initial population of candidate solutions is randomly created (the size of the population being proportional to the number of aircraft with a maximum of $N_{pop} = 200$ individuals). Then the fitness of each individual (representing a configuration of maneuvers) is evaluated. The best individuals are then reproduced and selected according to their adaptation (the selection technique used is the "stochastic reminder without replacement"). A part of the population (50 %) is then crossed: from two "parents," two "children" are created; they replace the parents in the population. Then a part of the population undergoes mutation (15 %). The mutation generally consists of modifying the maneuver of an aircraft in the cluster. The distance used to distinguish two configurations for the "sharing" operator is simple. Two maneuvers are considered equal if they are both vertical, speed or horizontal maneuvers and, in the later case, if they are carried out to the same side. To measure the distance between two configurations, the number of different maneuvers are computed. An elitist strategy is applied: at each generation, the best individuals of the population are preserved so that they do not disappear during a crossover or a mutation process.

Taking the temporal requirements imposed by the real-time traffic management into account, the termination criterion consists of stopping the optimization procedure at the end of a certain number of generations (generally 20 in the 1997 experiments). However, this number continues to increase if the algorithm is unable to find a solution without conflict (in the experiments, the maximum number of generations was limited to 40).

6.6.4.2. *The horizon effect*

The solver has only one short-term vision of the aircraft trajectories. With the cost function simply consisting of limiting the delay generated by a maneuver, the solver is sometimes tempted to defer a conflict beyond the temporal window without solving it. In order to counter this "horizon effect", we can measure the effectiveness of the resolution of a conflict and modify the fitness function of the algorithm for resolving the conflict.

For any pair of aircraft under consideration in a cluster:

– if the aircraft are not in conflict, it is not necessary to penalize the cost function;

– on the other hand, if the trajectory tracks between the current positions of the aircraft and their destinations cross, the cost function is penalized when the aircraft are still not crossing each other at the end of the time window.

6.6.4.3. *The fitness function*

For each configuration, a matrix F of size $(n \times n)$ is used to store the following information:

– the diagonal term $F_{i,i}$ measures the lengthening of aircraft i's trajectory. It is zero if no maneuver is given to aircraft i;

– the term $F_{i,j}$ with $i < j$ measures the separation violation between aircraft i and aircraft j. It is zero when the two aircraft are not conflicting;

– the term $F_{i,j}$ with $i > j$ measures the effectiveness of the conflict resolution between aircraft i and aircraft j.

The chosen fitness function is:

$$\exists(i,j),\ i \neq j,\ F_{i,j} \neq 0 \Rightarrow F = \frac{1}{2 + \sum_{i \neq j} F_{i,j}}$$

$$\forall(i,j),\ i \neq j,\ F_{i,j} = 0 \Rightarrow F = \frac{1}{2} + \frac{1}{1 + \sum_i F_{i,i}}$$

It guarantees that a configuration without conflict has a better fitness than a configuration with one or more conflicts remaining.

As described earlier, the genetic algorithm could hardly solve large clusters, but taking advantage of the partially separable structure of the denominator in the fitness function helps to define crossover and mutation operators adapted to the problem.

6.6.4.4. *Use of partial separability*

Let us consider the minimization problem of a function F of n variables $x_1, x_2, \ldots, x_n$, sum of m terms F_i, each of which depends only on a subset of the variables of the problem.

Such a function (that is denoted as partially separable) can be expressed as:

$$F(x_1, x_2, \ldots, x_n) = \sum_{i=1}^{m} F_i(x_{j_1}, x_{j_2}, \ldots, x_{j_{n_i}})$$

6.6.4.5. *The adapted crossover operator*

The intuitive idea is the following: for a completely separable problem, the global minimum is obtained when the function is separately minimized for each variable. In this case, the function to be minimized can be written as:

$$F(x_1, x_2, \ldots, x_n) = \sum_{i=1}^{n} F_i(x_i)$$

Minimizing each function F_i leads to the global minimum of the function.

A crossover operator that chooses, for each variable x_i, among the two parents, the variable that minimizes the function F_i, creates an individual that is better than the two parents (or at least equal).

This strategy can be adapted for partially separable functions. To create a child starting from two parents, for each variable, the idea is to choose among the two parents the one that minimizes the sum of the partial functions F_i in which it occurs.

First, let us define a *local fitness* $G_k(x_1, x_2, .., x_n)$ for variable x_k as follows:

$$G_k(x_1, x_2, .., x_n) = \sum_{i \in S_k} \frac{F_i(x_{j_1}, x_{j_2}, .., x_{j_{n_i}})}{n_i}$$

where S_k is the set of i such that x_k is a variable of F_i and n_i the number of variables of F_i.

The local fitness associated with a variable isolates the contribution of this variable in the global fitness.

When minimizing F, if:

$$G_k(parent_1) < G_k(parent_2) - \Delta$$

then child 1 will contain variable x_k of parent 1. Otherwise, if:

$$G_k(parent_1) > G_k(parent_2) + \Delta$$

then child 1 will contain variable x_k of parent 2. If:

$$|G_k(parent_1) - G_k(parent_2)| \leq \Delta$$

then variable x_k of child 1 will be randomly chosen or can be a random linear combination of the kth variable of each parent when dealing with real variables. If the same strategy is applied to child 1 and to child 2, children may be identical, especially if Δ is small. This problem can be avoided by taking a new pair of parents for each child.

Let us consider the following completely separable function:

$$F(x_1, x_2, x_3) = x_1 + x_2 + x_3$$

for x_1, x_2 and x_3 integers included in $[0, 2]$. Variable k's local fitness is: $G_k(x_1, x_2, x_3) = x_k$. Let us cross parents $(1\,, 0\,, 2)$ and $(2\,, 1\,, 0)$ that have the same fitness $F = 3$. With $\Delta = 0$, child 1 will be $(1\,, 0\,, 0)$: $F = 1$. With $\Delta = 1$, child 2 may be $(2\,, 1\,, 0)$, $(2\,, 0\,, 0)$, $(1\,, 1\,, 0)$ or $(1\,, 0\,, 0)$. The children's fitnesses are always better than the parents' fitnesses when $\Delta = 0$, which is not the case with a classical crossover operator.

As it is completely separable, this function is obviously too simple to demonstrate the benefits of the adapted crossover operator. In section 6.6.4.6, a simple partially separable function is introduced and the improvement achieved is theoretically measured.

6.6.4.6. *Theoretical study of a simple example*

Let us define the following function:

$$F(x_1, x_2, .., x_n) = \sum_{0<i\neq j\leq n} \delta(x_i, x_j) \qquad [6.1]$$

where $(x_1, x_2, .., x_n)$ is a bit string and $\delta(x_i, x_j) = 1$ if $x_i \neq x_j$ and 0 if $x_i = x_j$. It must be noticed that the function is only partially separable and has two global minima, $(1, 1, 1, ..., 1)$ and $(0, 0, 0, ..., 0)$.

For $x = (x_1, x_2, ...x_n)$, we define the local fitness $G_k(x)$ by:

$$G_k(x) = \frac{1}{2}\sum_{i=1}^{n} \delta(x_k, x_i)$$

We define $I(x)$ as the number of bits equal to 1 in x. Then, it is easy to establish that:

$$F(x) = I(x)(n - I(x))$$

$$G_k(x) = \frac{I(x)}{2} \quad if\ x_k = 0$$

$$= \frac{n - I(x)}{2} \quad if\ x_k = 1$$

In the following discussion, we use a classical n point crossover operator; A_1 and A_2 represent two parents randomly chosen in a population and C represents their child.

In section 6.6.4.7, the probabilities of increasing the fitness with the adapted or the classical crossover operator are compared. The interested reader will find a detailed study for this example in [DUR 98].

6.6.4.7. *Probability of improvement*

For function [6.1], the probabilities of increasing the fitness with the classical or the adapted operator can be mathematically computed for every possible couple of parents.

Let us define $P_{1-1}(i, j, k)$ as the probability to find k bits equal to 1 at the same position in both parents A_1 and A_2, with $I(A_1) = i$ and $I(A_2) = j$. As $P_{1-1}(i, j, k) = P_{1-1}(j, i, k)$, we will assume in the following discussion that $i \leq j$. It can be shown that:

– if $k > i$, then:

$$P_{1-1}(i, j, k) = 0$$

– if $k \leq i$, then:

$$P_{1-1}(i, j, k) = C_i^k \prod_{l=0}^{k-1} \frac{j-l}{n-l} \prod_{l=k}^{i-1} \frac{(n-l)-(j-k)}{n-l}$$

The classical crossover used is the n point crossover that randomly chooses bits from A_1 or A_2 (the order of the bit string has no influence on the fitness).

For the adapted crossover (respectively for the classical crossover), let us define $P_a(i, j, k)$ (resp. $P_c(i, j, k)$) as the probability that if $I(A_1) = i$ and $I(A_2) = j$ then $I(C) = k$. As $P_a(i, j, k) = P_a(j, i, k)$ and $P_c(i, j, k) = P_c(j, i, k)$, we will assume in the following discussion that $i \leq j$. Then, it can be shown that for the classical crossover:

$$P_c(i,j,k) = \sum_{l=\max(0,\frac{i+j+1-n}{2})}^{\min(k,i+j-k)} P_{1-1}(i,j,l)\,\frac{C_{i+j-2l}^{k-l}}{2^{i+j-2l}}$$

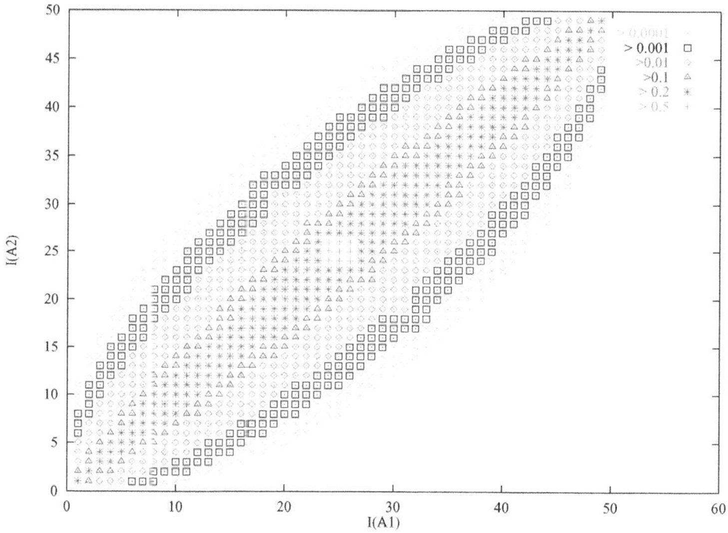

Figure 6.21. *Prob*$(F(C) > \max[F(A_1), F(A_2)])$ *according to* $[I(A_1), I(A_2)]$ *— traditional crossover —* $n = 50$*. For a color version of the figure, see www.iste.co.uk/durand/atm.zip*

For the adapted crossover (with $m = \min(k, n-k)$):

$$i+j < n : P_a(i,j,k) = P_{1-1}(i,j,k)$$

$$i+j > n : P_a(i,j,k) = P_{1-1}(n-i, n-j, n-k)$$

$$i+j = n : P_a(i,j,k) = \sum_{l=0}^{m} P_{1-1}(i,j,l)\,\frac{C_{i+j-2l}^{k-l}}{2^{i+j-2l}}$$

As $P_{1-1}(i,j,k) = 0$ if $k > \min(i,j)$, then:

– if $i+j < n$ and $k > \min(i,j)$, then $P_a(i,j,k) = 0$;

– if $i+j > n$ and $k < \max(i,j)$, then $P_a(i,j,k) = 0$.

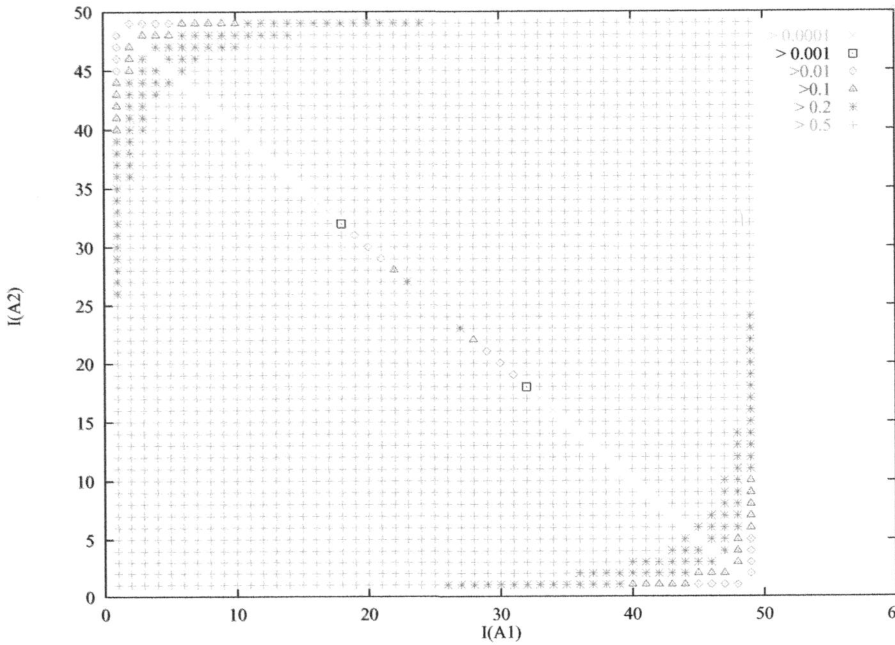

Figure 6.22. *$Prob(F(C) > max[F(A_1), F(A_2)])$ according to $[I(A_1), I(A_2)]$ — adapted crossover — $n = 50$. For a color version of the figure, see www.iste.co.uk/durand/atm.zip*

Consequently:

– if $i + j < n$ and $P_a(i, j, k) > 0$, then $k < \min(i, j, n - i, n - j)$;

– if $i + j > n$ and $P_a(i, j, k) > 0$, then $k > \max(i, j, n - i, n - j)$.

Thus, if $i + j \neq n$, then $F(C) \geq \max[F(A_1), F(A_2)]$. If $i + j = n$, local fitness of variables of each parent is equal and the adapted crossover behaves like a classical n points crossover.

Figures 6.21 and 6.22 present the probability for a child to have a better fitness than its parents (for all the possible combinations of the parents). In this example, the adapted crossover widely improves the crossover efficiency. The small square in the center of Figure 6.21 represents a probability of improvement larger than 0.5. It becomes a very large square in Figure 6.22.

6.6.4.8. *Application to conflict resolution*

For the conflict resolution problem, the "local fitness" associated with each aircraft is defined as follows:

$$F_i = \sum_{j=1}^{n}(F_{i,j})$$

The adapted crossover operator is described in Figure 6.23. For each aircraft i, if the local fitness of aircraft i of parent A is definitely lower than that of parent B, then the maneuver of aircraft i of parent A is chosen for both children. In the opposite case (e.g. for aircraft 3), the maneuver of aircraft i of parent B is chosen for both children. When the local fitnesses are close, a combination of both maneuvers is used.

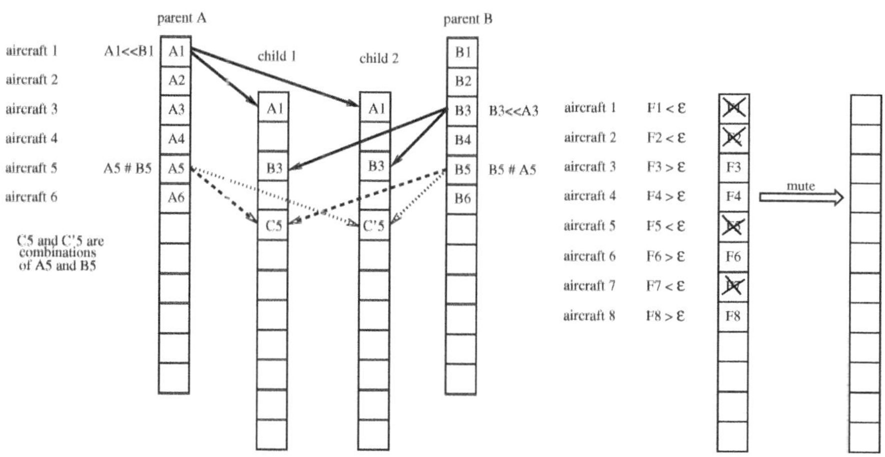

Figure 6.23. *The adapted crossover and mutation operators*

An adaptive mutation operator is also used (Figure 6.23). An aircraft is chosen among those whose local fitnesses are higher than a given threshold (e.g. the aircraft that are still in conflict).

6.6.5. *Alternative modeling*

Alternative models were derived from the previous model. In [GRA 01a], instead of maneuvering aircraft at specific time steps, we decided to add extra beacons on the aircraft routes corresponding to the turning points. Instead of modeling uncertainties with convex polygons in the horizontal plane, uncertainty was modeled by one or several segments as shown in Figure 6.24.

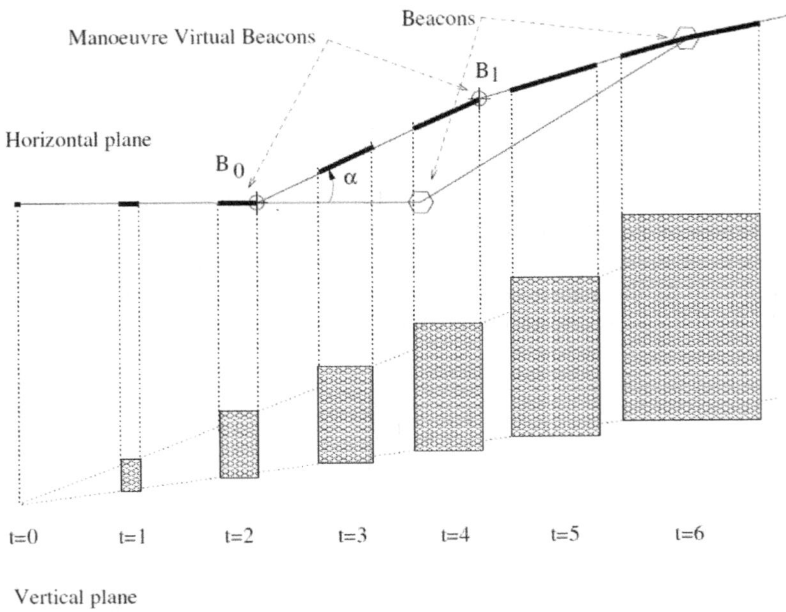

Figure 6.24. *Alternative uncertainty modeling*

6.6.6. *One-day traffic statistics*

In the late 1990s, simulation results were obtained throughout a day of traffic in the French airspace (Friday May 21, 1999: 7,540 flights carried out). More complete results can be found in [GRA 02]. The simulation was carried out with three levels of uncertainties:

– 2 % in the horizontal plane and 5 % in the vertical plane;

– 5 % in the horizontal plane and 15 % in the vertical plane;

– 10 % in the horizontal plane and 30 % in the vertical plane.

A total of 2,140 real conflicts are observed during the day above flight level 100 (10,000 ft) when the resolution process is not used.

For each level of uncertainty, the simulator was able to solve all the conflicts. The simulator added random noise to the real trajectories of the aircraft so that they did not precisely maintain the nominal trajectories. Table 6.3 shows the number of times the solver was called, the number of maneuvers, the average duration of the maneuvers, the proportion of the flight constrained by the maneuvers and the execution time of the simulation[4] for the various levels of uncertainties. It is observed that with a weak uncertainty, the number of maneuvers carried out (2,461) is slightly higher than the number of real conflicts (2,140). Hence, it can be assumed that uncertainty generates some useless maneuvers. With 10 % and 30 % of speed uncertainty, the number of maneuvers is almost three times higher than that with 2 % and 5 %, and the number of times the solver is called is more than doubled.

Uncertainty (%)	Number of clusters	Number of maneuvers	Mean duration by aircraft (s)	Proportion of constrained flight (%)	Duration of the simulation (mn)
2 and 5	8,539	2,461	34	1.27	26
5 and 15	12,831	3,881	78	2.85	35
10 and 30	19,390	6,819	236	8.43	55

Table 6.3. *Numerical results*

Table 6.4 shows the influence of uncertainty on the size of the clusters. The increase in uncertainty is observed to play a significant role in determining the size of the clusters to be solved and difficulty solving problems thus grows significantly.

Cut	2	3	4	5	6	7	8	9	10	11–17	18–37
2 %–5 %	7,205	1,021	224	56	23	6	3	1			
5 %–15 %	9,970	1,855	586	218	100	42	24	14	11	11	
10 %–30 %	12,859	3,326	1,317	741	388	245	153	81	77	157	46

Table 6.4. *Influence of the uncertainty on the size of the clusters*

6.6.7. *Introducing automation in the existing system*

The existing tactical control task relies completely on human expertise and introducing automation in the system is not simple for several reasons. First, a transitional system that can handle both equipped and non-equipped aircraft has to be imagined. This system should be able to assist the controllers in their task. We could imagine a system that reproduces the controllers' detection task and helps them to find solutions to conflicts. However, such a system would have to be trusted by controllers. In the transitional phase, if they detect conflicts that are not detected by the automated system, they might not trust the automated detection. But if the system

4 The simulations were carried out using 12 PCs; the most powerful one PC was a Pentium IV 2.53 MHz machine, the resolutions were carried out in parallel.

detects too many conflicts, controllers will not trust it either. Solutions found by the solver are very often hard to understand and might thus be useless for controllers.

Max speed decrease (%)	Max speed increase (%)	Remaining conflicts
0	0	4,031
3	2	1,939
6	3	1,355
10	5	804
15	10	482

Table 6.5. *Influence of the speed change on the number of remaining conflicts*

En Route Air traffic Soft Management Ultimate System (ERASMUS) was imagined in 2006 in order to avoid these problems. The idea was to slightly modify aircraft speeds to solve conflicts without altering the controllers mental picture of the traffic. The solver presented in this chapter was thus restricted to speed maneuvers. The α parameter previously defined becomes a speed change variable. Some simulation tests were carried out using data from a day of traffic (April 10, 2008). In order to simulate heavy traffic, time was squeezed by 70%. Without any resolution, 4,031 conflicts were detected during this day of traffic. The separation distance used was 8NM. It takes into account the 5NM separation standard and an error margin of 3NM for a 20mn prediction (which is quite low).

Table 6.5 gives the influence of the speed change on the number of remaining conflicts. The higher the speed change, the less the remaining conflicts.

Table 6.6 gives the influence of the proportion of ERASMUS equipped aircraft on the number of remaining conflicts. The speed can be changed from -6% to $+3\%$. The anticipation time is still $20\,mn$.

No. of aircraft (%)	Equipped aircraft (%)	Remaining conflicts	Solved conflicts (%)
8,166	0	4,031	0.00
8,166	25	3,225	20.00
8,166	50	2,541	36.96
8,166	75	1,878	53.41
8,166	100	1,355	66.39

Table 6.6. *Influence of the proportion of equipped aircraft on the number of remaining conflicts*

These results show that using speed modifications is less efficient than horizontal or vertical maneuvers. Speed changes are all the more efficient since the anticipation time is substantial and the speed change margin is high. Furthermore, 75% of aircraft would need to be equipped to solve 50% of the conflicts.

6.7. A global approach using ant colony optimization

In this section, ant colony optimization (ACO), as described by Dorigo *et al.* [DOR 96] and Dorigo and Caro [DOR 99], is used to solve large conflicts. This approach was published in [DUR 09].

6.7.1. *Problem modeling*

A toy problem described in Figure 6.25 was defined. n aircraft are located on a circle of radius R and flying to the center of the circle with the same speed. Their destination is the point of the circle located at the other end of the circle diameter they are flying on. The objective is to find new trajectories for every aircraft that solve every conflict and minimize the extra distance flown.

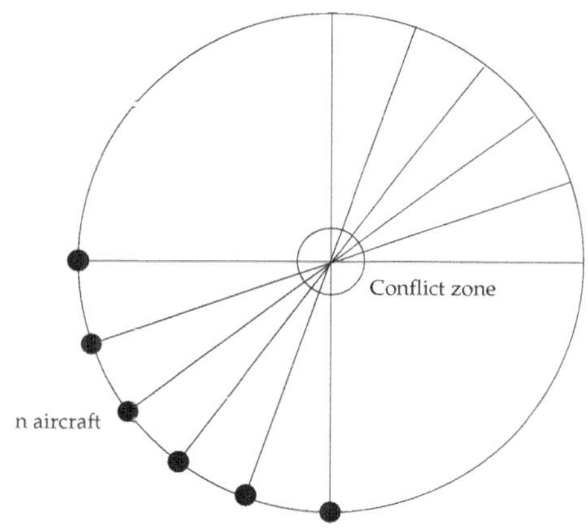

Figure 6.25. n *aircraft conflict problem*

Aircraft trajectories are modeled by a graph. Time is discretized in n_t time steps. A maneuver starts at some time T_1 and ends at some time T_2. Conflicts are only solved horizontally: a heading change of 10°, 20° or 30° right or left is given to the aircraft (see Figure 6.26).

The graph of the aircraft positions can be defined as follows: each node represents a time and an aircraft position. The transition from position i to position $i + 1$ is represented by an edge on which ants deposit pheromones.

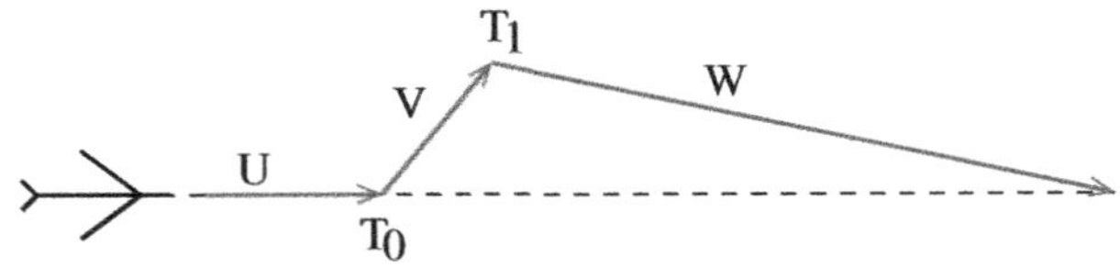

Figure 6.26. *Maneuver modeling*

An aircraft can be in three successive states. An aircraft is in state U before any maneuver. When a maneuver is started at T_1, it is in state V. Finally, when the maneuver is ended at T_2, aircraft is in state W. If U_i, V_i and W_i are the number of possible aircraft positions, respectively, in states U, V and W at time i, then:

$$
\begin{aligned}
U_{i+1} &= U_i \\
V_{i+1} &= V_i + 6 \\
W_{i+1} &= V_i
\end{aligned}
$$

with $U_1 = 1$, $V_1 = 6$ and $W_1 = 0$. It can be easily deduced that $U_i + V_i + W_i = 12\,i - 5$.

If we consider that one ant represents one conflict solution of an ACO (see Figure 6.27), then for n_a aircraft and n_t time steps, the number of possible trails at time i is $(12\,i - 5)^{n_a}$, and the total number of possible trails is $(12\,n_t - 5)^{n_a}$. For $n_a = 5$ and $n_t = 10$, more than 10^{10} trails can be obtained.

The modeling presented in this section considers a bunch of n_a ants to solve an n_a conflicting aircraft problem. Ants are treated independently, except to calculate the quantity of pheromones to deposit, which depends on the number of conflicts each ant of the bunch has been able to solve. This modeling reduces the number of trails to update to $n_a\,(12\,n_t - 5)$. For $n_a = 5$ and $n_t = 10$, the number of trails to update is 575, which is far less excessive than 10^{10}. For $n_a = 30$ and $n_t = 20$, the number of trails to update is only 7,050 instead of 10^{71} with the previous modeling.

6.7.2. *Algorithm description*

The ACO used in this section is a classical ACO as presented by Dorigo *et al.* [DOR 96] and Dorigo and Caro [DOR 99]. The only difference is that an ant is replaced by a bunch of n_a ants representing the n_a aircraft. Each ant of a bunch represents an aircraft. An ant can be in three different states as shown in Figure 6.28:

– before any maneuver the ant is in state U;

– after T_0, it changes its heading and moves to state V;

– after T_1, it changes its heading and moves to state W.

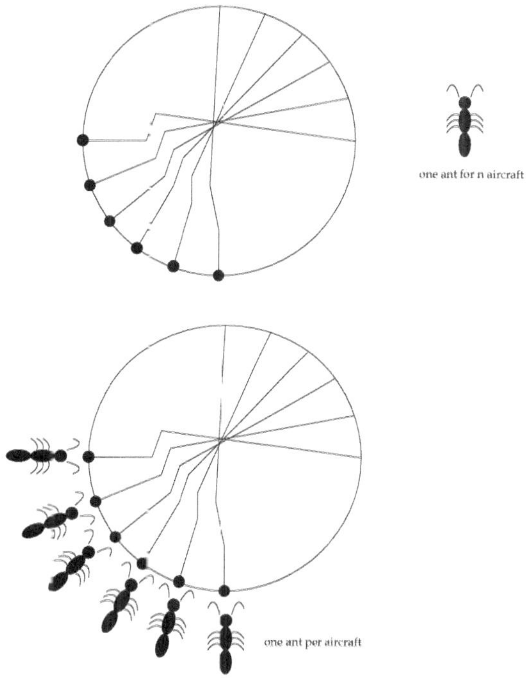

Figure 6.27. *One ant per cluster or one ant per aircraft*

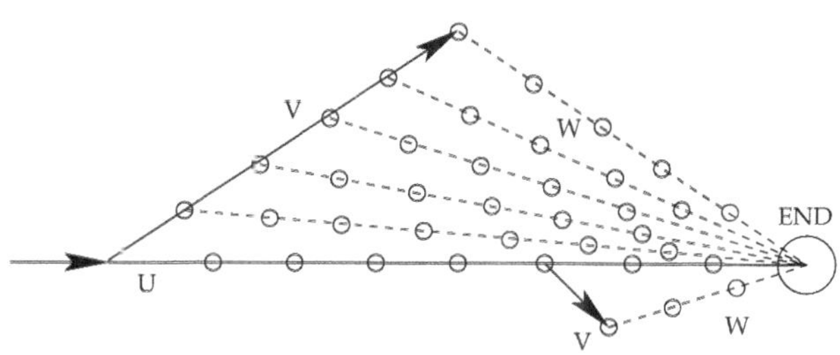

Figure 6.28. *Graph modeling*

At each node of the graph representing the possible trajectories of an aircraft, the ant chooses the next node with a probability depending on the quantity of pheromones left on the edge connecting the two nodes. The trajectories are then tested in order to check the existing conflicts. Ants representing conflicting aircraft do not deposit any pheromones whereas ants representing conflict-free aircraft deposit pheromones. The quantity of pheromones deposited decreases with the delay due to the aircraft maneuver.

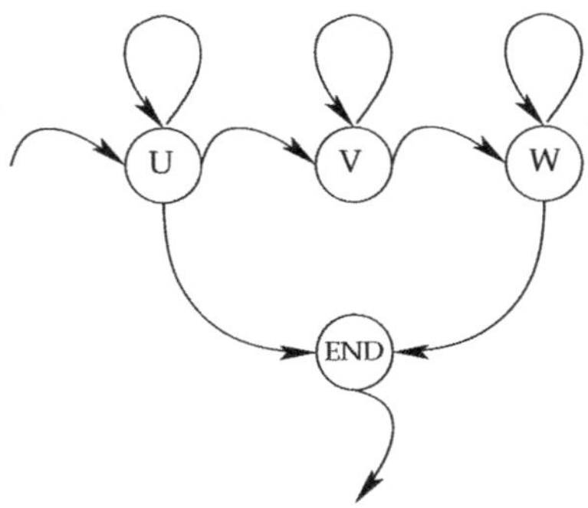

Figure 6.29. *Possible transitions*

The graph of possible paths is built in order to accept a maximum delay for each aircraft. At the beginning of the algorithm, initial pheromones are spread on the graph in order to ensure an equal probability for each path to be chosen. Figure 6.30 gives an example of the distribution of initial pheromones that ensures equal chance to every path. In this simple example, aircraft can turn left or right (30°) or go straight and only a few steps are represented. The amount of pheromones on each edge is thus proportional to the number of possible paths remaining after passing through this edge. Starting from the END, a state W is given a unit of pheromones, and then pheromones are added at each node in order to fill the whole graph.

If n_a is the number of aircraft, a bunch of n_a ants is created in order to represent each aircraft cluster at each generation of the optimization process. The process is repeated q times at each generation. In the following example, $q = 10 \times n_a$.

Each path is given a score. The smaller the score is, the better the path is. Because the straight line is the shortest path, getting through state U does not change the score. State V adds 2 points and state W adds 1 point. This scoring gives an advantage to maneuvers starting late: when aircraft are in state W, the score increases whereas in state U it does not.

At each node an ant chooses the next edge with a probability depending on the quantity of pheromones left on the next edge.

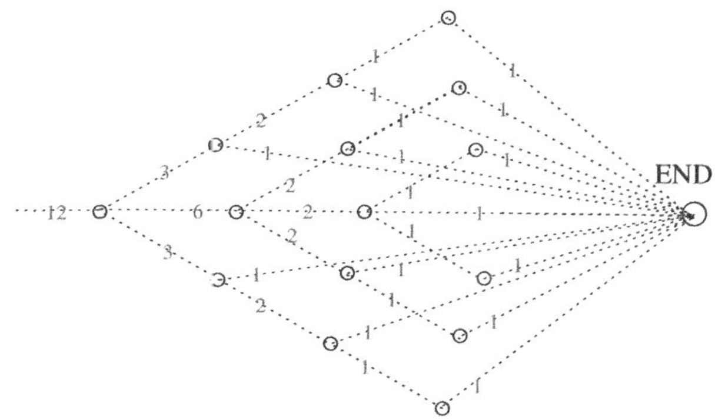

Figure 6.30. *Initial amount of pheromones on the graph*

If the ant is in conflict with another ant, it does not deposit any pheromones. However, when there is no conflict, it leaves behind a quantity of pheromones equal to:

$$\Delta\tau = \frac{n_a - n_{\text{out}}}{n_a} \cdot \frac{\tau_0}{s_{\text{path}}}$$

where n_{out} is the number of "conflicting" ants, τ_0 the original quantity of pheromones and s_{path} the score of the path followed by the ant. This amount takes into account the number of ants that finally found a valid path.

After each generation, and before starting a new generation, an evaporation principle is applied on the existing trails. The amount of pheromones is decreased by $x\%$ (in the examples $x = 10\%$) at the end of each generation.

The algorithm ends when the score obtained by each bunch of ants representing each aircraft does not decrease for a while or when the time allowed for the algorithm runs out.

6.7.3. *Algorithm improvement: constraint relaxation*

In high-density areas, conflicts might become difficult to solve and it may happen that a random generation of maneuvers cannot solve any conflict. This means that none of the ants might be able to solve every conflict. In such a case, there is no way to find even a bad solution for the problem. We propose to relax the conflict resolution constraint during the first generations in order to help the algorithm to find solutions with a small number of remaining conflicts. When solutions are found for a certain number of ants, the constraint is reinforced in order to move toward solutions that solve more conflicts and so on. For example at the first generation of the algorithm, we count the number n_c of ants having less than c conflicts for $c = 0, 1, 2, 3, ...(n_a - 1)$.

Let us define r as the maximum value of $\frac{n_a}{n_c}$ rounded to the higher integer. r gives the number of allowed conflicts per ant at the first generation. Each time the number of ants having less than r conflicts is higher than $\frac{n_a}{r}$ then r is reduced by one unit. This is repeated as long as $r > 0$.

There are lots of ways to choose r and to make it decrease. The choice made in this chapter is empirical and further work needs to be done to check it on different conflict sizes and configurations. Different strategies need to be compared.

6.7.4. *Results*

In this section, a difficult toy problem is solved with the ACO algorithm described in section 6.7.2. Figure 6.31 shows the best solution obtained after 18, 46 and 105 iterations of the algorithm for the five-aircraft problem. In this figure, we can see how the algorithm is able to deal with the combinatorial characteristics of the problem because the different solutions found at different steps of the algorithm do not give the same combinations of maneuvers to the aircraft. The scores obtained decrease with the generations. At generation 18 the score is 89, at generation 46 it is 78 and at generation 105 it is 50.

Figure 6.32 shows the best solution obtained for a 30-aircraft problem at different steps of the algorithm. The initial picture shows the best solution at the first generation. Only nine ants having four conflict or less are represented. The conflict constraint is reinforced because $\frac{30}{9} \leq 4$. Only ants having less than three conflicts now survive. At generation 14, 13 ants are having less than three conflicts. The conflict constraint is reinforced again because $\frac{30}{13} \leq 3$. At generation 15, despite the reinforcement 13 ants are still having less than two conflicts. This number increases to 20 at generation 44 and the conflict constraint is reinforced again because $\frac{30}{20} \leq 2$. At the next generation, the number of ants having less than one conflict is still 20 and increases to 30 at generation 47. The no-conflict constraint is applied at this step because $\frac{30}{1} \leq 1$. The first solution of the problem is found at generation 48. The solution is then improved and the ending criteria occur at generation 65.

6.7.5. *Conclusion and further work*

By modeling trajectories with a simple graph, we are able to adapt an ACO algorithm in order to deal with a reasonable number of trails: each aircraft cluster is represented by a bunch of ants that optimizes its trajectory. A relaxation principle is also added in order to help the algorithm find solutions when the conflict is complex to solve. When the algorithm starts to converge, it becomes possible to reinforce the constraint to find a no-conflict solution.

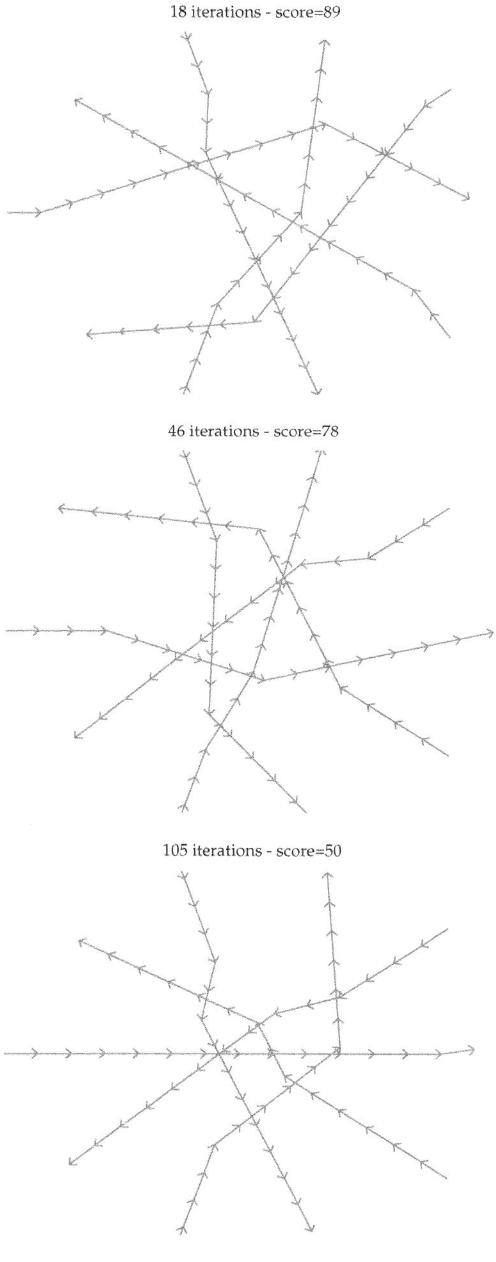

Figure 6.31. *Example of five-aircraft conflict resolution*

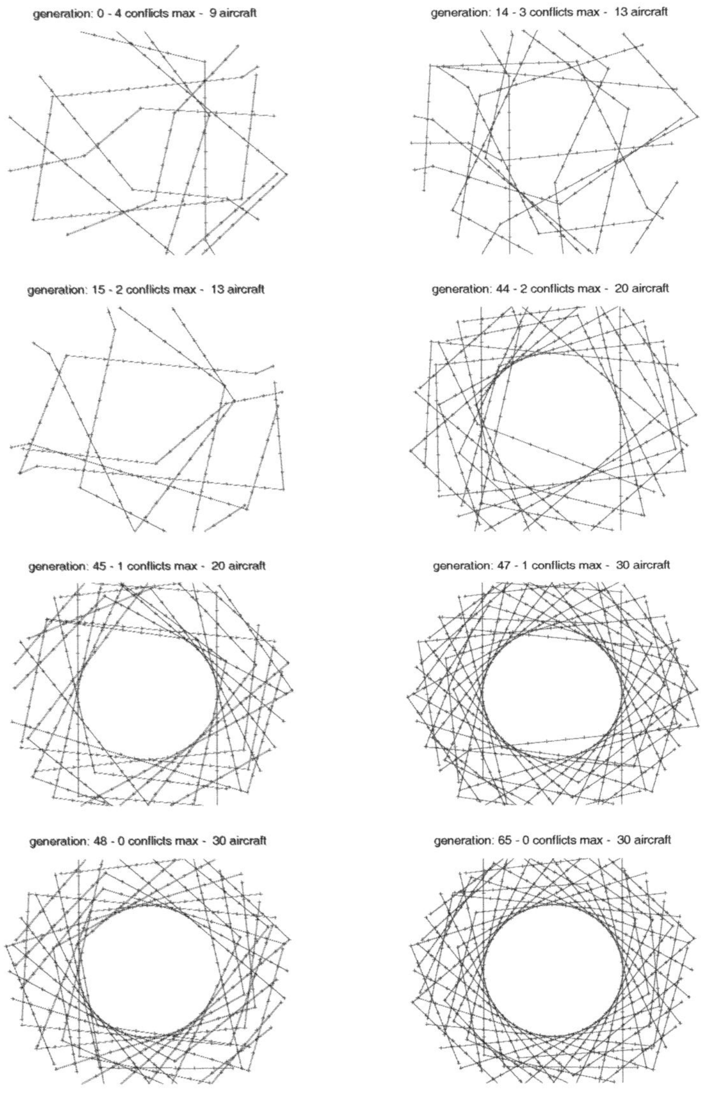

Figure 6.32. *Example of 30-aircraft conflict resolution*

This algorithm has not been tested on real examples yet and a lot of values have been empirically chosen. However, we showed that it was able to deal with very large problems. This approach has not been compared to other metaheuristics in terms of efficiency.

6.8. A new framework for comparing approaches

6.8.1. *Introduction*

Separating the model from the resolution tool is very useful to allow comparisons between resolution methods. In this section, we detail a new conflict resolution framework that can be treated with metaheuristics or exact methods such as CP. This approach was presented in [ALL 13]. For a problem involving n aircraft, we define for each aircraft i, n_{man} alternative trajectories T_{ik}, each alternative trajectory has a cost $cost_{ik}$. We build a 4D conflict matrix, where $C_{i,j,k,l} = 1$ if trajectory k of aircraft i is in conflict with trajectory l of aircraft j and $C_{i,j,k,l} = 0$ if not. With this modeling, the problem can be solved with classical CP techniques as well as various metaheuristics. The advantage of such a model is that the conflicts between trajectories are checked only once. For n aircraft, $\frac{n(n-1)}{2}n_{\mathrm{man}}^2$ trajectory pairs need to be checked to build the 4D matrix C. This can be done in parallel. The trajectory prediction model can be changed, uncertainties can be added or removed, more or less alternative trajectories can be used without changing the resolution tool.

Section 6.8.2 introduces the model that was chosen to build the trajectories that are used in the experimental results. We particularly detail the uncertainty model used in these examples and how the convex hulls of trajectories are built. Section 6.8.3 presents the detection algorithm that is used to build the 4D conflict matrix. Section 6.8.4 describes the method used to build conflict resolution benchmarks with different sizes and levels of uncertainties. Section 6.8.5 proposes two methods for the resolution of conflicts, namely an EA and CP. Section 6.8.5 4 gives some experimental results with a comparison of both approaches.

6.8.2. *Trajectory prediction model*

We give here an example of a trajectory prediction tool that can be used to build the aircraft positions at each time step according to the chosen maneuver options and the uncertainties taken into account. To constrain the search space to a "reasonable" size, only a limited number of maneuvers is defined for each aircraft involved in a conflict, then each pair of maneuvers for two different aircraft are tested to check if they are conflicting or not.

Moreover, our model is able to handle various degrees of uncertainties by considering the future positions of aircraft not simply as mere 2D points in the airspace but as growing convex hulls representing all its possible positions. Loss of separation between aircraft are then detected by computing the minimal distance between their two hulls.

6.8.2.1. *Maneuvers*

In our trajectory prediction model, a discretization of time into steps of duration τ is used to describe maneuvers. τ is chosen small enough to detect every conflict in the application. For example in section 6.8.4, $\tau = 3$ s because two facing aircraft flying at 600 kts (maximal speed) get only 1 NM closer every 3 s, so no conflict could be missed with such a small τ value (see [BAR 12] for a discussion on this topic).

Trajectories are defined in the horizontal plane, but the scenarios could be easily extended to the vertical dimension if we used a proper flight simulator. Initial routes are defined by a list of points. The first point O is the origin and the last point D is the destination. Aircraft fly from point to point and are able to correct the lateral error to the original trajectory thanks to their FMS. This means that in the further examples, the associated uncertainty does not increase with time.

However, various other sources of uncertainties cannot be reduced by current FMS functionalities and must be taken into account in our model. Aircraft speeds are hence subject to a ε_s error such that future positions of aircraft are spread over a range which grows with time.

In our trajectory model, maneuvers (i.e. heading changes) are engaged on a point of the initial trajectory referenced by the decision variable d_0, which represents the curvilinear distance from the origin O. Because of uncertainties on the exact location of the turn, a distance error ε_0 is added around this point. This means that the aircraft may start the maneuver ε_0 nautical miles before or after d_0.

An uncertainty ε_α is also associated to the heading change angle α at the turning point corresponding to d_0. Then the maneuver ends at a curvilinear distance d_1 from d_0 (i.e. at $d_0 + d_1$ from the origin O) with an associated error ε_1, when the aircraft returns toward its destination point D.

This kind of simple maneuvers, depicted in Figure 6.33, are representative of current air traffic control practice and can be easily implemented by pilots and current FMS technologies (see [GRA 01a]).

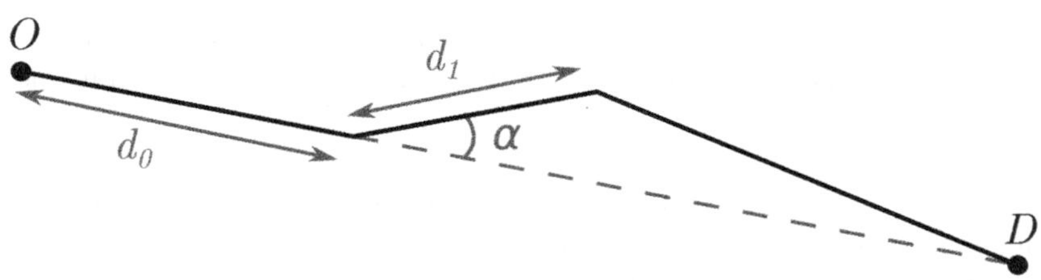

Figure 6.33. *Maneuver model*

In order to limit the number of maneuvers created, and thus the size of the search space, d_0 can only take a limited number n_0 of values (typically $n_0 = 5$ in the experimental benchmark presented in section 6.8.5.4). The heading change α can also take $n_\alpha = 7$ different values in our benchmark, that is $0°$, $10°$, $20°$ or $30°$ to the left or the right of the current heading, and the number of values for the distance of the returning point d_1 is also limited by n_1 (typically $n_1 = 5$).

If we consider five values for d_0, five values for d_1 and the six possible angles (there is no use to combine a null heading change $\alpha = 0$ with various d_0 and d_1 values, so that only one maneuver is added when the aircraft is not deviated), the number of maneuvers per aircraft is:

$$n_{\text{man}} = n_0 \times n_1 \times (n_\alpha - 1) + 1$$

so for the benchmark presented in section 6.8.4: $n_{\text{man}} = 5 \times 5 \times 6 + 1 = 151$.

For an instance with n aircraft, the search space is then of size n_{man}^n, that is $\approx 6 \times 10^{21}$ for a 10-aircraft instance (almost 4×10^{43} for 20 aircraft).

6.8.2.2. *Decision variables*

To simplify the access to the conflict matrix C and reduce the number of combinations to the useful ones (e.g. only one possible maneuver for $\alpha = 0$), the three decision variables d_0, α and d_1 associated with aircraft i are aggregated into a single decision variable m_i by a bijection from the allowed triples to interval $[1, n_{\text{man}}]$. We call M the set of decision variables of the problem:

$$M = \{m_i, i \in [1, n]\} \qquad [6.2]$$

6.8.2.3. *Cost*

The maneuver cost of our model is straightforwardly computed from the decision variables. Values of d_0 are enumerated by an index k_0 varying in $[1, n_0]$, values of d_1 by index k_1 in $[1, n_1]$ and angles α of value $10°$, $20°$ or $30°$ right or left, are, respectively, indexed by k_α in $[1, \frac{n_\alpha}{2}]$. For our benchmark problems, the cost of a maneuver m_i for aircraft i is then defined as follows:

$$\text{cost}_{\text{man}}(m_i) = \begin{cases} 0 & \text{if } \alpha = 0 \\ (n_0 - k_0)^2 + k_1^2 + k_\alpha^2 & \text{otherwise} \end{cases} \qquad [6.3]$$

where k_0, k_1 and k_α are the indexes corresponding to maneuver m_i. This cost is null whenever an aircraft is not maneuvered.

Furthermore, this cost function ensures the following properties:

– any maneuver is more costly than no maneuver;

– maneuvers should start as late as possible;

– maneuvers should be as short as possible;

– the angle should be as small as possible.

In a real environment, the cost function should be adapted to the aircraft performance model or to other criteria, including controllers' preferences and fuel consumption. We present here a framework that dissociates the solver method from the problem itself, so as to provide the scientific community (which may be unfamiliar with ATM and conflict resolution) with the simplest possible framework that enables to compare different solvers on our benchmark.

Given an instance with n aircraft, we define the cost of a solution as the sum of maneuvers' costs:

$$\text{cost} = \sum_{i=1}^{n} \text{cost}_{\text{man}}(m_i) \qquad [6.4]$$

6.8.2.4. *Handling uncertainties*

We shall now describe how the maneuver hulls are built in order to be able to detect conflicts between two maneuvers for two different aircraft, while taking various uncertainties into account.

In our framework, the maneuvers description are stored in a table that defines for each aircraft and each maneuver the possible future positions of the aircraft at every time step. These positions are represented by their convex hull, which is computed with Graham's algorithm [GRA 92].

Each aircraft position is described at multiples of the time step τ (i.e. 0, τ, $2\,\tau$, $3\,\tau, \ldots$) by three convex hulls corresponding to the three possible states of the aircraft:

– S_0 if it has not been maneuvered yet;

– S_1 if it is currently maneuvered;

– S_2 if it is heading toward its destination after a maneuver.

Once the three convex hulls are defined for every time step, they are merged in a single one whenever several envelops coexist for the same time step (around turning points of the trajectory).

We first start with one point representing the current position of the aircraft at $t = 0$. To build the possible positions at $t + \tau$, we take into account every extreme position of the three convex hulls at time t and calculate the future possible positions of each point. During this process, some points stay in the same state whereas others change near the turning points of the trajectory. Moreover, some points may generate two different future positions in two different states. For example, a point in state S_0 (before any maneuver) may reach $d_0 - \varepsilon_0$ at the next step if the aircraft flies at the fastest possible speed according to the amount of uncertainty taken into account by parameter ε_0. It will then change heading and be in state S_1. The same point may as well fly at the lowest possible speed and stay in state S_0. After each movement, the convex hull of the cloud of points created is computed for each state. At the very end of the process, the convex hull of the whole trajectory is calculated for each time step.

Figure 6.34 gives an example of maneuver with the different states. In red, the aircraft has not started any maneuver. In blue, the aircraft has changed its heading, and in green, it is heading back to the next point on its route (D). The gray line gives the convex hull of the three states. The conflicts will then be detected among such envelops by computing their minimal distance.

It is important to notice that any traffic simulator using any kind of uncertainty hypothesis could be used to build the trajectory prediction for the aircraft and for the maneuver options. Different aircraft could have different uncertainties and different maneuver options according to their ability to follow a route. We only need a convex hull of the possible future positions of an aircraft at every time step of the trajectory.

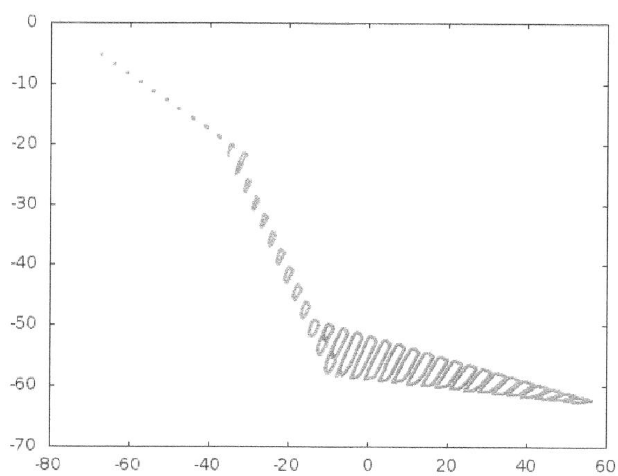

Figure 6.34. *An example of trajectory prediction. Red, green and blue correspond, respectively, to states S_0, S_1 and S_2; gray parts represent the convex hulls. For a color version of the figure, see www.iste.co.uk/durand/atm.zip*

This approach can easily be generalized to the third dimension (vertical plane), taking into account uncertainties on the climbing rate of the aircraft. Convex

3D-volumes would thus be defined and conflicts detected according to the distance between them.

6.8.3. *Conflict detection*

Once the trajectory predictions are computed and stored, the 4D conflict matrix C can be built. To simplify the access to the matrix and reduce the number of combinations to the useful ones (e.g. only one possible maneuver for $\alpha = 0$), the three decision variables d_0, α and d_1 are aggregated in a single decision variable by a bijection from the allowed triples to interval $[1, n_{\mathrm{man}}]$ (as explained in section 6.8.2.2). Then, for each pair of aircraft (i,j) and each pair of maneuver options (k,l) (where k is a maneuver option for aircraft i and l for aircraft j), we test if maneuvers k and l generate a conflict. In this case, $C_{i,j,k,l} = 1$, otherwise $C_{i,j,k,l} = 0$. Furthermore, we can consider that $i < j$ since a conflict between i and j is equivalent to a conflict between j and i. To detect a conflict, the distance between the two envelops representing the possible positions of aircraft i and j is computed and compared to the separation standard norm (5 NM).

For every time step, the algorithm is divided in to three stages:

– check if a vertex of convex hull k is inside convex hull l, or if a vertex of convex hull l is inside convex hull k;

– otherwise, check if two edges of convex hulls k and l intersect;

– otherwise, check the distance between every vertex of convex hull k and every edge of convex hull l, or every vertex of convex hull l with every edge of convex hull k. As soon as one of the distances is smaller than the separation standard, $C_{i,j,k,l}$ is set to 1.

This calculation is the most time-consuming aspect of the problem generation because the number of pairs tested is big. For example, a 20-aircraft conflict with 151 maneuvers per aircraft generates $\frac{20\times19}{2} = 190$ pairs of aircraft for which $151^2 = 22,801$ pairs of maneuvers must be tested. A total of $4,332,190$ pairs of maneuvers must be tested to build the conflict matrix.

However, this operation can be parallelized very easily. For instance, different processors can be used to test different pairs of maneuvers. The computation time can thus drastically be reduced. We will give different examples in section 6.8.4 of the time required to calculate $C_{i,j,k,l}$ as a function of the number of processors used for the calculation (see section 6.8.5.4). Furthermore, sweep-line techniques [DEB 98] could be used as well to lower the time complexity of the edge intersection checks performed during the second step of our convex hull distance algorithm.

6.8.4. *Benchmark generation*

In the experimental results presented in section 6.8.5.4, instances of four different sizes have been considered, involving 5, 10, 15 and 20 aircraft, with three levels of uncertainties. For each combination, 10 scenarios of aircraft converging to the center of the considered airspace volume were randomly built. For each scenario, speeds are chosen from 384 to 576 kts (i.e 20% variation around a typical speed of 480 kts). The aircraft initial positions are chosen on a 70-NM-radius circle and are noised within a 20-NM-side square. The initial heading is also noised with a value chosen in $[-1, 1]$ radians ($\approx \pm 60°$). Figure 6.35 illustrates these dimensions.

A total of 40 scenarios were built to compare the algorithms. For each scenario, three levels of uncertainty are defined. The lower level of uncertainty ε_{low} takes into account $\varepsilon_s = 1\%$ of error on the aircraft speed, $\varepsilon_0 = 1\,\text{NM}$ of error on the location of the turning point, $\varepsilon_\alpha = 1°$ on the angle of the turn and $\varepsilon_1 = 1\,\text{NM}$ of error on the location of the returning point. The medium level of uncertainty ε_{med} doubles every value: $\varepsilon_s = 2\%$, $\varepsilon_0 = 2\,\text{NM}$, $\varepsilon_\alpha = 2°$ and $\varepsilon_1 = 2\,\text{NM}$. Finally, the higher level of uncertainty $\varepsilon_{\text{high}}$ triples the lower uncertainty values: $\varepsilon_s = 3\%$, $\varepsilon_0 = 3\,\text{NM}$, $\varepsilon_\alpha = 3°$ and $\varepsilon_1 = 3\,\text{NM}$. A total of 120 scenarios are thus built and tested with two different approaches in section 6.8.5.

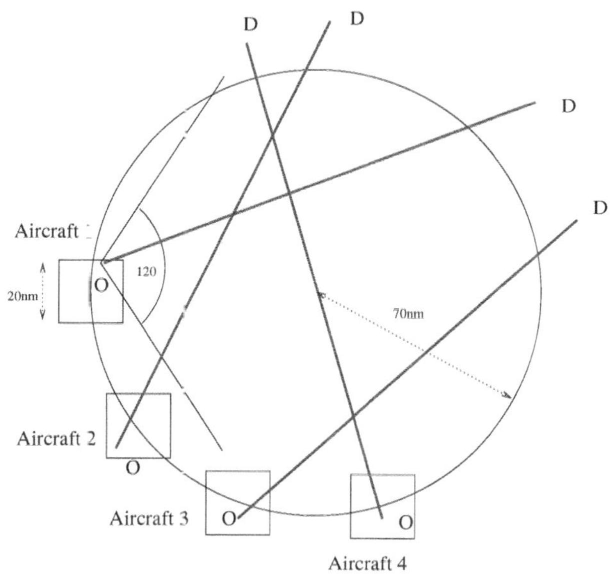

Figure 6.35. *Conflict scenario generation*

6.8.5. *Conflict resolution*

In this section, we propose two methods for the resolution of the generated conflicts. The first method, an EA (section 6.8.5.1). The second method, CP (section 6.8.5.2), is based on a systematic search of the solution space, which enables us to prove the optimality (or the absence) of a solution.

6.8.5.1. *Evolutionary algorithm*

6.8.5.1.1. Principles

The EA used is similar to the algorithm described in section 6.6.4. A sharing process is added to prevent from premature convergence to local optimum. We decided to use the sharing process introduced by Yin and Germay [YIN 93] because it has the great advantage to grow in $\Theta(p \log p)$ (instead of $\Theta(p^2)$ for classical sharing) if p is the size of the population. For the sake of simplicity, the distance implemented in our EA returns only two values: *true* if the elements (set of trajectories) are identical and *false* otherwise. The fitness of elements belonging to the same cluster is then divided by the size of the cluster to avoid an overrepresentation of a particular solution in the population and encourage diversification.

6.8.5.1.2. Fitness function

The fitness function of our EA is very basic and does not aim at taking into account fuel consumption or controllers' preferences. We just focus on finding a conflict-free set of heading changes starting as late as possible, with the smallest deviation length and heading change.

The fitness function is then defined by two cases depending on the presence (first case) or absence (second case) of remaining conflicts in the solution:

$$F = \begin{cases} \dfrac{1}{2 + \sum\limits_{i<j} C_{i,j,m_i,m_j}} & \text{if } \exists(i,j),\ i < j,\ C_{i,j,m_i,m_j} \neq 0 \\ \dfrac{1}{2} + \dfrac{1}{1 + \text{cost}} & \text{if } \forall(i,j),\ i < j,\ C_{i,j,m_i,m_j} = 0 \end{cases}$$

where cost, defined by equation [6.4] in section 6.8.2.3, represents the cost of a solution.

Moreover, this fitness function guarantees that if a chromosome value is larger than $\frac{1}{2}$, no conflict occurs, so as to strictly order the cost of proper solutions from conflicting ones. If a conflict remains, the fitness does not take into account the cost of the maneuvers, allowing the EA to focus the search for conflict-free solutions first, regardless of the quality of the maneuvers involved.

6.8.5.1.3. Adapted crossover and mutation

With this new formulation, the partial separability described in section 6.6.4.4 is preserved and the adapted crossover and mutation operators can be used. Non-specific classical operators used by Gruber, Alliot and Schoenauer in [ALL 92] did not produce satisfactory results on our benchmark. The crossover and mutation operators described in section 6.6.4.8 are used here.

These operators are more deterministic at the beginning of the optimization, when many conflicts remain in the population, so that a solution without conflict can be found very quickly. When conflict-free solutions become sufficiently numerous, these operators are less deterministic and other parts of the search space can be explored.

6.8.5.2. *Constraint programming*

CP is a versatile optimization technology based on the constraint satisfaction problem (CSP) formalism that emphasizes the satisfaction of combinatorial *constraints* (i.e. arbitrary relations over a set of decision variables). CP offers a clean separation between the modeling language and the resolution algorithms, enabling to quickly develop solvers in an incremental manner and to experiment with various search strategies without changing the model. See [VAN 95] for more details on the CP technology.

6.8.5.2.1. CSP model

The set M of decision variables of the CSP is the set defined by equation [6.2] in section 6.8.2, where each variable m_i is the index of the maneuver for aircraft i and thus takes a value in $[1, n_{\text{man}}]$.

The constraints are expressed as *binary constraints*, i.e. constraints involving exactly two variables. For a given couple of aircraft i and j $(i < j)$, the constraint c_{ij} between variables m_i and m_j is defined as the set:

$$c_{ij} = \{(m_i^k, m_j^l) \quad \text{s.t.} \quad C_{i,j,k,l} = 1\} \qquad [6.5]$$

where m_i^k and m_j^l are, respectively, the kth and the lth value of interval $[1, n_{\text{man}}]$ of the maneuvers available for aircraft i and j. c_{ij} therefore describes all couples of maneuvers that *cannot* be performed by aircraft i and j without resulting in a conflict.

We denote by $|c_{ij}|$ the cardinal of the constraint c_{ij}, that is the number of forbidden couples of maneuvers

6.8.5.2.2. Solution search

The exploration of the search space is based on an enhanced version of a systematic search algorithm called *backtracking*. We used a *weighted degree* [BOU 04] adaptive heuristic that learns from the failures during the search, so that the variables involved in the constraints that have failed the most so far are instantiated first. This heuristic proved to be particularly efficient on this problem, as it dynamically focuses on the hardest parts of the CSP first.

6.8.5.3. *Optimization*

The optimization criterion c simply is the sum of the costs of each single maneuver as defined in equation [6.4] of section 6.8.2.3. The optimization algorithm used to solve the CSP is an adaptation of the backtracking algorithm called *branch and bound*: each time a solution with cost c_s is found, the constraint $c < c_s$ is dynamically added to the CP model, and the search is resumed to look for a better solution. When every constraint fails, this *proves* that the best solution so far is optimal or that no solution satisfying all constraints exists. Moreover, our search strategy focuses on maneuvers that least increases the cost in order to quickly obtain solutions of good quality.

6.8.5.4. *Results*

The benchmark generation (section 6.8.4) and conflict resolution (section 6.8.5) were implemented using the FaCiLe constraint library [BAR 01a] for the CP model. The following results were obtained on a standard workstation consisting of an octocore Intel® Xeon® processor running at 3.4 GHz and equipped with 8 GB of memory.

6.8.5.4.1. Benchmark

A total of 120 instances were produced, based on situations with 5, 10, 15 and 20 aircraft in the same airspace volume and uncertainty levels of 1, 2 and 3 (see section 6.8.4), thus changing the density of the problem. Ten random instances were created for each set of parameters, in order to assess the reliability of the resolution algorithms.

The generation of a given instance is highly parallelizable (the computation of the constraint between two given aircraft is independent from other constraints in the problem), which made it possible to dramatically reduce the needed computation time. As an example, the biggest and toughest instances (20 aircraft with high uncertainty level) were produced in less than 3 min while the smallest ones only needed a few seconds.

Figure 6.36 shows the influence of the number of processors used on the benchmark generation time for a given instance. The time saving is quite huge, since only 10 s are necessary with 64 processors where it took more than 9 min for a single processor. However the gain becomes less and less interesting when the number of processors increases, because the communication between processes is taking a significant amount of time. For the type of instances we generated, 16 processors seemed to constitute a fair compromise.

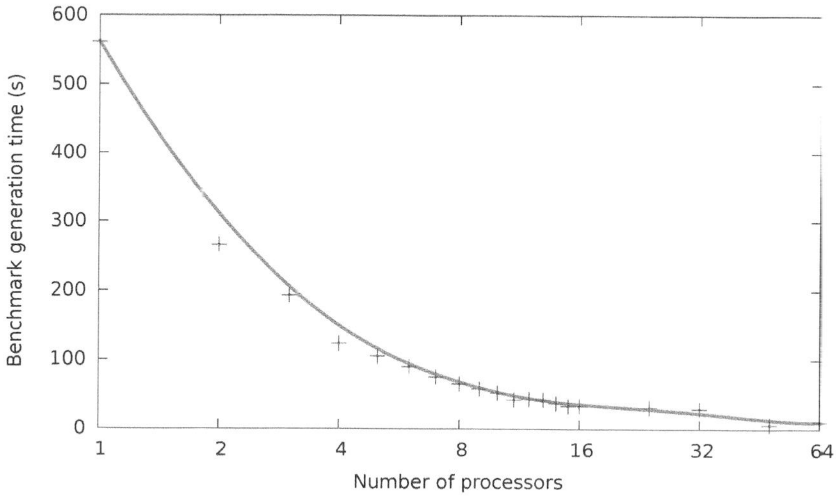

Figure 6.36. *Benchmark generation time w.r.t. number of processors. The horizontal scale is logarithmic*

6.8.5.4.2. Conflict resolution

The resolution algorithms were both limited to a 5 min execution time, in order to be compatible with the time constraints of an operational setting. In this context, all feasible instances were solved within seconds, and an optimality proof was obtained for most of them. Figure 6.37 shows a solution for a 10-aircraft conflict.

6.8.5.4.3. Computing times

In more detail, Table 6.7 provides the computation times (averaged over the 10 different instances for each set of parameters) for finding the best solution. Instances with 5 and 10 aircraft are efficiently solved (under 1 s) by both algorithms (CP being a bit faster than EA). Most 15-aircraft instances are solved within 1 min, while 20-aircraft instances often need a few minutes. Moreover, a proof of optimality is obtained (with CP only) on all instances with 5 and 10 aircraft and almost all instances with 15 aircraft. When 20 aircraft are involved, however, optimality proof is not reached within the 5 min time limit.

Particularly interesting is the fact that for instances with no solution, a proof of non-feasibility is obtained within 1 s. This could make it possible to generate, in a real-time setting, a new instance where, for the same situation, more maneuvers would be allowed, hopefully giving a resolution to the conflicting situation.

	n							
	5		10		15		20	
	CP	EA	CP	EA	CP	EA	CP	EA
ε_{low}	0.00	0.02	0.22	0.97	24.08	2.01	75.14	95.98
ε_{med}	0.00	0.02	0.27	1.44	45.17	32.60	79.61	184.61
$\varepsilon_{\text{high}}$	0.00	0.02	1.04	0.37	48.59	93.19	58.44	274.16

Table 6.7. *Average time (in seconds) for finding best solution with EA and CP algorithms, for each set of parameters*

Finally, in almost all instances, including the toughest ones, a first solution was found within seconds. This means that in a real-time operational context, it could be possible to quickly provide the controllers with a first set of maneuvers that solves the conflict, so that it could be their choice to transmit them right away or wait for a more efficient solution, depending on their current workload and the urgency of the situation.

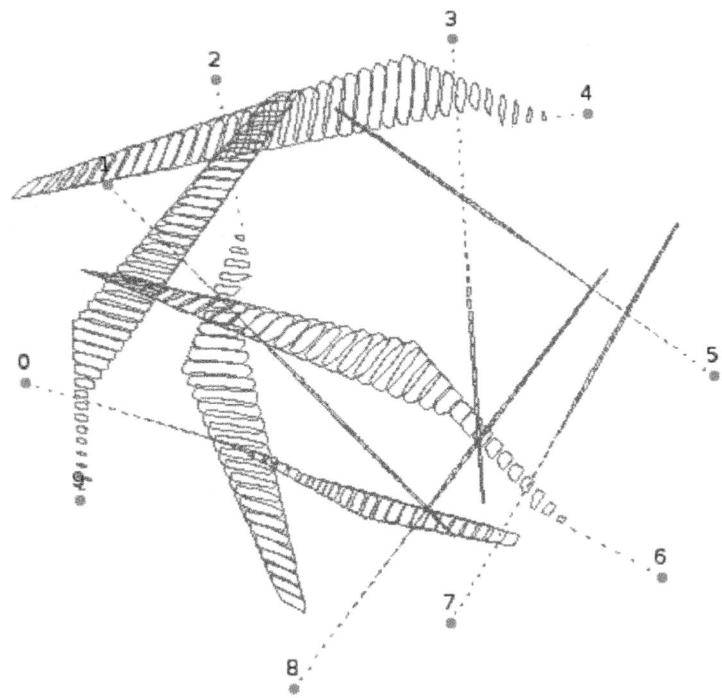

Figure 6.37. *A solution to a 10-aircraft conflict. Trajectories are depicted as sequences of convex hulls, representing the uncertainty*

6.8.5.4.4. Cost of solutions

Table 6.8 provides average costs for each set of parameters. According to the definition given in equation [6.3] (section 6.8.3), each maneuver has a cost belonging to the interval $[0, 50]$ for the investigated instances. As expected, the cost increases with the number of aircraft involved, because the density of aircraft and conflicts increases with this parameter for a given constant airspace volume (see section 6.8.4). The maneuver cost per aircraft varies from less than 1 for the smallest instances to 15 for the toughest ones.

	n					
	5	10	15		20	
	CP EA	CP EA	CP	EA	CP	EA
ε_{low}	5.3	29.8	86.3	86.8	185.8	176.9
ε_{med}	4.2	46.6	104.0	104.0	267.6	282.8
$\varepsilon_{\text{high}}$	5.1	45.7	170.4	156.3	299.0	305.0

Table 6.8. *Average cost of best solutions for each set of parameters. Red cells include solutions that were not proved optimal, 2-in-1 cells correspond to sets of parameters where both CP and EA reached optimal solution. For a color version of the table, see www.iste.co.uk/durand/atm.zip.*

Figure 6.38 depicts the cost of the best solution found with respect to the *intrinsic difficulty* ρ of the instance. The intrinsic difficulty is here defined as the total number of forbidden couples of maneuvers:

$$\rho = \sum_{\substack{i,j \in [1,n]^2 \\ i<j}} |c_{ij}|$$

where c_{ij} is the constraint between aircraft i and j, as defined in equation [6.5]. Clearly, the cost of the best solutions is closely correlated to the intrinsic difficulty of the problem, which could be used a priori to determine the expected efficiency of resolution.

In terms of cost, CP and EA are equivalently efficient: they both reach optimal solutions for almost all instances involving 15 or less aircraft, and give alternatively the best solution for 20-aircraft instances. It would therefore be interesting to run both algorithms in parallel for a given instance, in order to always get the best possible solution.

6.8.5.5. *Conclusion and further work*

Separating the model from the resolution is a good framework to compare different approaches and see how metaheuristics can compete with exact methods.

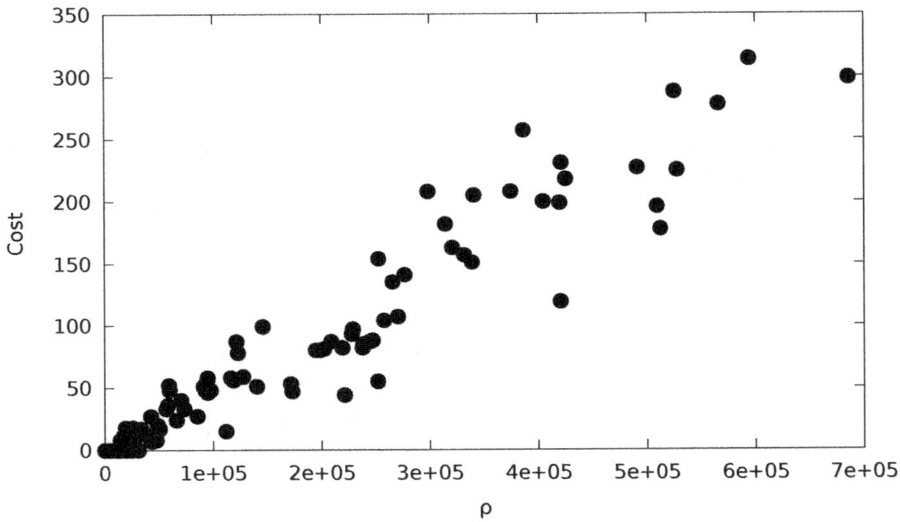

Figure 6.38. *Cost of the best solution found w.r.t. the intrinsic difficulty ρ of the instance*

The production of the benchmark presented is highly configurable: density of the conflict (controlled by the number of aircraft involved or the volume of the considered airspace), number of authorized maneuvers, level of uncertainty to be taken into account are the main parameters, but the tuning can be even finer, for example with the possibility of defining custom maneuvers. The output is a data file containing all precomputed trajectories and a list of maneuvers that cannot be performed simultaneously. This phase being highly parallelizable, this method can be used to generate an entire benchmark database within a reasonable computation time.

Two different approaches to the resolution of such problems, an EA and a CP were compared, as well as the results from their application to 120 instances of various difficulties. Most of these instances were solved in less than 1 s, the toughest ones needing a few minutes of computation. Optimality proofs were obtained (with the CP model only) in most cases, and instances without solution were proved inconsistent within 1 s. As expected, the cost of the solutions, the sum of maneuver costs defined in the conflict data, increases with the intrinsic difficulty of the instance.

Vertical maneuvers, such as flight level change, interrupted climb or anticipated descent, could be added thus increasing the configurability of the framework. In terms of efficiency, the detection phase could be enhanced by the use of a fastest algorithm for computing distances between the convex hulls that model the uncertainties.

6.9. Conclusion

In this chapter, we first showed how challenging conflict resolution is. The problem is combinatorial and cannot be solved with basic strategies. We described different models that were imagined: centralized or distributed, iterative or global. Because of problem inherent uncertainties, we focused on resolution methods able to handle objective functions based on simulations. Metaheuristics are adapted to such functions because they do not require any properties compared to other methods. We detailed different approaches: an NN trained by an EA for self-separation, an EA and an ACO algorithm for centralized global conflict resolution. We finally showed in section 6.8 that we could define models that separate the problem definition from the resolution while still handling realistic uncertainties. This latter approach has the great advantage to allow comparisons between metaheuristics and exact optimization tools.

Conclusion

In this book, we have presented several applications of metaheuristics to air traffic management (ATM) problems related to route network design, airspace management, takeoff slot allocation, airport management and conflict resolution for airborne aircraft. Whenever possible, we have tried to present different models and formulations for the problems being addressed and different methods to solve them. We have presented challenging problems, generally too complex and too big to be solved easily. Furthermore, most of these problems are interdependent and should ideally be solved simultaneously. Even considering problems separately, many of them remain very combinatorial, involving mixed variables. Because of uncertainties, there are usually no simple analytical expressions for the objective functions and constraints. This is why metaheuristics are often good candidates to tackle these difficult problems.

Unfortunately, it was rarely possible to compare different methods on exactly the same problem, with the same data. Such comparative studies are the basis of a scientific approach. There is a lack of public problems and data. ATM is a complex activity involving many actors. For a very long time, progress in ATM could be made just through a better coordination among the actors, improved operational procedures, reorganization and the deployment of new equipment.

As a consequence, the motivation for the ATM actors to formulate ATM problems as well-posed scientific problems and to make them available in public websites or databases has been low. Another reason for very few repositories of ATM problems is that the data are huge, often proprietary, and that these must be collected from different sources. Useful data concerning air traffic situations may include airspace sectors and airways descriptions, radar records, flight plans, weather data, aircraft onboard flight data and performance parameters, etc. These data are not always public, at least in Europe, and some of them are considered as valuable or sensitive by their owners[1]. Things are slowly changing, however. At the end of Chapter 6, we compared different resolution approaches on the same problem due to a framework that separates the problem from the resolution tool. Researchers in ATM might expect more and more benchmarks to become available in the future, such as the ENAC (*Ecole Nationale de l'Aviation Civile*) benchmark for conflict resolution algorithms (http://clusters.recherche.enac.fr/) that can be easily tested without any knowledge of the ATM context.

We have seen in this book that metaheuristics are powerful methods for solving difficult ATM problems. We have also seen a few cases where simple heuristics or exact methods could successfully compete with metaheuristics, on real-problem instances of limited difficulty. This sometimes required a slightly different formulation of the general problem being addressed. For example, on the 2D-route network design problem, geometrical methods can give good solutions on the nodes and edges positioning problem, even if their aim is not to find an optimal solution. Before using metaheuristics, it is always worth checking if other methods can be applied or not, and if they give good results.

In many cases, however, metaheuristics are the most efficient existing methods. They are sometimes the only applicable methods to deal with combinatorial and difficult ATM problems for which the evaluation of the criteria being optimized require to run traffic simulations. This is typically the case for the conflict resolution problem, at least when using a realistic model for uncertainties. We have to predict the future trajectories, and their uncertainties, to be able to detect conflicts and to evaluate the objective function. Metaheuristics require very few assumptions on the objective function being optimized, so ATM problems can be formulated and modeled in a realistic way instead of using a simplified mathematical model that is often unable to handle realistic constraints.

For several ATM problems presented in this book, hybridizing metaheuristics with problem-specific exact methods proved beneficial. This was the case when building separate 3D-tubes for the main flows. Hybridization was simply achieved by replacing the canonical mutation operator of an evolutionary algorithm by a specific operator embedding an A^* algorithm and an ad hoc local search method. In that respect, metaheuristics are very easy to adapt to specific problem representations and constraints. All of this makes metaheuristics flexible tools to solve difficult real-world problems.

---

1 For example, the cost index and aircraft mass are considered as competitive parameters by many airline operators. These parameters would be useful to improve ground-based trajectory predictors.

Bibliography

[ALI 08] ALI F., LEI X., XIAO X., "The aircraft departure scheduling based on particle swarm optimization combined with simulated annealing algorithm", *IEEE World Congress on Computational Intelligence*, 2008.

[ALL 92] ALLIOT J.-M., GRUBER H., SCHOENAUER M., "Genetic algorithms for solving ATC conflicts", *Proceedings of the Ninth Conference on Artificial Intelligence Application*, IEEE, 1992.

[ALL 97] ALLIOT J.-M., BOSC J., DURAND N., *et al.*, "CATS: a complete air traffic simulator", *Digital Avionics Systems Conference, 1997 (DASC 1997), AIAA/IEEE 16th*, 1997.

[ALL 03] ALLIOT J.-M., DE VERDIÈRE D.C., "ATM: 20 ans d'effort et perspectives", *Symposium de l'Académie Nationale de l'Air et de l'Espace: vers l'automatisation du vol et sa gestion*, 2003.

[ALL 11] ALLIGNOL C., Planification de trajectoires pour l'optimisation du trafic aérien, PhD thesis, INPT, 2011.

[ALL 13] ALLIGNOL C., BARNIER N., DURAND N., *et al.*, "A new framework for solving en-route conflicts", *Proceedings of the 10th USA/Europe Air Traffic Management Research and Development Seminar*, 2013.

[ARC 04] ARCHAMBAULT N., DURAND N., "Scheduling heuristics for on board sequential air conflict solving", *Digital Avionics Systems Conference, 2004 (DASC 2004), AIAA/IEEE 23rd*, 2004.

[ARC 08] ARCHIBALD J., HILL J., JEPSEN N., *et al.*, "A satisficing approach to aircraft conflict resolution", *IEEE Transactions on Systems, Man, and Cybernetics, Part C: Applications and Reviews*, vol. 38, no. 4, pp. 510–521, July 2008.

[ATK 07] ATKIN J.A.D., BURKE E.K., GREENWOOD J.S., *et al.*, "Hybrid metaheuristics to aid runway scheduling at London Heathrow Airport", *Transportation Science*, vol. 41, no. 1, pp. 90–106, 2007.

[ATK 08] ATKIN J., BURKE E., GREENWOOD J., *et al.*, "Online decision support for take-off runway scheduling with uncertain taxi times at London Heathrow airport", *Journal of Scheduling*, vol. 11, no. 5, pp. 323–346, 2008.

[BAR 01a] BARNIER N., BRISSET P., "FaCiLe: a Functional Constraint Library", *Colloquium on Implementation of Constraint and LOgic Programming Systems CICLOPS'01 (Workshop of CP'01)*, Paphos, Cyprus, December 2001.

[BAR 01b] BARNIER N., BRISSET P., RIVIÈRE T., "Slot allocation with constraint programming: models and results", *International Air Traffic Management R&D Seminar ATM-2001*, Santa Fe (NM), USA, December 2001.

[BAR 02a] BARNIER N., BRISSET P., "Graph coloring for air traffic flow management", *CPAIOR'02: Fourth International Workshop on Integration of AI and OR Techniques in Constraint Programming for Combinatorial Optimisation Problems*, Le Croisic, France, pp. 133–147, March 2002.

[BAR 02b] BARNIER N., Application de la programmation par contraintes à des problèmes de gestion du trafic aérien, PhD thesis, INPT, 2002.

[BAR 12] BARNIER N., ALLIGNOL C., "Trajectory deconfliction with constraint programming", *The Knowledge Engineering Review*, vol. 27, no. 03, pp. 291–307, 2012.

[BEN 09] BENCHEIKH G., BOUKACHOUR J., EL HILALI A., *et al.*, "Hybrid method for aircraft landing scheduling based on a job shop formulation", *International Journal of Computer Science and Network Security*, vol. 9, no. 8, pp. 78–88, 2009.

[BEN 11] BENNELL J., MESGARPOUR M., POTTS C., "Airport runway scheduling", *4OR: Quarterly Journal of Operations Research*, vol. 9, no. 2, pp. 115–138, 2011.

[BIC 04] BICHOT C.-E., ALLIOT J.-M., DURAND N., *et al.*, "Optimisation par fusion et fission. Application au problème du découpage aérien européen", *Journal Européen des Systèmes Automatisés*, vol. 38, no. 9–10, pp. 1141–1173, 2004.

[BIC 07a] BICHOT C.-E., Élaboration d'une nouvelle métaheuristique pour le partitionnement de graphe: la méthode de fusion-fission, Application au découpage de l'espace aérien, PhD thesis, INPT, 2007.

[BIC 07b] BICHOT C.-E., DURAND N., "A tool to design functional airspace blocks", *Proceedings of the 7th USA/Europe Air Traffic Management Research and Development Seminar*, 2007.

[BIS 96] BISHOP C.M., *Neural Networks for Pattern Recognition*, Oxford University Press, 1996.

[BLU 05] BLUM C., SOCHA K., "Training feed-forward neural networks with ant colony optimization: an application to pattern classification", *Fifth International Conference on Hybrid Intelligent Systems*, 2005.

[BOL 00] BOLAT A., "Procedures for providing robust gate assignments for arriving aircraft", *European Journal of Operational Research*, vol. 120, no. 1, 2000.

[BOL 01] BOLAT A., "Models and a genetic algorithm for static aircraft-gate assignment problem", *Journal of the Operational Research Society*, vol. 52, no. 10, pp. 1107–1120, 2001.

[BOU 04] BOUSSEMART F., HEMERY F., LECOUTRE C., *et al.*, "Boosting systematic search by weighting constraints", *European Conference on Artificial Intelligence – ECAI*, pp. 146–150, 2004.

[BOU 14] BOURAS A., GHALEB M.A., SURYAHATMAJA U.S., *et al.*, "The airport gate assignment problem: a survey", *The Scientific World Journal*, vol. 2014, 2014.

[BUR 09] BURGAIN P., FERON E., CLARKE J., "Collaborative virtual queue: benefit analysis of a collaborative decision making concept applied to congested airport departure operations", *Air Traffic Control Quarterly*, vol. 17, no. 2, pp. 195–222, 2009.

[CAI 12] CAI K., ZHANG J., ZHOU C., *et al.*, "Using computational intelligence for large scale air route networks design", *Applied Soft Computing*, vol. 12, no. 9, pp. 2790–2800, September 2012.

[CFM 00] CFMU, *Basic CFMU Handbook – General & CFMU Systems*, 6.0 edn, Eurocontrol CFMU, Brussels, February 2000.

[CHE 12] CHENG C.-H., HO S.C., KWAN C.-L., "The use of meta-heuristics for airport gate assignment", *Expert Systems with Applications*, vol. 39, no. 16, 2012.

[CHI 97] CHIANG Y.-J., KLOSOWSKI J., LEE C., *et al.*, "Geometric algorithms for conflict detection/resolution in air traffic management", *Proceedings of the 36th IEEE Conference on Decision and Control*, vol. 2, pp. 1835–1840, December 1997.

[CHR 08] CHRISTODOULOU M.A., KONTOGEORGOU C., "Collision avoidance in commercial aircraft free flight via neural networks and non-linear programming", *International Journal of Neural Systems*, vol. 18, no. 5, pp. 371–387, 2008.

[COM 07] COM S.E., The ATM target concept, Report, SESAR Consortium, September 2007.

[CON 92] CONN A.R., GOULD N.I.M., TOINT P.L., *LANCELOT: A Fortran Package for Large-Scale Nonlinear Optimization (Release A)*, Springer-Verlag, 1992.

[CON 07] CONSORTIUM S., Milestone deliverable D3: the ATM target concept, Report, SESAR, 2007.

[COO 04] COOK A.J., TANNER G., ANDERSON S., Evaluating the true cost to airlines of one minute of airborne or ground delay: final report, Eurocontrol, Brussels, May 2004.

[DAL 97] DALICHAMPT M., PETIT E., JUNKER U., *et al.*, Innovative slot allocation (ISA), Report, Eurocontrol, Brussels, 1997.

[DEA 09] DEAU R., GOTTELAND J.-B., DURAND N., "Airport surface management and runways scheduling", *Proceedings of the 8th USA/Europe Air Traffic Management Research and Development Seminar*, 2009.

[DEA 10] DEAU R., Optimisation des séquences de pistes et du trafic au sol sur les grands aéroports, PhD thesis, INPT, 2010.

[DEB 98] DE BERG M., VAN KREVELD M., OVERMARS M., *et al.*, *Computational Geometry – Algorithms and Applications*, Springer, 2nd edn, 1998.

[DEL 94] DELAHAYE D., ALLIOT J.-M., SCHOENAUER M., *et al.*, "Genetic algorithms for partitioning airspace", *Proceedings of the Tenth Conference on Artificial Intelligence Application*, IEEE, 1994.

[DEL 95a] DELAHAYE D., Optimisation de la sectorisation de l'espace aérien par algorithmes génétiques, PhD thesis, ENSAE, 1995.

[DEL 95b] DELAHAYE D., ALLIOT J.-M., SCHOENAUER M., *et al.*, "Genetic algorithms for automatic regroupment of air traffic control sectors", *Evolutionary Programming 95*, 1995.

[DEL 98] DELAHAYE D., SCHOENAUER M., ALLIOT J.-M., "Airspace sectoring by evolutionary computation", *IEEE International Congress on Evolutionary Computation*, 1998.

[DEL 06] DELAHAYE D., PUECHMOREL S., "3D airspace sectoring by evolutionary computation: real-world applications", *Proceedings of the 8th Annual Conference on Genetic and Evolutionary Computation,GECCO'06*, New York, NY, USA, ACM, pp. 1637–1644, 2006.

[DEL 08] DELAHAYE D., PUECHMOREL S., "3D airspace design by evolutionary computation", *Digital Avionics Systems Conference, 2008 (DASC 2008), IEEE/AIAA 27th*, pp. 3.B.6-1–3.B.6-13, 2008.

[DIN 05] DING H., LIM A., RODRIGUES B., *et al.*, "The over-constrained airport gate assignment problem", *Computers and Operations Research*, vol. 32, no. 7, pp. 1867–1880, 2005.

[DOR 96] DORIGO M., MANIEZZO V., COLORNI A., "The ant system: optimization by a colony of cooperating agents", *IEEE Transactions on Systems, Man, and Cybernetics – Part B*, vol. 26, pp. 29–41, 1996.

[DOR 99] DORIGO M., CARO G.D., "Ant colony optimization: a new meta-heuristic", *Congress on Evolutionary Computation*, vol. 2, 1999.

[DOR 07] DORNDORF U., DREXL A., NIKULIN Y., *et al.*, "Flight gate scheduling: state-of-the-art and recent developments", *Omega*, vol. 35, pp. 326–334, 2007.

[DUR 96a] DURAND N., Optimisation de Trajectoires pour la Résolution de Conflits en Route, PhD thesis, ENSEEIHT, Institut National Polytechnique de Toulouse, 1996.

[DUR 96b] DURAND N., ALLIOT J.-M., NOAILLES J., "Automatic aircraft conflict resolution using genetic algorithms", *Proceedings of the Symposium on Applied Computing*, ACM, Philadelphia, 1996.

[DUR 96c] DURAND N., ALLIOT J.-M., NOAILLES J., "Collision avoidance using neural networks learned by genetic algorithms", *The Ninth International Conference on Industrial & Engineering Applications of Artificial Intelligence and Expert Systems (IEA-AEI96 Nagoya, Japan)*, 1996.

[DUR 97] DURAND N., ALLIOT J.-M., "Optimal resolution of en route conflicts", *Séminaire Europe/USA, Saclay*, June 1997.

[DUR 98] DURAND N., ALLIOT J.-M., "Genetic crossover operator for partially separable functions", *Proceedings of the Third Annual Genetic Programming Conference*, 1998.

[DUR 03] DURAND N., GRANGER G., "A traffic complexity approach through cluster analysis", *Proceedings of the 5th USA/Europe Air Traffic Management Research and Development Seminar*, 2003.

[DUR 04] DURAND N., Algorithmes Génétiques et autres méthodes d'optimisation appliqués à la gestion de trafic aérien, PhD thesis, Thèse d'habilitation, 2004.

[DUR 09] DURAND N., ALLIOT J.-M., "Ant colony optimization for air traffic conflict resolution", *Proceedings of the 8th USA/Europe Air Traffic Management Research and Development Seminar*, 2009.

[DUR 15] DURAND N., BARNIER N., "Does ATM need centralized coordination? Autonomous conflict resolution analysis in a constrained speed environment", *Proceedings of the 11th Air Traffic Management Research and Development Seminar*, 2015.

[EBY 99] EBY M., KELLY W.E.I., "Free flight separation assurance using distributed algorithms", *Proceedings of the IEEE 1999 Aerospace Conference*, vol. 2, pp. 429–441, 1999.

[EIB 03] EIBEN A., SMITH J., *Introduction to Evolutionary Computing*, Springer, 2003, ISBN: 3-540-40184-9.

[ERZ 97] ERZBERGER H., PAIELLI R., ISAACSON D., *et al.*, "Conflict detection and resolution in the presence of prediction error", *Proceedings of the 1st Air Traffic Management Research and Development Seminar*, 1997.

[EUR 10] Eurocontrol, AMAN status review 2010, Report, Eurocontrol, Brussels, 2010.

[EUR 11] Eurocontrol, A-SMGCS Implementation Manual, Eurocontrol, Brussels, 2011.

[EUR 12] Eurocontrol, CDM Implementation Manual, Eurocontrol, ACI, IATA, 2012.

[FLE 07] FLENER P., PEARSON J., ÅGREN M., *et al.*, "Air-traffic complexity resolution in multi-sector planning using constraint programming", in PUSCH C., SAUNDERS-HODGE S. (eds.), *Proceedings of the 7th USA/Europe Research and Development Seminar on Air Traffic Management*, Barcelona, Spain, July 2007.

[FOR 95] FORTUNE S., "Voronoi diagrams and Delaunay triangulations", in DU D.-Z., HWANG F. (eds.), *Computing in Euclidean Geometry*, World Scientific, Singapore, 1995.

[FRA 01] FRAZZOLI E., MAO Z.-H., OH J.-H., *et al.*, "Resolution of conflicts involving many aircraft via semidefinite programming", *AIAA Journal of Guidance, Control and Dynamics*, vol. 24, no. 1, January-February 2001.

[FRO 93] FRON X., MAUDRY B., TUMELIN J.-C., Arc 2000: automatic radar control, Report, Eurocontrol, 1993.

[GAR 05] GARCÍA J., BERLANGA A., MOLINA J., *et al.*, "Optimization of airport ground operations integrating genetic and dynamic flow management algorithms", *AI Communications*, vol. 18, no. 2, pp. 143–164, 2005.

[GAR 09] GARIEL M., FERON E., "3D conflict avoidance under uncertainties", *Digital Avionics Systems Conference, 2009 (DASC 2009), IEEE/AIAA 28th*, pp. 4.E.3-1–4.E.3-8, Oct 2009.

[GIA 02a] GIANAZZA D., ALLIOT J.-M., "Optimal combinations of air traffic control sectors using classical and stochastic methods", *The 2002 International Conference on Artificial Intelligence IC-AI'02*, Las Vegas, 2002.

[GIA 02b] GIANAZZA D., ALLIOT J.-M., "Optimization of air traffic control sector configurations using tree search methods and genetic algorithms", *Digital Avionics Systems Conference 2002 (DASC 2002), IEEE/AIAA 21st*, 2002.

[GIA 04a] GIANAZZA D., Optimisation des flux de trafic aérien, PhD thesis, Institut National Polytechnique de Toulouse, 2004.

[GIA 04b] GIANAZZA D., DURAND N., "Separating air traffic flows by allocating 3D- trajectories", *Digital Avionics Systems Conference, 2004 (DASC 2004), IEEE/AIAA 23rd*, 2004.

[GIA 04c] GIANAZZA D., DURAND N., ARCHAMBAULT N., "Allocating 3D trajectories to air traffic flows using A* and genetic algorithms", *Proceedings of the International Conference on Computational Intelligence for Modelling, Control, and Automation (CIMCA04)*, 2004.

[GIA 05a] GIANAZZA D., "Algorithme évolutionnaire et A* pour la séparation en 3D des flux de trafic aérien", *Journal Européen des Systèmes automatisés*, vol.38, no. 9-10/2004, 2005.

[GIA 05b] GIANAZZA D., DURAND N., "Assessment of the 3D-separation of air traffic flows", *Proceedings of the 6th USA/Europe Seminar on Air Traffic Management Research and Development*, 2005.

[GIA 06a] GIANAZZA D., GUITTET K., "Evaluation of air traffic complexity metrics using neural networks and sector status", *Proceedings of the 2nd International Conference on Research in Air Transportation, ICRAT*, 2006.

[GIA 06b] GIANAZZA D., GUITTET K., "Selection and evaluation of air traffic complexity metrics", *Digital Avionics Systems Conference, 2006 (DASC 2006), IEEE/AIAA 25th*, 2006.

[GIA 08] GIANAZZA D., "Smoothed traffic complexity metrics for airspace configuration schedules", *Proceedings of the 3rd International Conference on Research in Air Transportation, ICRAT*, 2008.

[GIA 09] GIANAZZA D., ALLIGNOL C., SAPORITO N., "An efficient airspace configuration forecast", *Proceedings of the 8th USA/Europe Air Traffic Management Research and Development Seminar*, 2009.

[GIA 10] GIANAZZA D., "Forecasting workload and airspace configuration with neural networks and tree search methods", *Artificial Intelligence Journal*, vol. 174, May 2010.

[GOL 89] GOLDBERG D., *Genetic Algorithms in Search, Optimization and Machine Learning*, Addison-Wesley, 1989.

[GOT 04] GOTTELAND J.-B., Optimisation du trafic au sol sur les grands aéroports, PhD thesis, INPT, 2004.

[GRA 92] GRAHAM R.L., "An efficient algorithm for determining the convex hull of a finite planar set", *Information Processing Letters*, 1992.

[GRA 01a] GRANGER G., DURAND N., ALLIOT J.-M., "Optimal resolution of en route conflicts", *Proceedings of the Fourth USA/Europe Air Traffic Management Research and Development Seminar*, 2001.

[GRA 01b] GRANGER G., DURAND N., ALLIOT J.-M., "Token allocation strategy for free-flight conflict solving", *International Joint Conference on AI (IJCAI'01)*, Seattle, WA, 2001.

[GRA 02] GRANGER G., Détection et résolution de conflits aériens: modélisations et analyse, PhD thesis, Ecole Polytechnique, 2002.

[GRA 06] GRAHAM R., YOUNG D., Preparing an initial Assessment of the SESAR Concept of Operations "EP3: Single European Sky implementation support through validation", Report, Eurocontrol Experimental Centre, France, 2006.

[GU 99] GU Y., CHUNG C., "Genetic algorithm approach to aircraft gate reassignment problem", *Journal of Transportation Engineering*, vol. 125, no. 5, 1999.

[GUD 03] GUDISE V., VENAYAGAMOORTHY G., "Comparison of particle swarm optimization and backpropagation as training algorithms for neural networks", *Proceedings of the 2003 IEEE Swarm Intelligence Symposium*, 2003.

[HER 05] HERING H., Air traffic freeway system for Europe, Report, Eurocontrol Experimental Centre, France, 2005.

[HIL 04] HILBURN B., Cognitive complexity in air traffic control, a literature review, Report, Eurocontrol Experimental Centre, France, 2004.

[HOE 03] HOEKSTRA J., RUIGROK R., VAN GENT R., "Free flight in a crowded airspace", *Proceedings of the Air Traffic Management 2003*, 2003.

[HOL 75] HOLLAND J., *Adaptation in Natural and Artificial Systems*, University of Michigan Press, 1975.

[HU 02] HU J., PRANDINI M., NILIM A., *et al.*, "Optimal coordinated maneuvers for three-dimensional aircraft conflict resolution", *AIAA Journal of Guidance, Control and Dynamics*, vol. 25, p. 2002, 2002.

[HU 07] HU X., DI PAOLO E., "An efficient genetic algorithm with uniform crossover for the multi-objective airport gate assignment problem", *IEEE Congress on Evolutionary Computation 2007 (CEC'07)*, pp. 55–62, 2007.

[HU 09a] HU X.-B., DI PAOLO E., "A ripple-spreading genetic algorithm for the airport gate assignment problem", *IEEE Congress on Evolutionary Computation, 2009 (CEC'09)*, pp. 1857–1864, 2009.

[HU 09b] HU X.-B., DI PAOLO E., "An efficient genetic algorithm with uniform crossover for air traffic control", *Computers and Operations Research*, vol. 36, no. 1, pp. 245–259, January 2009.

[HWA 07] HWANG I., KIM J., TOMLIN C., "Protocol-based conflict resolution for air traffic control", *ATC Quarterly*, vol. 15, pp. 1–34, 2007.

[INT 01] INTERNATIONAL CIVIL AVIATION ORGANIZATION, Annex 11 to the Convention on International Civil Aviation, Air Traffic Services, 13th ed. 2001.

[INT 08] INTERNATIONAL CIVIL AVIATION ORGANIZATION, Manual on Air Traffic Management System Requirement, Doc 9882, 1st ed. 2008.

[JAS 11] JASON A.D.A., BURKE E.K., RAVIZZA S., "A more realistic approach for airport ground movement optimisation with stand holding", *Multidisciplinary International Scheduling Conference (MISTA)*, 2011.

[KIC 09] KICINGER R., YOUSEFI A., "Heuristic method for 3d airspace partitioning: genetic algorithm and agent-based approach", *Ninth Aviation Technology, Integration, and Operations (ATIO) Conference, AIAA Paper*, vol. 7058, 2009.

[KIM 14] KIM S.H., FERON E., "Impact of gate assignment on departure metering", *IEEE Transactions on Intelligent Transportation Systems*, vol. 15, no. 2, 2014.

[KIR 83] KIRKPATRICK S., GELATT C., VECCHI M., "Optimization by simulated annealing", *Science*, vol. 220, no. 4598, pp. 671–680, May 1983.

[KOS 98] KOSECKA J., TOMLIN C., PAPPAS G., *et al.*, "2-1/2 D conflict resolution maneuvers for ATMS", *Proceedings of the 37th IEEE Conference on Decision Control*, pp. 2650–2655, 1998.

[KRE 89] KRELLA F., et al., Arc 2000 scenario (version 4.3), Report, Eurocontrol, April 1989.

[LEE 14] LEE H., Airport surface traffic optimization and simulation in the presence of uncertainties, PhD thesis, Massachusetts Institute of Technology, 2014.

[LEI 08] LEI X., ALI F., SHI A., "The aircraft departure scheduling based on second-order oscillating particle swarm optimization algorithm", *IEEE World Congress on Computational Intelligence*, 2008.

[LEN 10] LE NY J., PAPPAS G., "Geometric programming and mechanism design for air traffic conflict resolution", *Proceedings of the 2010 American Control Conference (ACC)*, Baltimore, MD, pp. 3069–3074, June 2010. 2010.

[LEU 03] LEUNG F., LAM H., LING S., *et al.*, "Tuning of the structure and parameters of a neural network using an improved genetic algorithm", *IEEE transactions on Neural Networks*, vol. 14, no. 1, pp. 79–88, January 2003.

[LIA 06] LIANG J., QIN A., SUGANTHAN P., *et al.*, "Comprehensive learning particle swarm optimizer for global optimization of multimodal functions", *IEEE Transactions on Evolutionary Computation*, vol. 10, no.. 3, pp. 281–295, June 2006.

[MAJ 02] MAJUMDAR A., OCHIENG W.Y., "Factors affecting air traffic controller workload: multivariate analysis based on simulation modeling of controller workload", *Transportation Research Record: Journal of the Transportation Research Board*, vol. 1788, no. 1, pp. 58–69, 2002.

[MAN 85] MANGOUBI R.S., MATHAISEL D.F.X., "Optimizing gate assignments at airport terminals", *Transportation Science*, vol. 19, no. 2, 1985.

[MAU 98] MAUGIS L., GOTTELAND J.-B., ZANNI R., *et al.*, TOSCA-II – WP3: assessment of the TMA to TMA hand-over concept, Report no. T0SCA/S0F/WPR/3/03, SOFREAVIA, 1998.

[MEC 94] MECKIFF D.C., GIBBS D.P., PHARE: highly interactive problem solver, Report, Eurocontrol, 1994.

[MEH 00] MEHADHEBI K., "A methodology for the design of a route network", *Proceedings of the Third Air Traffic Management Research and Development Seminar (ATM-2000)*, Napoli, Italy, Eurocontrol & FAA, June 2000.

[MIC 92] MICHALEWICZ Z., *Genetic Algorithms+Data Structures=Evolution Programs*, Springer-Verlag, 1992.

[MOG 95] MOGFORD R., GUTTMAN J.A., MORROW S.L., *et al.*, The complexity construct in air traffic control: a review and synthesis of the literature, Report, FAA Technical Center, Atlantic City, 1995.

[NIE 89a] NIEDRINGHAUS W., Automated planning function for AERA3: manoeuver option manager, Report, DOT/FAA/DS-89/21, FAA, 1989.

[NIE 89b] NIEDRINGHAUS W., A mathematical formulation for planning automated aircraft separation for AERA3, Report, D0T/FAA/DS-89/20, FAA, 1989.

[OH 97] OH J.-H., SHEWCHUN J., FERON E., "Design and analysis of conflict resolution algorithms via positive semidefinite programming [aircraft conflict resolution]", *Proceedings of the 36th IEEE Conference on Decision and Control*, vol. 5, pp. 4179–4185, December 1997.

[PAL 01] PALLOTTINO L., BICCHI A., FERON E., "Mixed integer programming for aircraft conflict resolution", *AIAA Guidance Navigation and Control Conference and Exhibit*, 2001.

[PAL 02] PALLOTTINO L., FERON E., BICCHI A., "Conflict resolution problems for air traffic management systems solved with mixed integer programming", *IEEE Transactions on Intelligent Transportation Systems*, vol. 3, no. 1, pp. 3–11, March 2002.

[PES 01] PESIC B., DURAND N., ALLIOT J.-M., "Aircraft ground traffic optimisation using a genetic algorithm", *Proceedings of the Genetic and Evolutionary Computation Conference (GECCO 2001)*, 2001.

[RIV 04] RIVIERE T., "Redesign of the European route network for sector-less", *Digital Avionics Systems Conference, 2004 (DASC 2004), IEEE/AIAA 23rd*, 2004.

[ROL 08] ROLING P., VISSER H.G., "Optimal airport surface traffic planning using mixed-integer linear programming", *International Journal of Aerospace Engineering*, vol. 2008, 2008.

[ROL 09] ROLING P.C., "Airport surface traffic planning optimization: a case study of Amsterdam Airport Schiphol", *Proceedings of the 9th AIAA Aviation Technology, Integration, and Operations Conference (ATIO)*, 2009.

[SID 73] SIDDIQUEE M., "Mathematical aids in air route network design", *IEEE Conference on Decision and Control including the 12th Symposium on Adaptive Processes*, December 1973.

[SIM 12] SIMAIAKIS I., SANDBERG M. BALAKRISHNAN H., *et al.*, "Design, testing and evaluation of a pushback rate control strategy", *Proceedings of the 5th International Conference on Research in Air Transportation (ICRAT)*, 2012.

[SLO 08] SLOWIK A., BIALKO M., "Training of artificial neural networks using differential evolution algorithm", *Conference on Human System Interactions*, 2008.

[SNA 10] SNAPE J., MANOCHA D., "Navigating multiple simple-airplanes in 3D workspace", *IEEE International Conference on Robotics and Automation (ICRA)*, pp. 3974–3980, 2010.

[SWE 06] SWENSON H., BARHYDT R., LANDIS M., Next generation air transportation system (NGATS) air traffic management (ATM)-airspace project, Report, National Aeronautics and Space Administration, 2006.

[TRA 03] TRAN DAC H., BAPTISTE P., "Airspace sectorization by constraint programming", *Proceedings of the First RIVF'03 International Conference*, 2003.

[VAN 95] VAN HENTENRYCK P., "Constraint solving for combinatorial search problems: a tutorial", in MONTANARI U., ROSSI F. (eds.), *Principle and Practice of Constraint Programming CP'95*, vol. 976 of Lecture Notes in Computer Science, Cassis, France, Springer, pp. 564–587, September 1995.

[VAN 11] VAN DEN BERG J., GUY S.J., LIN M.C., *et al.*, "Reciprocal n-body collision avoidance", *Proceedings of the 14th International Symposium on Robotics Research*, pp. 3–19, 2011.

[XU 01] XU J., BAILEY G., "The airport gate assignment problem: mathematical model and a tabu search algorithm", *Proceedings of the IEEE 34th Annual Hawaii International Conference on System Sciences*, 2001.

[XUE 09a] XUE M., "Airspace sector redesign based on Voronoi diagrams", *Journal of Aerospace Computing, Information and Communication*, vol. 6, 2009.

[XUE 09b] XUE M., KOPARDEKAR P., "High-capacity tube network design using the Hough transform", *Journal of Guidance, Control, and Dynamics*, vol. 32, no. 3, pp. 788–795, 2009.

[YAN 01] YAN S., HUO C.-M., "Optimization of multiple objective gate assignments", *Transportation Research A: Policy and Practice*, vol. 35, no. 5, 2001.

[YIN 93] YIN X., GERMAY N., "A fast genetic algorithm with sharing scheme using cluster analysis methods in multimodal function optimization", in ALBRECHT R.F., REEVES C.R., STEELE N., (eds.), *Proceedings of the Artificial Neural Nets and Genetic Algorithm International Conference*, Innsbruck, Austria, Springer-Verlag, 1993.

[ZEG 98] ZEGHAL K., "A comparison of different approaches based on force fields for coordination among multiple mobiles", *1998IEEE/RSJ International Conference on Intelligent Robots and Systems*, vol. 1, pp. 273–278, October 1998.

[ZEL 09] ZELINSKI S., "A comparison of algorithm generated sectorization", *Proceedings of the 8th USA/Europe Air Traffic Management Research and Development Seminar*, 2009.

Index

G, H, I

M, N

R, S

T

V, X

Other titles from

ISTE

in

Computer Engineering

2015

CHEN Ken
Performance Evaluation by Simulation and Analysis with Applications to Computer Networks

CLERC Maurice
Guided Randomness in Optimization

MUNEESAWANG Paisarn, YAMMEN Suchart
Visual Inspection Technology in the Hard Disk Drive Industry

WERTZ Harald
Object-oriented Programming with Smalltalk

2014

BOULANGER Jean-Louis
Formal Methods Applied to Industrial Complex Systems

BOULANGER Jean-Louis
Formal Methods Applied to Complex Systems: Implementation of the B Method

GARDI Frédéric, BENOIST Thierry, DARLAY Julien, ESTELLON Bertrand, MEGEL Romain
Mathematical Programming Solver based on Local Search

KRICHEN Saoussen, CHAOUACHI Jouhaina
Graph-related Optimization and Decision Support Systems

LARRIEU Nicolas, VARET Antoine
Rapid Prototyping of Software for Avionics Systems: Model-oriented Approaches for Complex Systems Certification

OUSSALAH Mourad Chabane
Software Architecture 1
Software Architecture 2

QUESNEL Flavien
Scheduling of Large-scale Virtualized Infrastructures: Toward Cooperative Management

RIGO Michel
Formal Languages, Automata and Numeration Systems 1: Introduction to Combinatorics on Words
Formal Languages, Automata and Numeration Systems 2: Applications to Recognizability and Decidability

SAINT-DIZIER Patrick
Musical Rhetoric: Foundations and Annotation Schemes

TOUATI Sid, DE DINECHIN Benoit
Advanced Backend Optimization

2013

ANDRÉ Etienne, SOULAT Romain
The Inverse Method: Parametric Verification of Real-time Embedded Systems

BOULANGER Jean-Louis
Safety Management for Software-based Equipment

DELAHAYE Daniel, PUECHMOREL Stéphane
Modeling and Optimization of Air Traffic

FRANCOPOULO Gil
LMF — Lexical Markup Framework

GHÉDIRA Khaled
Constraint Satisfaction Problems

ROCHANGE Christine, UHRIG Sascha, SAINRAT Pascal
Time-Predictable Architectures

WAHBI Mohamed
Algorithms and Ordering Heuristics for Distributed Constraint Satisfaction Problems

ZELM Martin *et al.*
Enterprise Interoperability

2012

ARBOLEDA Hugo, ROYER Jean-Claude
Model-Driven and Software Product Line Engineering

BLANCHET Gérard, DUPOUY Bertrand
Computer Architecture

BOULANGER Jean-Louis
Industrial Use of Formal Methods: Formal Verification

BOULANGER Jean-Louis
Formal Method: Industrial Use from Model to the Code

CALVARY Gaëlle, DELOT Thierry, SÈDES Florence, TIGLI Jean-Yves
Computer Science and Ambient Intelligence

MAHOUT Vincent
Assembly Language Programming: ARM Cortex-M3 2.0: Organization, Innovation and Territory

MARLET Renaud
Program Specialization

SOTO Maria, SEVAUX Marc, ROSSI André, LAURENT Johann
Memory Allocation Problems in Embedded Systems: Optimization Methods

2011

BICHOT Charles-Edmond, SIARRY Patrick
Graph Partitioning

BOULANGER Jean-Louis
Static Analysis of Software: The Abstract Interpretation

CAFERRA Ricardo
Logic for Computer Science and Artificial Intelligence

HOMES Bernard
Fundamentals of Software Testing

KORDON Fabrice, HADDAD Serge, PAUTET Laurent, PETRUCCI Laure
Distributed Systems: Design and Algorithms

KORDON Fabrice, HADDAD Serge, PAUTET Laurent, PETRUCCI Laure
Models and Analysis in Distributed Systems

LORCA Xavier
Tree-based Graph Partitioning Constraint

TRUCHET Charlotte, ASSAYAG Gerard
Constraint Programming in Music

VICAT-BLANC PRIMET Pascale *et al.*
Computing Networks: From Cluster to Cloud Computing

2010

AUDIBERT Pierre
Mathematics for Informatics and Computer Science

BABAU Jean-Philippe *et al.*
Model Driven Engineering for Distributed Real-Time Embedded Systems 2009

BOULANGER Jean-Louis
Safety of Computer Architectures

MONMARCHE Nicolas *et al.*
Artificial Ants

PANETTO Hervé, BOUDJLIDA Nacer
Interoperability for Enterprise Software and Applications 2010

PASCHOS Vangelis Th
Combinatorial Optimization – 3-volume series
Concepts of Combinatorial Optimization – Volume 1
Problems and New Approaches – Volume 2
Applications of Combinatorial Optimization – Volume 3

SIGAUD Olivier *et al.*
Markov Decision Processes in Artificial Intelligence

SOLNON Christine
Ant Colony Optimization and Constraint Programming

AUBRUN Christophe, SIMON Daniel, SONG Ye-Qiong *et al.*
Co-design Approaches for Dependable Networked Control Systems

2009

FOURNIER Jean-Claude
Graph Theory and Applications

GUEDON Jeanpierre
The Mojette Transform / Theory and Applications

JARD Claude, ROUX Olivier
Communicating Embedded Systems / Software and Design

LECOUTRE Christophe
Constraint Networks / Targeting Simplicity for Techniques and Algorithms

2008

BANÂTRE Michel, MARRÓN Pedro José, OLLERO Hannibal, WOLITZ Adam
Cooperating Embedded Systems and Wireless Sensor Networks

MERZ Stephan, NAVET Nicolas
Modeling and Verification of Real-time Systems

PASCHOS Vangelis Th
Combinatorial Optimization and Theoretical Computer Science: Interfaces and Perspectives

WALDNER Jean-Baptiste
Nanocomputers and Swarm Intelligence

2007

BENHAMOU Frédéric, JUSSIEN Narendra, O'SULLIVAN Barry
Trends in Constraint Programming

JUSSIEN Narendra
A to Z of Sudoku

2006

BABAU Jean-Philippe *et al.*
From MDD Concepts to Experiments and Illustrations – DRES 2006

HABRIAS Henri, FRAPPIER Marc
Software Specification Methods

MURAT Cecile, PASCHOS Vangelis Th
Probabilistic Combinatorial Optimization on Graphs

PANETTO Hervé, BOUDJLIDA Nacer
Interoperability for Enterprise Software and Applications 2006 / IFAC-IFIP I-ESA'2006

2005

GÉRARD Sébastien *et al.*
Model Driven Engineering for Distributed Real Time Embedded Systems

PANETTO Hervé
Interoperability of Enterprise Software and Applications 2005

Printed and bound by CPI Group (UK) Ltd, Croydon, CR0 4YY

13/09/2026

14961017-0001